warp
labels unlimited

warp

Rob Young
With contributions by
Adrian Shaughnessy

labels unlimited

Black Dog Publishing

6	**I Smell Quality** The colour purple: Warp Records overview and origins of Warp's house style
28	**Evolution Of The Bleep** Forgemasters to LFO: Pioneers of the hypnotic groove
50	**Artificial Intelligence** How electronic music moved from dancefloor to armchair
70	**Ultravisitors** Fed with weird things: Aphex Twin, Autechre, Squarepusher
98	**Children At Play** Brand new retro, nostalgia for the future: Blech, Mira Calix, Broadcast, Boards Of Canada
120	**A Second Decade** Warp goes global. Tenth anniversary and beyond. Lex Records: The hiphop connection
144	**Q&A: Steve Beckett**
154	**Warp Artists A-Z**
186	**Label Discography**
190	**Acknowledgements**

Stills from *I Smell Quality*, a short promotional film made by director David Slade for Warp in 1994.

The colour purple: Warp Records overview and origins of Warp's house style

I smell quality

It all nearly ended up Warped. That was the name at the top of the list drawn up in 1989 by Steve Beckett and Rob Mitchell, two Sheffielders in their early 20s just out of college, and Robert Gordon, a 23 year old studio engineer, dreaming up possible futures for the record label they were planning to set up and run from the FON record shop and studio complex in Sheffield's city centre where they worked. Steve Beckett remembers the words "dry ice" written on his to-do list every weekend at the time, which he constantly needed to procure for the smoky, strobe-lit indoor raves that were central the scene they hung out in. The nightclubs of Sheffield (and further afield in Leeds and Bradford), with names like Occasions and Kiki's, may still have been decorated with tacky 1980s glamour signifiers – glitter balls, smoke machines and cocktail Tropicaña – but the music spun on their dancefloors was beginning to mutate into startling new patterns. DJs displayed a wide knowledge base, mixing older rare groove, funk and disco into the newer abstract electronic minimalism on anonymous 12"s arriving on import from Chicago and Detroit. Although most of the music was made by black producers, the anonymity of the abstract sound made it leap across traditional racial divides. It was an optimistic moment in a Britain on the cusp of recession: the clubs were racially mixed, the music policy expressed a new harmony. As Robert Gordon puts it, "You'd go to raves and you'd see rastas and rave kids in the same clubs, just there for the music. It was anti-racial, united music – it worked."

In the dawn hours, the revellers would spill out onto the pavement under pallid purple skies. It's been rumoured that the mauve canopy was the source of the distinctive Warp 'house colour' and generic 12" record sleeves that have survived throughout the history of the label. Designers Republic's Ian Anderson, who devised the colour scheme, denies that was the reasoning, but even if it's not strictly true, that colour has remained a constant link with the origins.

But the name they eventually chose didn't lock the enterprise into that particular time and milieu. As they soon discovered, the word 'Warped' was too easily misheard and didn't transmit well over the phone. So they called it Warp.

WE ARE REASONABLE PEOPLE

Spelling it out: the sticker that has graced a thousand DJ boxes.

The name was perfect: it declared futurist leanings, and gave a clue to the soundworld the label would promote. Warp has overtones of science fiction: Captain Kirk's regular instructions to engineer Scotty to crank the Starship Enterprise up to warp drive in *Star Trek*. It carries the sense of distortion, to be physically or mentally twisted out of shape. So there's this twin meaning of fast forward motion and something bent out of the ordinary, unrecognisable. The word also occurs in the terminology of loom weaving and canal tow ropes, which imaginatively connects Warp to the industrial landscape of Sheffield. And finally, it stood as an acronym for a phrase with a quintessentially English ring: "We Are Reasonable People".

In 1989 Sheffield was one of the largest cities in the north of England still suffering under the divisive policies of Margaret Thatcher's Conservative government. Sheffield itself was popularly known as the 'Republic of South Yorkshire'; its left wing council had been generous funders of local arts projects, and the city possessed several venues and local community initiatives to encourage young people to become involved in the arts. During the 1970s the Meatwhistle theatre

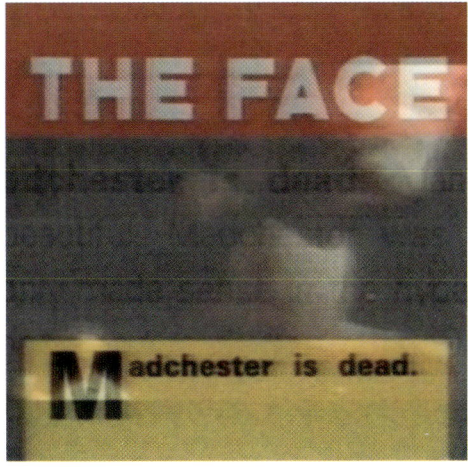

left: Warp co-founders Steve Beckett and Rob Mitchell, appearing on Yorkshire Television's *PS* arts report in 1991.
right: From the same programme, *The Face* announces the demise of the North of England's previously most significant musical city, paving the way for a Sheffield resurgence.

company became a magnet for anyone who was anyone in the first wave of Sheffield electronic pop such as The Human League, Cabaret Voltaire, Heaven 17 and ABC. In the late 80s, the Red Tape complex was instigated as a hub for local music and arts practitioners. Coal mines, steelworks and factories were disappearing, and as the town's old industrial backbone crumbled away, a new 'cultural industry quarter' was being installed in its place. Today the Red Tape site at 1 Brown Street is transformed beyond recognition, but in the late 80s it housed the studios of The Human League and the FON Records label, plus the amalgamated stations of the Yorkshire Radio Network. There was talk of Sheffield becoming the base of a new national fifth TV channel, although that never materialised. But it was from this tangle of activity that Warp emerged in 1989, its roots in the FON studio and shop partnership.

In Warp's first years, the label tended to push the notion of supporting a particularly homegrown talent in Sheffield. A short feature segment of 1991 TV culture show *PS* displayed a headline in *The Face* magazine that screamed, "Madchester is dead – it's official".

"Probably an exaggeration", continues reporter Steve McLaren, "but the word on the music grapevine is that the reign of Manchester as club city may be coming to an end. Across the Pennines there's a serious new pretender – a club scene inspired by rave culture but influenced by the city's industrial surroundings. This is the sound of Sheffield...."

Defined against a Manchester scene that had largely bloated into a herd following baggy self-parody, the leaner, crisper sound of Sheffield Techno, with a dash of Northern Soul, provided a refreshing alternative.

LFO's bedroom studio in Leeds.

DJ Parrot, a member of early Warp acts Sweet Exorcist and The Step, is interviewed in a club backroom for the TV report: "Sheffield's always had a history, how our heritage is like electronic dance music, The Cabs, The Human League, people like Hula and Chakk, so it'll always have some of that in it, but it'll always have some Northern Soul in it, it'll always have some heavy industry in it, cos that's our town, that's why records from Chicago and Detroit have been so important to us, because they're like steel towns."

An early magazine article quoted Robert Gordon, the long time FON producer who, as one of the Forgemasters, was on the first Warp release: "There's talent seeping from the fingernails of Sheffield, but for a while there was no real access to the release button for this new power. We had the ability to solve the problem, hence the birth of Warp. There's no hype, no scam, no gimmick, the talent was there, and now it has an outlet."

As the 90s took off, and a millennial search for the future of music took hold, the sounds stamped with the Warp imprint largely set the pace in the UK. The artists and producers associated with the first phase – Forgemasters, Sweet Exorcist, Nightmares On Wax, The Step, Tricky Disco, Tuff Little Unit, etc. – trod an exhilaratingly precarious line between the animated body music of funk and disco, and a colder and harder animatronic machine music that derived its momentum from Kraftwerk, electro and hiphop. Not so much rare groove as pared groove: funk as mechanised routine that tuned into the dancefloor's pleasure principle. The 1990s were remarkable for their sequence of rapidly mutating dance music microtrends, beginning with breakbeat-driven 'ardkore' Techno. But Warp's next generation of artists – LFO, Aphex Twin, Autechre, B12,

clockwise from top: The first three releases on Warp: The Forgemasters' "Track With No Name", 1989 (WAP1), Nightmares On Wax's "Dextrous", 1989 (WAP2), and the remixes of Sweet Exorcist's "Testone", 1990 (WAP3). The distinctive purple outer bag and logo, conceived by Sheffield's Designers Republic, have remained unchanged ever since. On the Forgemasters 12" can be seen an original alternative version of the logo.

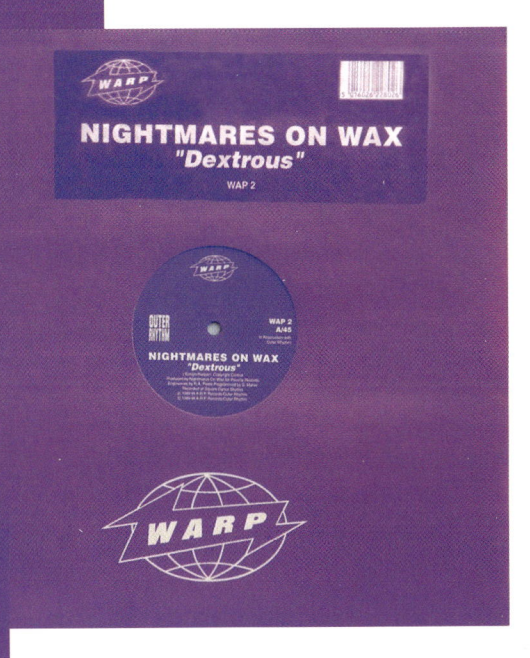

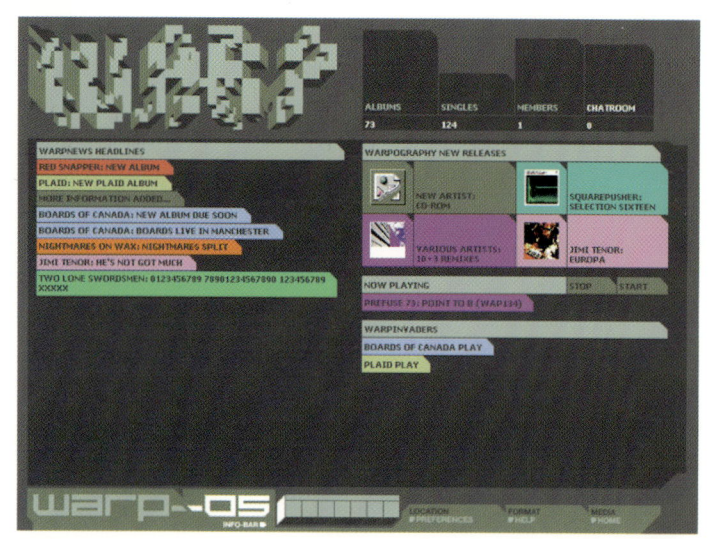

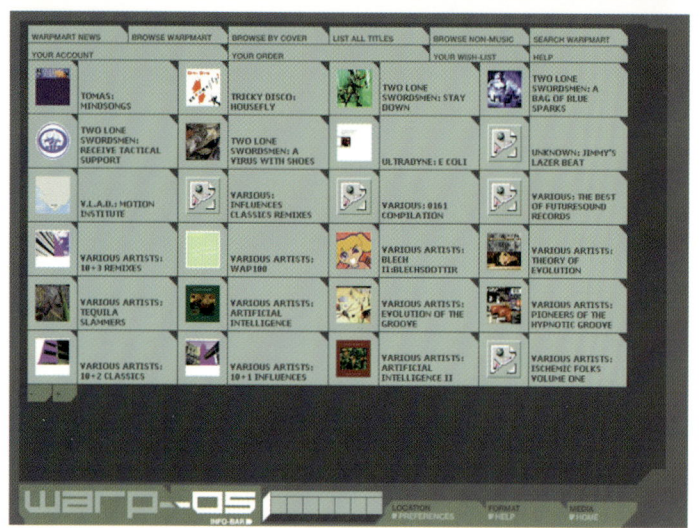

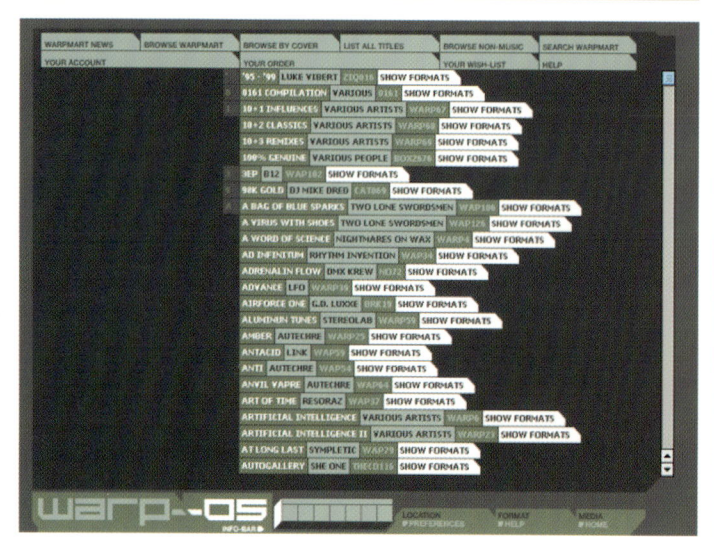

Warp was one of the first high profile record labels to realise the power of the Internet, and the distinctive 'Lego-brick' feel of www.warprecords.com acts as a portal to an industrious, tech-savvy label environment.

Steve Beckett and Rob Mitchell, photographed in the late 1990s.

The Black Dog, FUSE, Speedy J – largely bypassed that tendency, playing up the 'scientific' aspects of the new electronic music. Instead of bodies, flesh and the physical communion of the dancefloor, the predominant issues at play were robotics, computers, synthetics, science fiction, and cybernetics, culminating in the notorious *Artificial Intelligence* album series of 1992-1994. Appropriately, these younger practitioners appeared reclusive, experimenting in private domestic situations, with recording, production and remixing the central activities, and 'live' performance at best a chore, at worst a necessary evil. In my own experiences interviewing various Warp related artists during the 1990s, I have encountered a general sense of impatience with the demand to analyse the creative process or engage with external critical interpretations.

Artificial Intelligence helped to cement Warp's reputation worldwide, but has remained something of a millstone ever since. Because it defined a brief era in electronic music, and was coupled with the brilliance of the artwork by the Designers Republic, it is still difficult for many observers to separate the modern Warp from the one set in place in the early 90s. Warp has gone on to diversify immeasurably from that period, and although many of the artists are still contracted, a common reaction to Warp is a knee-jerk 'they're not as good as they used to be', or a sense that much of the initial momentum has been lost. It's an unfortunate but inevitable consequence of early success. Fighting the tensions between underground credibility and wider exposure has formed the backdrop to Warp's entire lifespan. In reaction to the self-promoting height of the 1980s' visible pop culture, many Warp artists were slippery, almost invisible. Detroit's Drexciya never grant interviews; ditto Vincent Gallo and comedian Chris Morris, both of whom released material on the label; B12 flit above: Gift artists V and Various Vegetables – two groups that would prove incompatible with Warp's early focus on electronic music. opposite: In 1991 Warp's short lived subsidiary, Gift Records, was set up primarily to help develop Pulp's career, as this press photo from the archives proves. Although the association would not last, the group's Jarvis Cocker directed several videos for Warp artists including Sweet Exorcist, Nightmares On Wax, and Aphex Twin.

behind shadowy aliases and Boards Of Canada stay remote in their Scottish retreat. Richard James, aka Aphex Twin, told an interviewer in 2003 that he holds back the music he considers his best, fearing that it will become tainted by imitation or overexposure in the public domain: "You end up hating your own music. So you have to protect it."[1]

That wariness about the music's reception may have been inevitable. On Warp's watch, electronica largely voyaged into total abstraction. It held out few analytical toeholds, no lyrics, titles often in an invented or computerised language, or carrying the loosest of associations with the music. Postmodern theory talks of language as nothing more than a play of signifiers detached from the things they purport to represent. In the same way, electronica can feel like a dance of pure texture, tone and pulse, 'about' nothing more (or less) than its structural form, or its own relationships with other electronic music past and present across a web of interconnected sound marks and reference points. The slew of tracks, churned out in their hundreds by Autechre, Aphex, Squarepusher, Luke Vibert, etc., taken together, are like those software applications that generate huge strings of anagrams of a particular word or sentence – with Aphex and Vibert having actually used such anagrams as track titles. With such camera shy personalities, and so little material for strong critical traction and interpretation, it's little wonder much of this music has faded out of the mainstream music press.

But Warp has not been the sole preserve of electronic music. Even back in 1990, Steve Beckett set up the Gift subsidiary, a shortlived rock/pop operation which initially gave Pulp a leg-up to their later success with Island Records, as well as being home (briefly) to a handful of marginal Sheffield groups like V and Various Vegetables. In 1994 indie shoegazers Seefeel joined the label and their presence

1. James, Richard, quoted in David Stubbs, "Protection Racket", *The Wire*, no. 237, November 2003.

Pulp

warpfashion guidance
purple is the new black

One of a series of slogan cards created by Designers Republic.

helped inscribe the *Artificial Intelligence* sector as a wider arc than is usually remembered. Later years have seen Warp signing groups and artists that don't fit the mould of the bedroom electronic producer: Red Snapper, Broadcast and Stereolab, Jimi Tenor's lurid orchestral/electro sleaze, Tortoise's post-rock, !!!'s No Wave funk, Gravenhurst's new folk rock, Chok Rock's live electro, Maxïmo Park's angular passion, Jamie Lidell's 'godson of soul' stance. A general broadening of the label's content has also included setting up Lex Records in 1999, run by Tom Brown and dedicated to uncovering new, experimental hiphop, which continues a strain that's been inscribed in Warp ever since the early output of Nightmares On Wax, and picked up later in the 90s when they signed Antipop Consortium, their vocalist Beans, and Scott Herren aka Prefuse 73.

As the label consolidated and developed its core roster through the mid 90s, the pressures on the business mounted. Logistics became difficult: more time needed to be spent in London and on the road; the music's outreach went global; and the Warp vision expanded into the domain of film and video with the foundation of Warp Films. This expansion necessitated a wholesale revision of Warp's infrastructure. Following the celebration of Warp's 100th release in 1998, and its tenth anniversary in 1999, it was announced that the ancestral home in Sheffield would be abandoned for new premises in London.

Such changes can easily provoke hostile reactions, but in business terms if nothing else, Warp hit the south at an opportune moment, when the 'dotcom' boom was on an upward curve and there was enough investment cash flying around to be able to develop not only Warp Films but also the label's website, which has always been a key factor in encouraging and nurturing relationships between itself and its fans and customers. Early adopters of the potential of the internet, Warp's site has always been one of the most sophisticated independent label pages, generous with information and features. The addition of Bleep.com in 2004, a separate enterprise selling an enormous quantity of Warp back catalogue and other electronic labels as downloadable MP3s, defied all expectations. Unlike many pay sites, Bleep.com innovated by treating its customers as fans and not potential criminals, offering sound files with no anti-piracy encoding – an attitude surely originating in that culture of trust in an audience that's treated more like an 'extended family'.

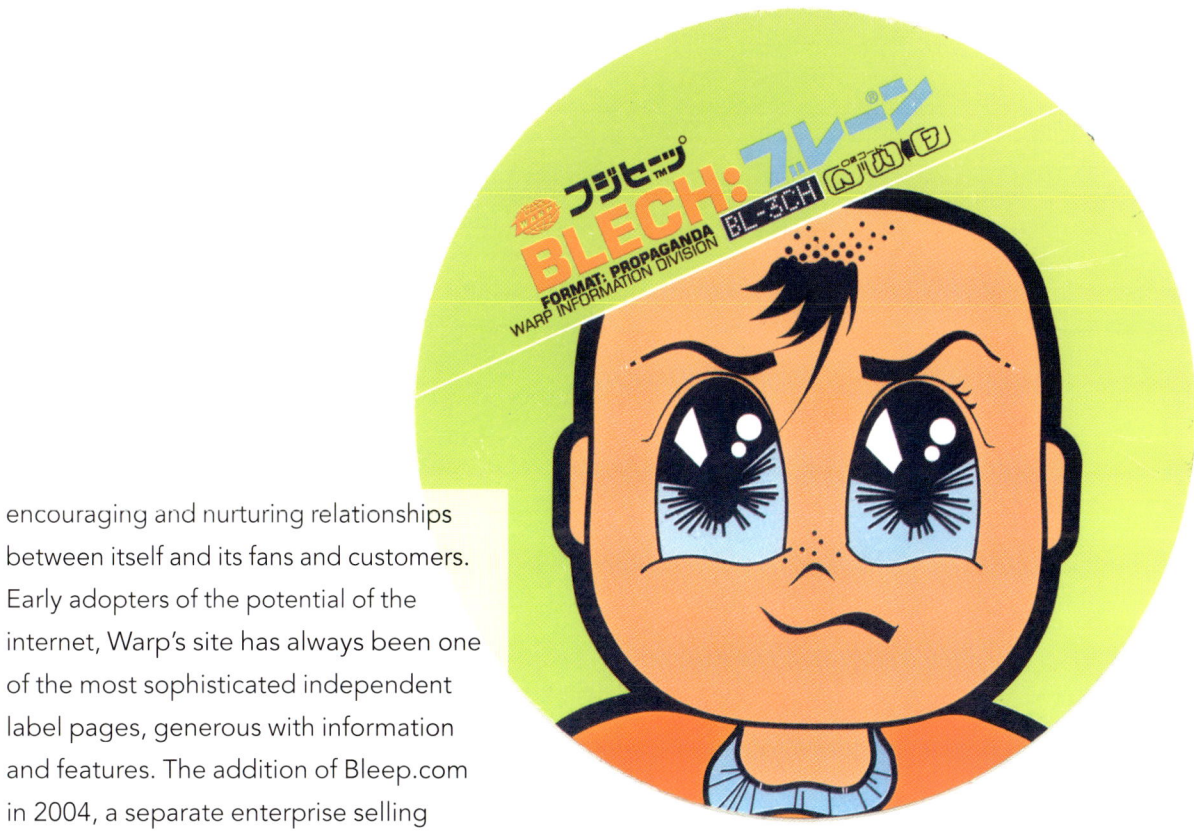

Set up in 1996 to portray a more human, fun side of electronica, Warp's Blech club and compilation album ushered in a new phase in the design aesthetic inspired by Japanese commercial packaging.

By the late 90s it was no longer possible to talk about a 'Warp sound' – it was more about a Warp state of mind. If the label's strong brand sometimes eclipsed its artists' individuality, Warp later concentrated on building their unique identities. A distinguishable new phase begins around 1996, after the setting up of Blech, the club night in Sheffield and attendant CD compilation, where the Designers Republic replaced their earlier stark and dense style with a more human, user friendly and fun logotype and cartoony vibe influenced by Japanese packaging and graphic design. Warp has always been about reinvention, futurism, anticipating the next move and reshaping to meet it. This can be read in different ways. For those left behind in its wake, it's a form of hypocrisy, of cynical surfing on the market zeitgeist. For those closer to the hub, it's a pragmatic strategy without which the entire operation might cease to exist entirely. There's hardly a record label that doesn't have to apply the approach, to some extent. But there will never be any reconciliation between those opposed mindsets.

While preparing to establish its new offices in Gospel Oak, North London, Warp celebrated its tenth anniversary with a lavish series of records collecting its influences, early singles catalogue and newly commissioned remixes, all of which demonstrated a new self-awareness of the label as a participant in a specific music continuum and history. Shortly afterwards, Rob Mitchell was diagnosed with cancer. The disease was too far advanced for preventative treatment, and he died on 8 October 2001. Warp had thrived on the chemistry between Mitchell and Steve Beckett. As Mitchell once said, running a label is gambling on your own taste.

Gambling inevitably will entail certain losses, though Warp has at least remained 100 per cent independent, solvent and as of 2005, in a state of expansion. It's worth remembering that during Warp's lifespan, the 'big five' major record companies have reduced to the 'big three', with thousands of jobs lost during various mergers. Some of Warp's core press supporters have also gone under, including such magazines as *Muzik*, *Jockey Slut*, *Melody Maker*, *The Face*, and *Sleazenation*.

Cash in the chips: Phil Wolstenholme's digitally rendered image, produced for 1991's *Pioneers Of The Hypnotic Groove* compilation, typified the emerging fascination with computer technology and its effect on music production and reception in the early 1990s.

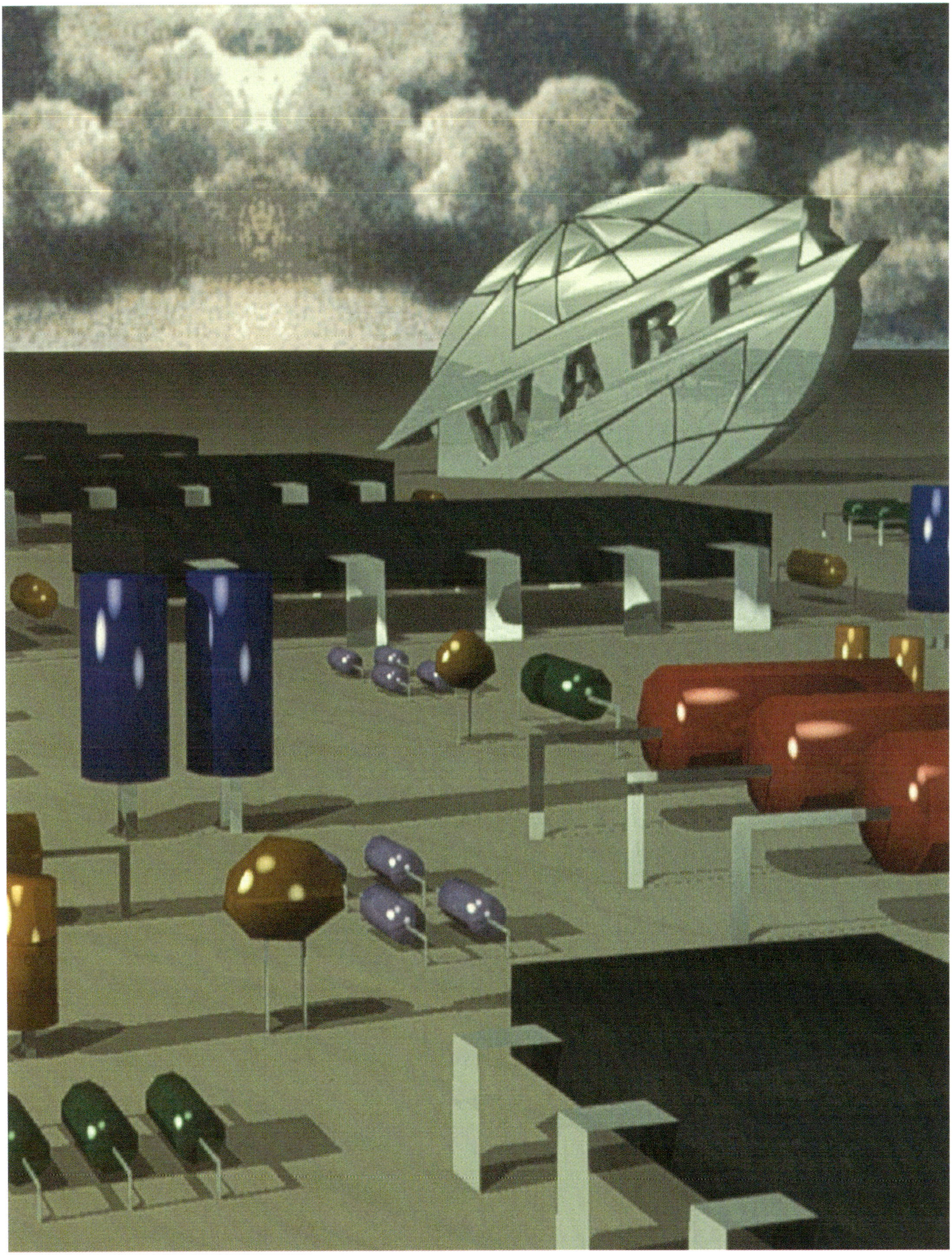
WARP

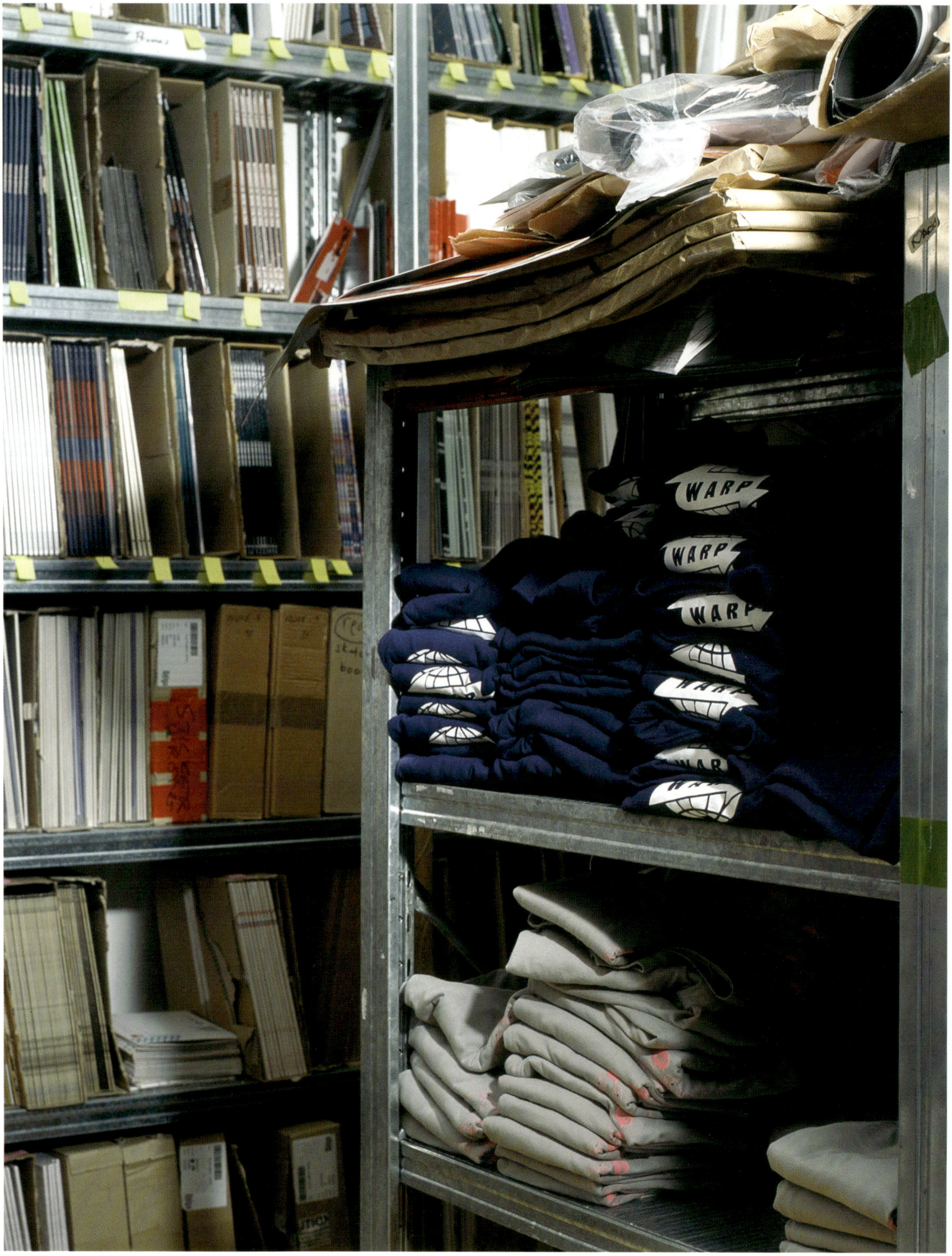
WARP

above: A wall of Warp artists (left to right): Aphex Twin, Squarepusher, Autechre's Sean Booth and Rob Brown, George Evelyn of Nightmares On Wax.
opposite: With a catalogue of 200 singles and 150 albums released between 1989-2005, Warp has amassed an enormous archive. One corner of the company's Warpmart mail order operation gives a sense of the scale of operations. Photo: Alessandra Rebagliati.

Warp has been home to nearly 100 different artists, and with such diversity it is impossible to pin down a single 'philosophy' through its releases alone. The idea of this book, and the Labels Unlimited series, was always to give a portrait of a label equally through words and images, and while it inevitably focuses on the more prominent artists, an A-Z on page 166 itemises every single artist that has released anything on Warp, and I have attempted at least to shine a torch into most corners of its output, including Warp's film and video work. I have been given access to Warp's own comprehensive archive of images, press cuttings and other documents, and wherever possible new quotes have been obtained from artists and relevant observers. The detailed story of the early days of the label is told here for the first time, and, threaded throughout the text, graphic design expert Adrian Shaughnessy supplies commentaries on various aspects of Warp's design philosophy and sleeve art.

> A surprisingly common view of Warp is that it has become a ghost of its original self; that it abandoned the original dream of a utopian electronic music and became diluted in a sea of random diversity and stylistic eclecticism. I don't entirely share that view. Survival is a process of mutation and adaptation, but Warp's DNA was always encoded with the tendency to look forward, keep ahead of the curve and avoid fossilisation. As it approaches institutional status, the tension between its reputation and legacy, and its futuristic drive, becomes increasingly acute. The goal is still in view, as Rob Mitchell expressed it many years ago: originate, not replicate.

Warp Design: Origins
Adrian Shaughnessy

For graphic designers, Warp record covers represent a sort of Shangri-La. Admiration for Warp sleeves is, of course, not confined merely to earnest, hardcore graphistas, but graphic designers are bound to look at Warp sleeves differently. They look at them with a kind of sad, admiring envy. They see the same graphic inventiveness and audacious rule-breaking that everyone else does: they see the same spectacular successes and the same doodlesome failures. But designers' perceptions of Warp sleeves (and other successful forms of unfettered visual expression) is coloured by the remorse that they feel when they recall how often their own work is diluted by clients who regard graphic design as merely a tasteless and odourless sandwich spread, to be smeared over products and services, imparting the uniformity and glutinous sameness that is considered desirable in modern commercial life.

Warp's best covers act as vivid signifiers of the label's strand of sonic wizardry, as well as its maverick status as an independent entity in the increasingly corporate music industry. Yet there's no Warp house style. Yes, there's the distinctive Jetsons-meets-Captain Scarlet logo, unchanged since the label's inception, and in the early days, the label released its records in uniform 'house bags' swathed in Warp purple and deploying, with unexpected typographic rigour, the high Modernist font Helvetica. But today, the defining element found in Warp sleeves is diversity: just as the label's roster of artists has diversified since its beginnings as a home for intelligent Techno ('electronic listening music', to use the label's own description), so too has Warp's vision of what a record cover should be. Today you are as likely to find an artist's photograph as a Techno illustration on a Warp record cover.

Yet, despite the absence of a house style, and the current stylistic diversity of the sleeves, there *is* a 'Warp look'. It's a fairly ramshackle and inconsistent look, often twisted and dysfunctional, with as many failures as successes, but it's nevertheless an identifiable visual presence – a graphic atmosphere – that forms part of the label's DNA code. Warp allows its visual constituent parts – album covers, music videos, websites – to carry the same chemical make-up as its music, and in doing so creates a label 'identity' that is always the same, yet, paradoxically, always different.

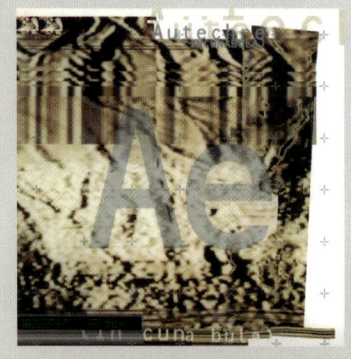

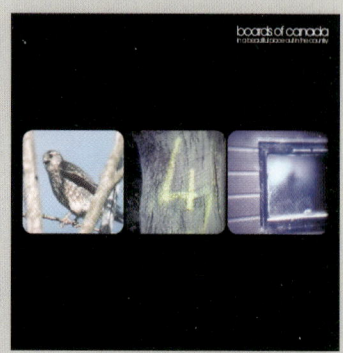

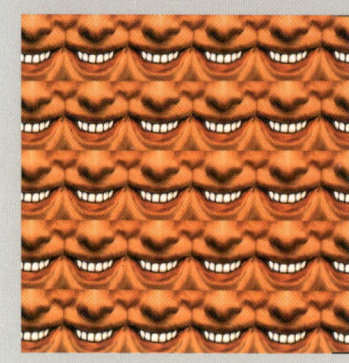

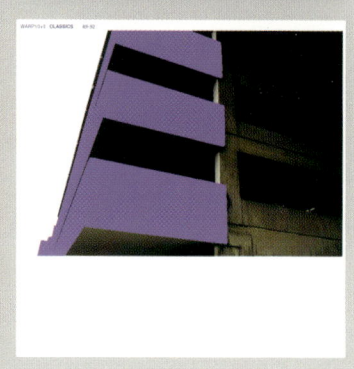

Factory and 4AD set the graphic benchmark in this area. Both labels achieved a near magical fusion of sound and visual expression. In his book, *24 Hour Party People*, a compelling rearview mirror 'novelisation' of Michael Winterbottom's film of the same name, label founder and Mancunian iconoclast Tony Wilson explains the Factory design 'philosophy': "And since the music was great, then the packaging in which the customer received said art would have to have the same attention to perfection." Many Factory sleeves did indeed reach a state of graphic perfection, yet all Factory sleeves were different. Even the central core of sleeves designed by Peter Saville that forms the Factory canon managed to retain an instantly discernable aesthetic homogeneity while offering fresh visual delights with every new sleeve.

Warp have had their own Peter Saville in Designers Republic, and it's tempting – especially for the design company's numerous and zealous fans – to imagine that the story of Warp cover art is inseparable from Designers Republic. But that would be wrong. They were around at Warp's start, imparting a steely, made-in-Sheffield aesthetic to the label's sleeves, and to outsiders it's almost as if Designers Republic are 'signed' to Warp, enjoying equal status with the musicians on the label's roster. But many key Warp sleeves are not designed by Designers Republic. DR (as they are routinely referred to) might be woven into the 'warp and weft' of the label – but they are not the sole custodians of the Warp look, and following the work they did for Warp's tenth anniversary series of box set compilations in 1999, their involvement has reduced considerably.

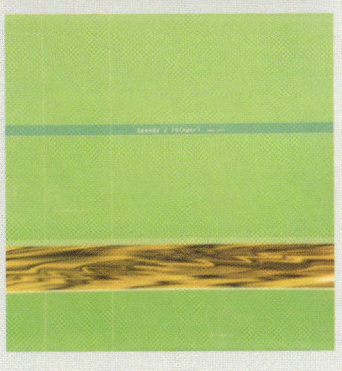

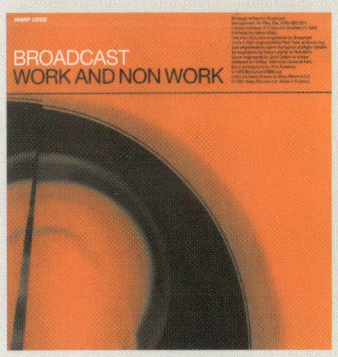

Designers Republic founder Ian Anderson met Warp founders Steve Beckett and Rob Mitchell on the Sheffield music scene prior to Warp starting up. "It wasn't as if they were strangers who rang up and said can we come in and talk about artwork," notes Anderson, in a conversation with Rob Young. "My background was in managing bands. I had a background in the music industry, and so even before the question of artwork appeared, they came tapping me for any knowledge that I had, which I gave willingly. I mentioned this to someone in an interview once and they wrote about it as if I'd been their mentor. It wasn't like that at all. If you were starting a record label and you wanted a bit of advice you'd go and ask anybody and everybody that you knew, so I was just one of a lot of people they spoke to. But the conversation was had, and obviously we said, 'Well, if you need any design…'."

A commitment to intelligent cover design was built into Warp's label ethos from the outset. As Steve Beckett noted in Simon Reynolds's rave-culture book *Energy Flash*: "From our point of view, it also felt like a lot of the dance music around had gotten really throwaway, just white labels from people jumping on the bandwagon to make a quick five hundred or thousand quid out of it. It felt like somebody should start paying attention to the production and the artwork – the whole way the music was presented."[1]

The search for ways to 'present the music' began with the creation of a logo. "The logo was designed because they wanted something that was futuristic," Anderson recalls. "But they didn't want something that would date, so what I did was a kind of 60s-looking thing. It was actually based on two things; there's a logo in an old logo book that is basically a globe with a sort of flash across it, and I combined this with a sort of *Star Trek/Dan Dare*/NASA futuristic thing. What we were trying to do was have something that looked futuristic that was, in some way, already dated, but dated to the degree where it kind of matured. So much stuff came out around that time that dated after about a year because people were trying too hard to be modern, which is always a massive mistake really. I think if you do something that's created with modern thinking then it will be, by default, modern. If you try to create something specifically modern then all you're doing is emulating the surface."

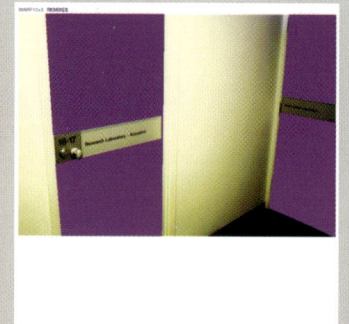

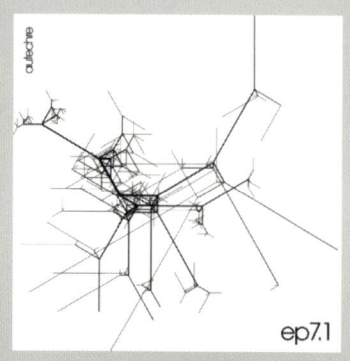

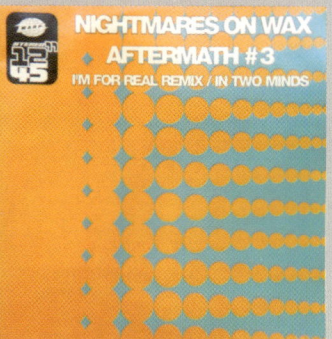

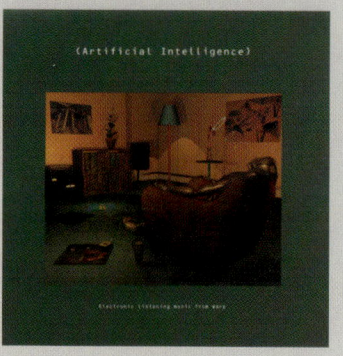

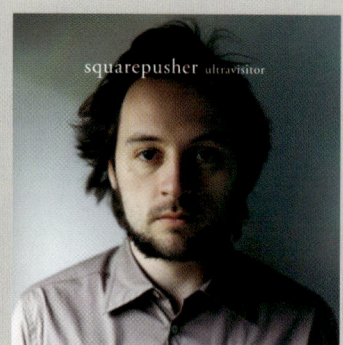

From the logo, attention passed to the creation of a label identity. "We showed them what we'd done for FON Records," explains Anderson. "We had this thing where you could do almost anything on the cover, but there were just black and white stripes down the spine and the first ten millimetres of the cover on the front and on the back, so that when you had them on your shelves you'd always spot a FON cover straight away." Beckett and Mitchell liked the idea of instant recognition for their fledgling label. Anderson recalls recommending the use of a colour: "I told them they needed a colour that other people weren't using, to give them some kind of point of difference… I wouldn't have said 'point of difference', because that's a late 90s branding term, but that idea of having something that's instantly recognisable."

Warp purple was to become emblematic of the nascent label. It is rumoured to have been chosen to represent the colour of the sky at 4am when clubbers emerge into the dawn, a notion that the voluble Anderson refutes: "I'd never heard that before," he says. "If you look at a lot of Designers Republic artwork around that time, there's lots of purple being used. We did the Cabaret Voltaire single 'Hypnotise', 1989, and that was purple, and there was other stuff too that used purple. It wasn't a primary colour, and it was a really intense purple. Originally, it was going to be a one-colour print, so I don't think it was an arbitrary choice, it wasn't just 'I like that colour so we'll do that'."

Even in their early stages, Warp covers would often veer off from the 'house' uniformity into hidden paths and meandering byways. "I don't think Rob or Steve would ever have wanted there to be a cohesive Warp look," claims

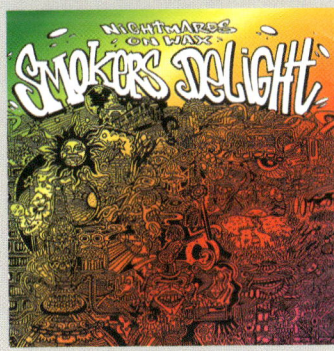

Anderson. "They didn't really want to have a Warp sound – although there kind of was one – in the same way that I don't think of Designers Republic as having a DR look. But I'm aware that there is one – kind of – and no matter how different the things that we do are, if you put one thing next to another, you might say, 'I didn't know you did that'."

"But if you put 30 things together that were all individually – or in ones and twos and threes – quite different, if you put them all together there'll be a sort of sensibility. And I think that Warp could have done that, I think they should have said to artists: 'You can do what you want, but we're putting this record out and we take pride in our artwork, and I think that that would have been better'."

Anderson's comments highlight one of the central issues in sleeve design: namely the commissioning of cover art by musicians – or even, in some cases, musicians creating their own album cover artwork. Most artists have it written into their recording contracts that they retain control over the design of their sleeves. In most cases this extends only as far as approving what the record companies decide is suitable artwork. And since record companies invariably pay for the cost of producing artwork, and then deduct the cost in its entirety from musician's earnings (unlike music videos, where the cost is shared between label and artist), it is little wonder that artists might want to retain control of the design process. This industry convention has resulted in some of the best record covers in pop's short history. It is also fundamental to the continuing presence of high-quality record covers, especially at a time when, due to the escalating use of digitally downloadable music, the album cover is widely considered by major record labels to be redundant – or at best, far less important than it once was. In truth, today it is often only the demands of musicians that guarantees meaningful cover art: if it was left to record labels, most covers would feature a glitzy artist photograph and be designed by the label's in-house studio to a rigid formula.

1. Reynolds, Simon, *Energy Flash*, London: Picador, 1998.

Steve Beckett photographed at the Warp Records shop on Division Street, Sheffield, in the early 90s. The original logo hanging above the shop, carved from a block of wood, survived the move to Warp's London office in 2000.

Evolution Of The Bleep

Forgemasters to LFO: pioneers of the hypnotic groove

Some time in the 1940s, an anonymous left wing activist painted the letters FON on a prominent wall in Sheffield city centre. At the time the acronym stood for 'Fear Of Nazis', a slogan of the campaign against Oswald Mosley's British blackshirts. The graffiti was still visible 40 years later, by which time people assumed it stood for 'Fuck Off Nazis'. And by the mid 80s, the name FON had become a byword for state of the art music production.

In 1984, DoubleVision, the video label associated with Sheffield's most famous Industrial music export Cabaret Voltaire, had bankrolled the release of the debut single by Industrial funk outfit Chakk, "Out Of The Flesh". Chakk were managed by local scenester Amrik Rai, an *NME* contributor who used to flog off his promo copies in Shock Horror, the shop he ran with Chakk's then manager Dave Taylor on Division Street above a clothes shop called Frock Horror. Chakk were propelled prematurely onto the paper's cover – and into a reputed £600,000 deal with MCA in 1985. But, insistent on creative autonomy, and inspired by the example of Cabaret Voltaire's Western Works, they swiftly invested around a third of the money in a rehearsal room and 24-track studio. This was the first FON complex, housed in an enormous Victorian warehouse on Sheldon Row, to the north of the city centre near the Wicker, which has since been demolished. Warp's origins lie in the coming together of several individuals variously connected to FON's studio and record shop.

As a teenager, Robert Gordon produced the first (unused) version of Chakk's debut album *Ten Days In An Elevator*. Born into a Jamaican family, he had worked as a musician and producer with reggae and punk groups, and was involved with local community music projects at Darnall Music Factory. In addition, he had established a reputation as something of a technical genius, conspicuous around Sheffield because he always lugged around a cumbersome brick of a mobile phone. "My pet hobby as a child was electronics," he says. "In the black world I was the chief pre-amp builder."

Chakk's Mark Brydon at the mixing desk of FON Studios circa 1987. At this desk Warp co-founder Robert Gordon created his pioneering grooves and remixes. FON, with its record shop and label, was the hub around which Warp Records eventually formed. Photo: David Bocking.

At FON during the late 80s he produced tracks by the likes of Cabaret Voltaire, The Human League, Age Of Chance, Richard Hawley's first group Treebound Story and others. When Chakk were dropped by MCA in late 1986, manager Dave Taylor's Shock Horror shop went into liquidation. The notion of setting up a new retail operation in collaboration with FON was mooted, but Dave Taylor, who reverted to managing Chakk once Rai had abandoned them to move to London, hesitated over the idea of getting involved in another shop. Two enthusiastic members of a local group, just out of university, persuaded him to change his mind.

Rob Mitchell was spending his working days as a salesman, hawking that gift for the elderly, the Stannah stair lift. With his friend Steve Beckett, a drummer, he had formed a group called Lay Of The Land in 1987. The name was taken from a song that appears on the album *The Wonderful And Frightening World Of The Fall*. LOTL's singer was Stephen Havenhand, briefly a bass player in local heroes Pulp. The group changed their name to Aitch in 1987, but neither of these two groups seem to have left any recorded traces.

With Taylor struggling with the financial nightmare of Chakk's demise, he caved in to Mitchell and Beckett's enthusiasm and desire to take on the task of relaunching the shop and "have an attempt at releasing some underground dance 12"s."[1]

1. Taylor, Dave, quoted in Martin Lilleker, *Beats Working For A Living: Sheffield Popular Music 1973-1984*, Sheffield: Juma Books, 2005.

'THE FEELING REMAINS...'

'Suddenly we were excited. H' turned up the music, grabbed Marylou and held her tight. We hit every city with unrivalled energy, never slowing down. From conception in autumn 1986 to new horizons, confidence in confidence.'

So speak **AITCH**; if you don't recognise this name, maybe you'll be more familiar with **LAY OF THE LAND**, for they are one and the same band. The line-up remains exactly as before, but the name has been changed because they 'got sick of it', so their drummer, Steve Beckett, informs me. 'It was too Indie sounding, and everyone associated it with The Fall song. A couple of years ago it was all The Smiths and jangly guitars, and we've moved on from that now. Our new songs are harder and dancier.

Indeed, material such as 'Tunbridge Wells' and 'Who's Fooling Who?' were voted 'CUT Demo of the Month' in November.

The name **AITCH** was conceived after spending 6 hours sitting round a table, locked in deadly debate. Eventually, the 400 or so alternatives were narrowed down to one: **AITCH** was chosen because 'it doesn't strike an image, so people can't categorize us. The music speaks for itself.' But, as you may or may not know, **AITCH** is also the brand name of a certain type of shiny acrylic jumper, of the variety sold in dubious jeans shops. It was only after they'd picked it that they found out, but this did not deter them. In fact, Steve was quite pleased about it. 'If they do make a fuss, we'll just change it to the letter "H", but I hope they do sue us, so we can get some publicity out of it!'

Besides metamorphosing into **AITCH**, the band are setting up their own studio in a Broomhill basement where they are writing new material in preparation for their imminent 'It's a Small World' tour. According to Steve, the entire stage show is 'guaranteed to give the audience an out of body experience'. Jumpers permitting, **AITCH** will be on the road in January – don't miss them!

LD

First and possibly only mention in print of Lay Of The Land and Aitch, the groups whose members included Warp's Steve Beckett (second from top) and Rob Mitchell (second from bottom). From Sheffield student magazine *Arrows*, no. 145, 1987.

Opened in 1987 at 40 Division Street, FON Records was run by Mitchell, who eventually secured a controlling stake in the operation over Dave Taylor. Beckett assisted with restructuring the business, streamlining the stock and honing it down to a choice selection of dance and Techno 12"s. By now a coterie of ambitious independent labels, releasing electronic music and progressive alternative sounds, were based in Sheffield, including The Orb's Wau! Mr Modo, Native and FON itself. Links were being forged between newer and older music producers, with rumoured collaborations between The Human League and Robert Gordon, and Cabaret Voltaire – by now signed to Virgin – reactivated as a glossier dancefloor friendly unit with expensive videos to match. In hindsight, the moment seems peculiarly transitional between opposed modes of negotiating celebrity and integrity, a tension that has remained part of Warp's fabric.

FON's imports buyer, Winston Hazel, was always known at school as the Funkmaster General. He DJed for his schoolmates in the late 70s, and when Acid House "crept up" on him around 1984-1985, he became resident at a large number of Sheffield club nights, licensed and unlicensed, such as The Steamer, Club Superman, Funky Precedent and Deep. Hazel recalls these as being "Packed

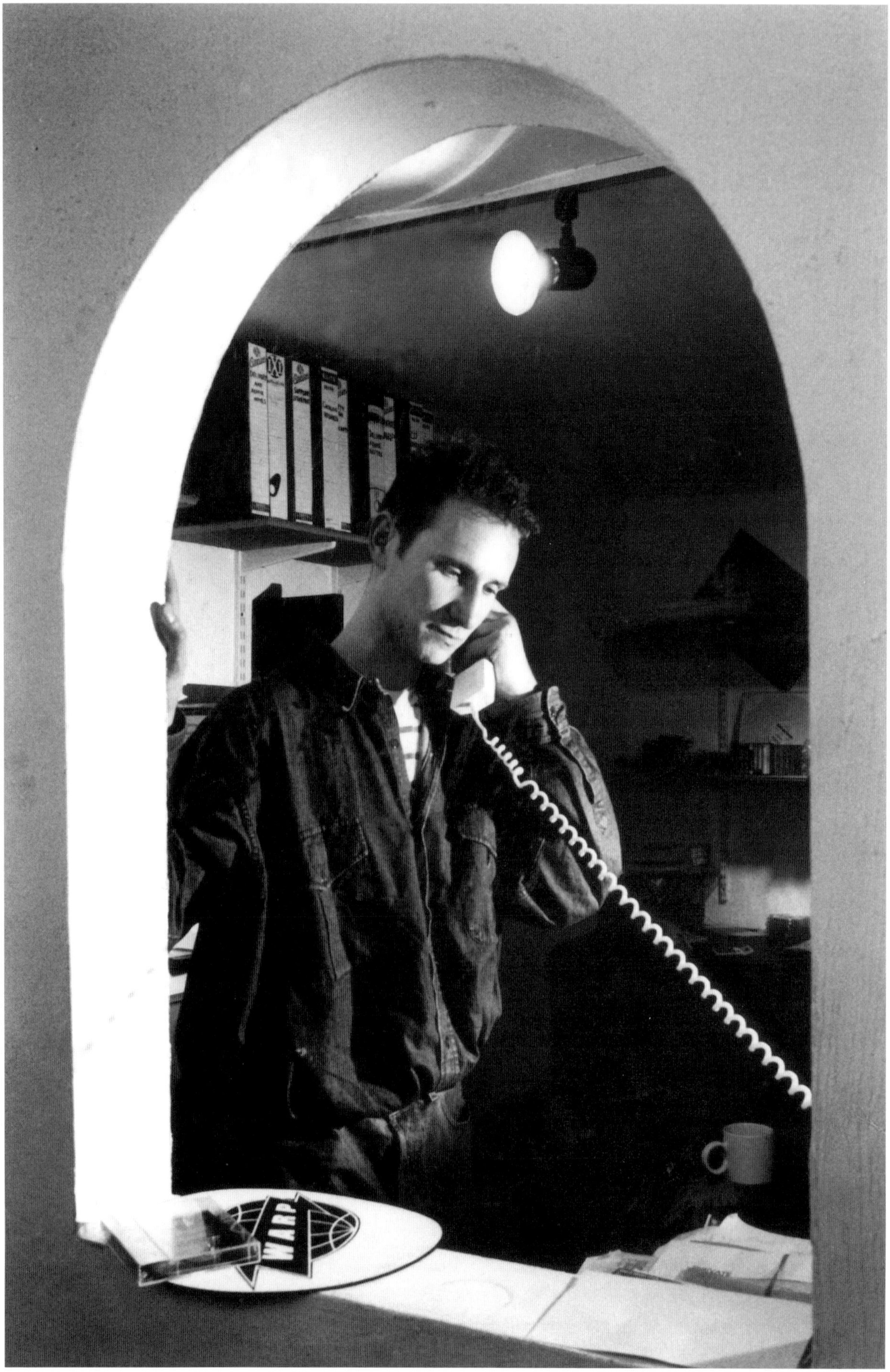
WARP

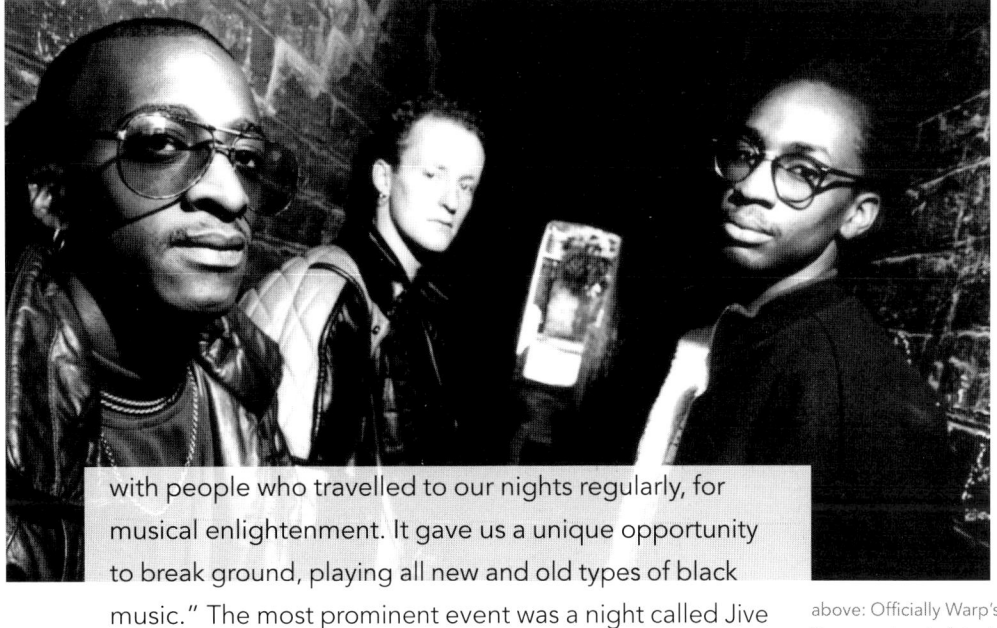

with people who travelled to our nights regularly, for musical enlightenment. It gave us a unique opportunity to break ground, playing all new and old types of black music." The most prominent event was a night called Jive Turkey, where he played out with Richard Barratt (aka DJ Parrot) at a sweatbox called Occasions.

Another club, Cuba, at Kiki's on Wednesday nights, acted as a sonic laboratory. In case anyone might think he wasn't working hard enough, Hazel also hosted three radio shows on the pirate station SCR. He claims to have been "the first DJ to blend soul, House, Techno, hiphop, electro and jazz on the airwaves" – at any rate his transmissions ranged far over the North of England, reaching other industrial cities like Manchester, Leeds, Hull and Nottingham. On his radio shows, Hazel would exhort listeners to bring their homemade tapes to the club: "The first breed of bedroom producers started bringing recordings to the Cuba club to hear their tracks played on a club sound system and to gauge a dancefloor response," he says. "Nearly all the early Warp tracks were first given dancefloor air and tested on a well-versed crowd. LFO, The Step, Tomas and Tuff Little Unit were all given maximum rotation."

In 1989 his day job was at the FON record shop, where he found a natural partner in Robert Gordon. "I knew Robert from childhood as the guy no one sees," says Hazel, "because he was into his electronics – building and fixing." Hazel remembers Gordon inviting him into his house one day to make a track on a roomful of studio equipment he'd just had delivered – paid for with the proceeds of his production work on Yazz's *Wanted* LP at FON Studios. "I took along Manu Dibango's 'Abele Dance' for sampling. Our friend Sean Maher was also present. It took us six hours from start to finish and Rob recorded it on to a TDK Metal Tape cassette so that I could play it on the radio to get a response."

above: Officially Warp's first artists: The Forgemasters. Left to right: Winston Hazel, Sean Maher, Robert Gordon.
opposite: Rob Mitchell works the phones at Warp's first, cramped office behind the record shop at Division Street. Photo: David Bocking.

WARP FACTORY

There's a buzz about Sheffield like there hasn't been for years, and this time around it's not industrial funk or glossy pop, but hardcore dance that has brought about the feeling of togetherness. Be you in Leeds, Manchester or London, you hear the same name time and time again, WARP. Warp is a record shop, Warp is a label, Warp is three guys with their finger on the pulse of a city sound. But who are they?

Steve Beckett and Rob Mitchell run the shop and label with the help of famed producer Robert Gordon, who, as well as being Warps production head honcho, and part of the acclaimed Fon Force unit, is half of the Forgemasters. It was their debut, Track With No Name, which kicked off the fledgling label with a 500-run white label issue that reputably sold out in a week at a mere handful of Northern dance music shops.

Robert Gordon "There's talent seeping from the fingernails of Sheffield, but for a while there was no real access to the release button for this new power. We had the ability to solve the problem, hence the birth of Warp. There's no hype, no scam, no gimmick, the talent was there, and now it has an outlet. There are other good labels like Mr Modo, Native and so on, but what they release doesn't overlap with our material."

Sheffield is a city geared towards the production of quality sounds. The musical infrastructure was set up in the late 70's and early 80's by bands like Cabaret Voltaire, Clock DVA and so on, who set up studios in the city for almost the first time. People saw numerous pop stars like ABC and Heaven 17 down at their local pub, normal Joe's, just like them. Why, as I write these notes an old timer called Phil Oakey just walked into the cafe. Thus was bred an inborn belief that you didn't need to leave town to get on. Sheffield is self-contained in a musical/media sense. It has all the contacts, all the facilities, all the self-confidence necessary. Beyond that it has a local government which supports its peoples wishes.

The latest innovation is the setting up of the massive Red Tape media complex down by the station, where they've encouraged anyone and everyone involved in music, radio, TV, film and design to relocate. The Human League, Chakk/Fon, Warp and other studios are all to be found here, as is the new Yorkshire Radio Network, (an amalgam of Radio Aire from Leeds, Hallam Radio, and all the ILR stations). The idea is that the Government will make Sheffield the base for Channel 5, though Conservative Bradford is the chief rival.

Steve Beckett "The City Council are admirable and far-sighted. It was a way-out idea, brought to fruition without any obvious cock-ups. Plus a commercially viable operation that will benefit everyone."

The importance of the Warp shop shouldn't be overlooked either. Originally they were based in the tiny FON shop, (an organisation they are unconnected to) but have just opened in much larger premises a few yards down the road at 40 Division Street, the old shop now being devoted to selling CD's. The new Warp outlet is, as usual, specialising in dance and independent music, a pure enthusiasts shop for people who are interested enough to walk the 200 yards up from the city centre. It was in this environment that the links with the like-minded dance community were forged. George, of Nightmares On Wax, the Leeds act whose 'Dextrous' re-recording became the second Warp release, actually walked into the shop trying to sell some of his own white labels of the track and was jumped upon by Steve, who'd heard it at a club the week before and had been searching desperately for it everywhere.

Meanwhile Rhythm King, the dance giants of the independent scene, wanted in on the action.

Rob Mitchell "They originally wanted to just licence The Forgemasters off us, but we weren't into that idea, so they said 'Let us support you as associates, and you use our structure as necessary' which was amazing. We wouldn't have dreamed of asking for that kind of deal in our position; a single white label release to our credit. We liked their attitude, they've accepted us as an autonomous organisation who find, develop, produce and release our own talent, with a active role in the marketing, and basically, total control over all

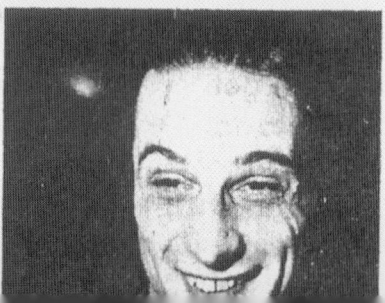

SHEFFIELD

the aspects that make a record label distinctive. We use the Rhythm King structure in areas like publicity and international negotiations."

The deal elevated Warp from minor league to major players with access to pressing plants and video budgets if the need arises. Yet, remember, there are still only two records available, and one of those a re-release. So how come the buzz?

Rob "People realise that we know what we're doing. We've got very strong connections with most Northern club deejays and dance specialists, they've heard the white label stuff we put out. We've got the right people and they know it. Nightmares On Wax have led us indirectly to two more great Leeds acts, and even today we signed another lot from up there, LFO, a trio with tons of incredible house sounds."

"I first heard LFO at Cuba (the hot hot hot night club run by Jive Turkey)", pumps in Robert Gordon, "It was so good I asked the DJ, Winston, what the record was, and he said it was a C90 tape that someone had handed to him. We didn't waste much time after hearing that."

Cuba, at KiKi's on Wednesday nights, acts like a mixture of testing ground and A & R department for Warp. DJ's Parrot and Winston are Robert Forgemasters partners, (not forgetting Parrot's flirtation with chart stardom in his Funky Worm guise). In Sheffield they are very particular about their dance music, they like it hard. Cuba don't play no pop, and it's people don't want none, you dig? You soon discover if a track can cut it or not.

The current floor crusher is the potential Sheffield dance anthem, (or so they kept telling me) Testone. a jerky hardcore sound that James Hamilton might refer to as a percolating, zippity spunker, or maybe not. More heard about than heard, everyone will be pleased to know that it fully justifies its legendary reputation. Apparently the first time it was aired, the dancefloor halted spontaneously to applaud. Of course, all this is helped by the fact that Testone was produced by Parrot and Richard Kirk of Cabaret Voltaire.

Robert "About 30% of the stuff played at Cuba is Sheffield originated. A lot of demo tapes are tried out, it's total hardcore dance. People never appreciate the direct parallel of Acid and Punk, the same methods of getting new ideas and sounds across to people are being used, there's a similar energy. The old punks should realise that their heroes would be into house if they were starting out today. Dance music is the cutting edge."

Steve "I can't believe people who say 'This house stuff will die out.' Of course it bloody will. Everything has its time, and this is NOW, this is where innovation is happening."

Robert "So many people jumped on the House bandwagon that I thought it would be killed off, but something strange happened, it split into two distinct strains, chart house and original. The peoples feeling for dance music wouldn't let it die."

For the immediate future, you'll find Warp remix work on Outer Rhythm's Man Machine release and there's talk of working over the next Stone Roses single to name but two. However, remix mania is beginning to bug the Sheffield boys, Mark Brydon, the ex-funky bassist of Chakk, and Robert Gordons partner in his Fon Force producer form, says that he's sick and tired of giving away his original work to other acts in this way. A moan echoed by Warp, who fear becoming a flavour of the month to the big companies. From their own acts look out for LFO material, a Forgemasters album, and a new single called ("Oooh! Can we tell him? No!") 'Computer Warrior',(Shhhh! Why did you tell him? That's a World exclusive that is Ronnie.') Also, new Nightmares On Wax tracks. More secretive muttering produces the name Sweet Exorcist, ('Our biggest secret') which may or may not be the Testone moniker. Either way, rare white labels aside, Outer Rhythm will be bringing it all to a shop near you.

A combination of good taste, good fortune and cool heads has brought the Warp trio a long way in a few short months, any two from three is sure to keep them there. **Words and pics by Ronnie Randall**

city beat

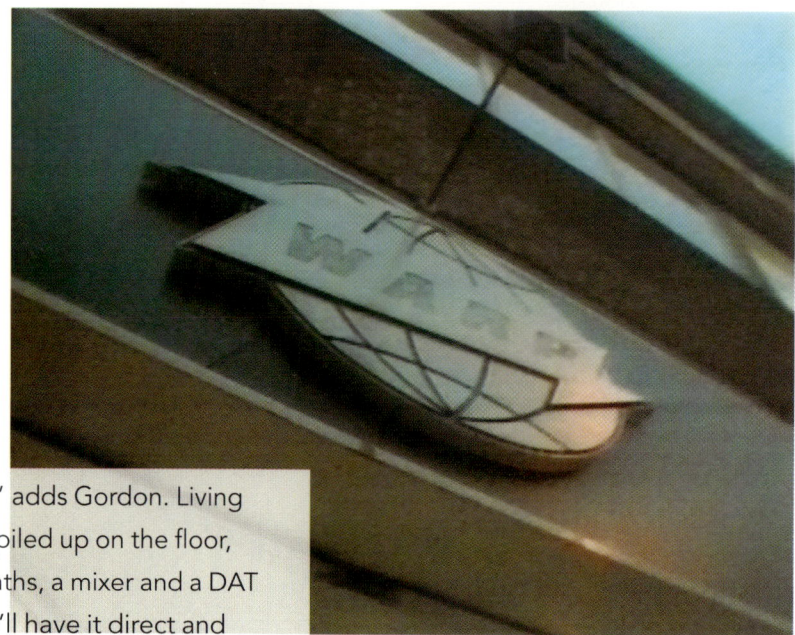

"It was extremely casual," adds Gordon. Living room floor, all the synths piled up on the floor, with one sampler, two synths, a mixer and a DAT machine. No effects. We'll have it direct and cheap, with no special effects, but let's also have it punchy, meaty, good bass."

Hazel: "We got so excited but couldn't think of a title for it, so we decided 'Track With No Name' would do for now. Then we realised that we needed to have an artist name too. We agreed the track was tuff like wrought iron, and named ourselves after Sheffield Forgemasters steelworks. The next day I played it on my radio show and the response was awesome – tons of phone calls."

Forgemasters played at clubs around the country and, in Hazel's extended industrial metaphor, "tore them up and left them for scrap". Robert Gordon remembers Hazel phoning him from a club, begging him to come down immediately. "He said, 'Rob, you've got to come to the club', because he and Parrot were DJing, and when I got to the club, the cassette of 'Track With No Name' was the biggest track of the night. Winston said, 'I'm gonna play it, now watch…'."

As Gordon watched the crowd went mental to the tune's popping electro-percussion suckers and frenetic synthetic hi-hats, he decided to press up 1000 white label copies. They sold out in a week. A self-confessed "audiophile-style producer", by this time he had worked on high profile production and remix projects for (among others) Jaki Graham, Afrika Bambaataa, UB40 and Joyce Sims, as part of the FON Force team. The popularity of the Forgemasters cut pointed towards a new future for his own music, production skills and the experience he had gained in the industry thus far. This is how he recalls what happened next:

Images of the Warp shop, from a 1991 TV report on the rise of Warp and the Sheffield 'bleep' revolution.

"I went back to the shop and suggested the idea: let's start a label, I've got this record, as you know it's selling; let's start a label all together. I suggested the name Warp, I suggested the colour purple, I suggested the thing with the lightning running through it, you name it. They were basically juniors who'd just left university running their little record shop."

Still, "Track With No Name", officially released on 17 August 1989, couldn't have been a more apt way for Warp Records to launch itself on the ocean of sound. The business grew rapidly, with Mitchell and Beckett manning the shop and fielding many of the calls and visits from prospective artists dropping off demo tapes, and Gordon holding down his job at the FON production desk and bringing to the Warp table his experience of contracts, publishing rights and mastering. "There's no appreciation for the amount of research that went into those records," he complains. "It's not a fluke, why they were good. All the Warp records at that time were cut at Virgin's Townhouse. I insisted on that. There was a guy there, Kevin Metcalfe, who cut the whole of the Greensleeves catalogue. Listen to any Greensleeves record: there's never anything wrong with it."

In September 1989 Mitchell said, "It may be that we can have chart successes without doing any lightweight stuff, but there could be less hardcore things we find that we realise can still be good records. However, they would probably be on something of ours with a different name, so that the identity of Warp will remain hardcore dance and hopefully its successes will be as a result of the charts waking up to what a lot of people are listening to."[2]

2. Mitchell, Rob, quoted in interview with Ian McGregor, *Echoes*, 30 September, 1989.

Beckett agreed, adding the terse projection of Warp becoming a "recognised, credible, uncompromising hard dance label". They were in an advantageous position, as Beckett noted, "We're selling music to people every day. The shop is our market research department."[3]

" I remember the period as being quite exciting, with many warehouse parties, loads of people discovering MDMA for the first time. A bit like casting off the past in the same manner as punk. Very DIY. Warp often came to the Cabaret Voltaire studio, Western Works, to listen to mixes and blag other favours, and I think they kind of enjoyed the connection with Sheffield's electronic heritage."
Richard H Kirk

Richard H Kirk, a founder member of the legendary Sheffield group Cabaret Voltaire, found himself increasingly sucked into the nocturnal world of Sheffield's underground club scene during the 1980s. CV had existed since 1974 and had already laid down many of the blueprints for DIY electronic music, specialising in paranoid cut-up sampling influenced overtly by WS Burroughs. Remembering Jive Turkey and Cuba, Kirk recalls those nights as: "Pretty crowded, everyone seemed to be 'on one', great atmosphere and excellent music – Detroit, New York, Chicago, Leeds/Bradford/Sheffield. Also very mixed ethnically – black, white, Asian, males, females, and no violence. When they first dropped [Sweet Exorcist's] 'Testone', spontaneous applause broke out! At the end, they used to play Soul II Soul's 'Back To Life' – people stood on tables singing along, and then went on to another party."

Rob Gordon, says Parrot, "helped me and Kirky when we were fighting with the Atari over 'Testone'", remixing it to a standard fit for official release. He had given the same treatment to "Dextrous", the second Warp single, another lo-fi production by Leeds outfit Nightmares On Wax

3. Beckett, Steve, quoted in Ronnie Randall, "Sheffield: City Beat", *Jocks*, February 1990.

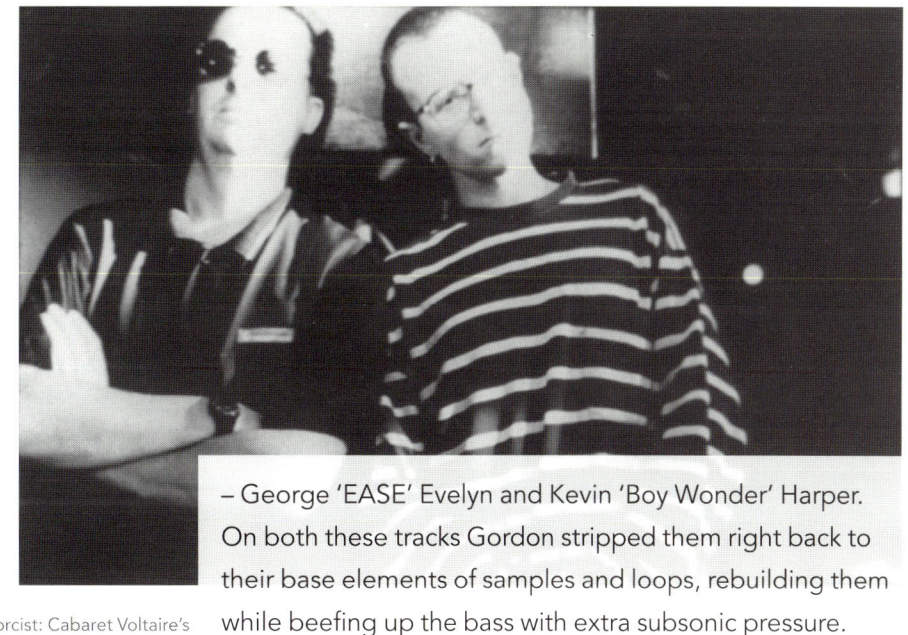

– George 'EASE' Evelyn and Kevin 'Boy Wonder' Harper. On both these tracks Gordon stripped them right back to their base elements of samples and loops, rebuilding them while beefing up the bass with extra subsonic pressure.

Sweet Exorcist: Cabaret Voltaire's Richard H Kirk (left) and DJ Parrot.

Signed to Virgin since 1983, Cabaret Voltaire had increasingly pushed into a more dance orientated production style much cleaner than their early gritty subversive cut-ups like "Nag Nag Nag" or "Do The Mussolini (Headkick)".

"Cabaret Voltaire kind of split for a while after [1987's] *Code* album," says Kirk. "I had known DJ Parrot since the mid 80s from the Sheffield club scene and we had planned to work on a project together, which eventually became Sweet Exorcist. We started to work on some tracks, which were put on hold after Parrot had some chart success as The Funky Worm [the track 'Hustle']. After Funky Worm had finished, Parrot approached me to help make a dance record using studio test tones, which we did. This record was aimed specifically at the crowd who went to Jive Turkey. With a nod of the head to Unique 3's 'The Theme' [generally considered the archetypal 'bleep' Techno track], a sensibility taking in Detroit Techno, dub-style bass, and a general vibe of electronic weirdness in the Sheffield vein. Cabaret Voltaire did become a little too mainstream for me at the time – too many outside influences pulling in the wrong direction! So 'Testone' was payback time."

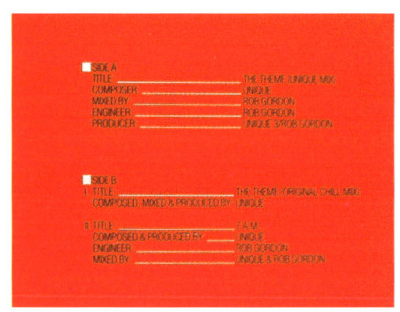

Bradford outfit Unique 3's track "The Theme" (10/Virgin 1989): the original British 'bleep' Techno tune, and a big influence on the first wave of Warp singles. Rob Gordon's engineering and remixing credits are stamped over many crucial underground dance releases around this time.

Stills from the video for Sweet Exorcist's "Testone", 1990, directed by Martin Wallace and Jarvis Cocker: low-res sci-fi that perfectly mirrors the track's production values.

A disembodied voice, preparing to signal to the alien mothership with a Moog synthesizer in *Close Encounters Of The Third Kind*, opens the third track to appear on Warp. Sweet Exorcist's "Testone" is a lo-fi and urgent take on the prefab House of 808 State, although its yearning chords have a sense of mystery and evocation, of *reaching*, that much of the Acid scene failed to provide. Rhythm boxes puff away like pistons or steam engine components. A video used jerky samples of clunky Space Invaders blips and the BBC testcard girl twiddling with an analogue synth.

The process of recording it was "quite slow and we did lots of mixes/edits before we had the right one", Kirk recalls. "We were mainly trying to make a record that would work at Jive Turkey, but I guess minimal works better for dance music. I think we spent a lot of time trying to get the bass to sound right, which was, and still is, very important for dance tracks – you need to physically feel it as well as hear it."

Interviewed on television at the time, Parrot commented, "Proper Techno is really intricate stuff, like if you listen to Derrick May's records – they're like symphonies, so well arranged. The stuff from up here is really simple, I don't know why they call it Techno at all, it's much closer to House, maybe people are equating those bleeps on the records with Techno."[4]

Two years before, an electronic revolution had reached its apex in British music. Several industrial metropolises around the world – namely Detroit, Chicago, Manchester, the triple Pennine cities of Sheffield/Bradford/Leeds and Frankfurt, had crosswired in a thicket of twining connections, and appeared to be sending coded signals between themselves in the form of bleeps and beats. In the American rustbelt, Detroit was deeply depressed, crime waves and dead urban nonplaces opening up a vacuum in which, along with the spread of lawlessness, left the Motor City's drive belt idling

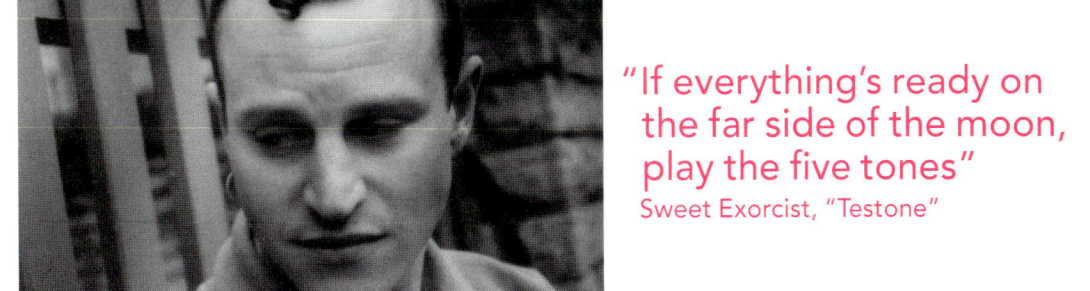

> "If everything's ready on the far side of the moon, play the five tones"
> Sweet Exorcist, "Testone"

and looking for traction on some new engine. In the vacated factory warehouses, the city's young people were gathering under the sign of the new trance Techno played by Juan Atkins (formerly Cybotron, active since the early 80s in the wake of German acts like Kraftwerk), Derrick May's Rhythim Is Rhythim, Theo Parrish, Jeff Mills, Kenny Larkin, Stacey Pullen, and the uncompromising, paranoid outfit Underground Resistance, that conducted itself more like an urban sonic guerrilla squad than a party collective. Similar shifts were occurring in Chicago, where a trio called Phuture had gotten hold of a Roland TB-303 Bass Line. This slim chrome-cased box was drily marketed as a musical tool: "Take a bass synthesizer that is programmable (in real time or not) like a sequencer," said an early advert. "Make it transposable across 3 octaves, add accent and slide. Leave resonance and envelope modulation control to be varied at pleasure."

But they didn't know how deep that pleasure would reach. Young Chicagoans like Phuture, Marshall Jefferson, Larry Heard aka Mr Fingers, Armando and Lil'Louis wrenched it into a totally new world of tortured squelches and sarcastic belchings, twining it with mechanical programmed beats. The characteristic of the Roland product was its license to transform sounds in real time, with unusually tactile control knobs, which meant that electronic music was not just a locked up system of preprogrammed outcomes but a dynamic sound that could be shifted and mutated right in front of an audience and played intuitively with a certain degree of virtuosity.

top: DJ Parrot (aka Richard Barratt), a prolific DJ on Sheffield's club scene and half of Sweet Exorcist. As The Step, he released "Yeah You!", 1991 (WAP8).

4. DJ Parrot quoted in Dele Fadele, "Warp! What Is It Food For?", *NME*, 25 August, 1990.

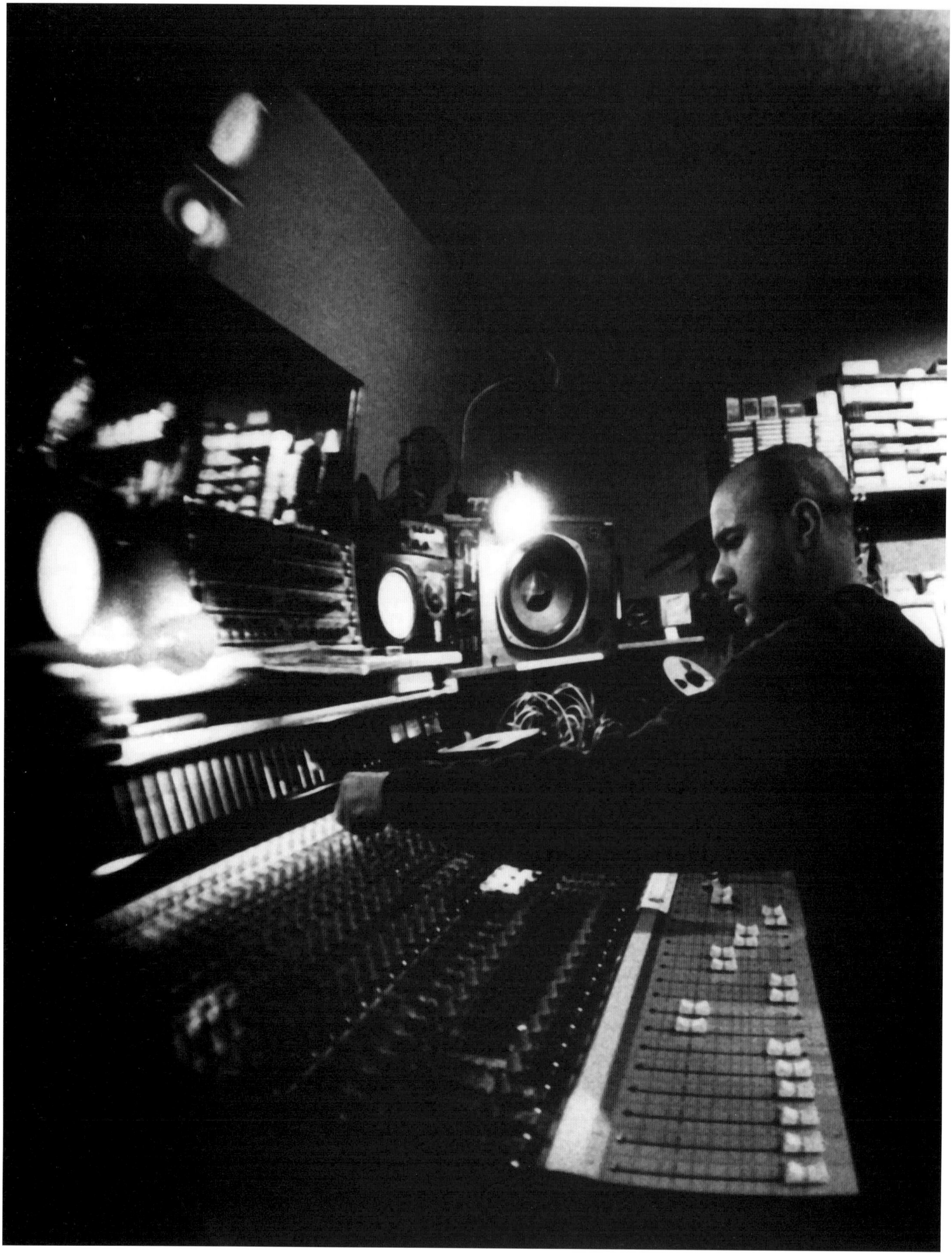

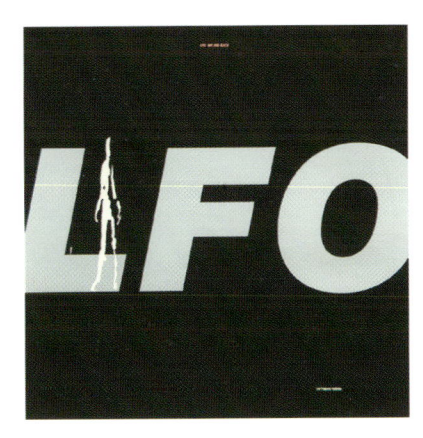

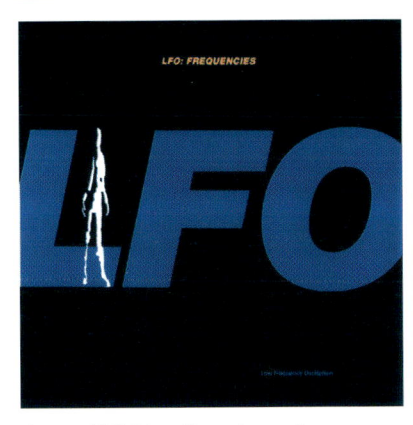

above: LFO's big selling releases from 1990-1992, "We Are Back" (WAP14), "What is House?" EP (WAP17) and the *Frequencies* album (WARP3).
opposite: George 'EASE' Evelyn of Nightmares On Wax drops some studio science.

In Huddersfield, went the rumour, a DJ was playing a track from an unlabelled cassette, that contained a subsonic bass so heavy, it was blowing up club sound systems and shattering everything from windows to punters' ear canals. Beckett and Mitchell began to sleuth down this sonic marvel. They ended up in a car park outside a club in Leeds, sitting in a motor vehicle with two teenagers who handed them a tape. Mark Bell and Gez Varley, from Leeds, had danced at Nightmares On Wax's Downtempo nights during the late 80s where they would have soaked up a cunning mix of hiphop, electro, 70s funk and House. As the duo LFO (low frequency oscillators), they came up with "LFO" on a Casio SK1 synth, handed it to Nightmares On Wax, who in turn passed it to Warp. In a few weeks the track was out on Warp and became their biggest hit – charting at number 12, with total sales of 130,000. It was so successful, even LFO's progenitors sat up and took notice: both Afrika Bambaataa and members of Kraftwerk requested their collaboration in the aftermath of the hit.

The opening track on their 1991 album, *Frequencies*, is "What Is House?". The question showed that dance music had reached a new level of sophistication and self-awareness, acknowledging its dues to an established canon while simultaneously critiquing and advancing it. Heavily muffled by a vocoder, a voice at the beginning asks, "What is House? To me House is Phuture, Pierre, Fingers, Adonis, Brian Eno, Kraftwerk, Depeche Mode and The Yellow Magic Orchestra… this album is dedicated to you."

— We are both 21   [LFO]

When Warp told us that Karl + Wolfgang had sent them a fax saying that they'd like to meet us we thought Warp were lying, we just couldnt beleive it. We went to Dusseldorf to do a trak with them (Elektric), which was really interesting, using keyboards + drum machines that we've never seen before. Most electronic Music at the moment you can tell exactly where all the sounds are from, but the noises that we used on 'Information' were created from old keyboards which have been modified so the noises are just so different. Karl, Emil, Wolfgang + lothar are really nice people as well, we thought they'd be really arrogant but they were just normal normal with a wierd sense of humour.

When we start a track it all begins + in my bedroom then depending on the quality of the samples etc. we decide wether to record it at my house or the studio.

Both of us play the guitar keyboards and clarinet. We're not very good at the clarinet yet.

We speak to anyone who listens to our music. A lot of it hasn't any lyrics but different tones make feel me sad or happy. We hope other people can feel it to.

I thought the Mix was okay. there was some clever little bits like the Cyber Choir on Autobahn but everyone's heard all those ideas before and other people have sampled the old kraftwerk tunes and used them more creastivley.

When we start developing a trak we try to make it sound beautiful or moving in some way then make it danceble.

On the new album there are four or five traks with acoustic instruments (Sitar, koto, guitar, Clarinet) I've no idea why there isn't any women common to techno bands.

previous pages: LFO's handwritten interview faxed to a Japanese magazine circa 1992. this page: Tricky Disco (Michael Wells and Lee Newman), and their singles "Tricky Disco", 1990 (WAP7), and "Housefly", 1991 (WAP11).

As the pre-Grunge early 90s arrived with a wave of gloom about the future of independent rock – the pillar of the indie community, Rough Trade, went into receivership in mid 1991 – Warp was firing on all cylinders, boosted by a financing deal with US label Rhythm King. By November 1990, the *Sheffield Star* was reporting that "A recent survey shows that Warp ... now claims 1.4 per cent of record sales in Britain, only a slight way behind long established labels like Chrysalis, Sire and Mercury, and above others with a higher media profile."

Nightmares on Wax's "Aftermath", which charted in late 1990, would be the last hit for another two years. In 1991, singles by The Step, Sweet Exorcist's "Clonk" (trumpeted as a successor style to the bleep), Tomas, Tricky Disco and Nightmares On Wax failed to follow through on the previous year's advance. At the same time, an unbridgeable rift opened up within Warp as Gordon fell out with Beckett and Mitchell. According to Gordon, they had first clashed over Tricky Disco, a side project by the GTO duo of London based Lee Newman and Michael Wells. When they visited the group in London, they heard two tracks. Gordon wanted to sign up both, but the other partners preferred the signature tune "Tricky Disco", which would eventually provide Warp with a number 14 hit. Soon after, Gordon suggested paying a nominal sum to license Chicago House track "Can't Stop", by Plez, which had just transfixed a crowd during a Winston Hazel DJ set. "Some tiny little label in America," says Gordon, "they'll respect 500 quid for this, they'd no idea how big it was in Sheffield. So I went into the office, I was like, 'I think we should sign Plez. [They replied] 'We don't license records!' I say, we do now: let's license Plez! 'We can't afford it!' Of course we can, phone them up, ask them… Massive argument."

Legend has it that Gordon's chunky phone was thrown during the exchange. "Shortly after that, Rob [Mitchell] says, what we've decided is, we're 66 per cent of the company and you're only 33 per cent of the company – we're voting you out." Aside from the negotiation of a release contract, that would be Robert Gordon's final face to face meeting with his erstwhile partners.

With Gordon's influence gone, the Warp sound began to change. Two compilation albums tell the story of Warp at this time: the title of *Pioneers Of The Hypnotic Groove*, released in mid 1991, sought to stake a claim on the heart of the electronic revolution slowly taking shape. A year later, *Evolution Of The Groove* collected nine tracks sourced by Warp over the previous 12 months, but in retrospect has the ring of a swansong for this phase of the label. It led off with "Feel It", an anthem by Coco, Steel & Lovebomb, the studio alias of Chris 'Coco' Mellor, who ran a regular night at Brighton's Zap Club.

"It was like a big extended family," Mellor says. "Obviously it had a lot to do with Ecstasy, but the whole atmosphere, there was a sense of togetherness: 'It's us, we've got this thing, and not a lot of other people know about it'. It was our secret, our shared, fantastic experience."

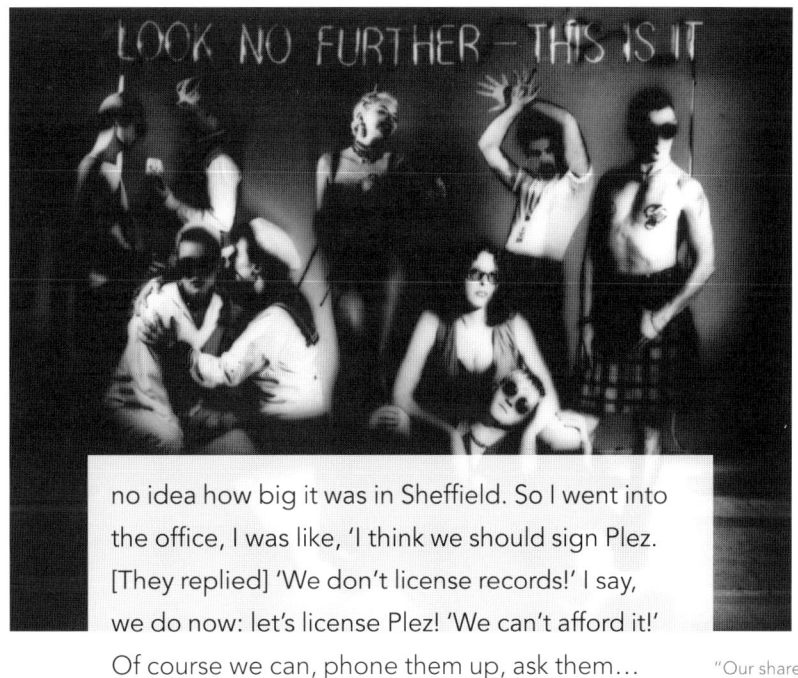

"Our shared fantastic experience": Coco, Steel & Lovebomb camp it up circa 1992 (Chris Coco reclining in foreground).

> "The nice people at Warp HATE the word bleep because they reckon it's going to kill off everything in the so-called Northern scene before it gets a chance to breathe."
> Anonymous TV presenter

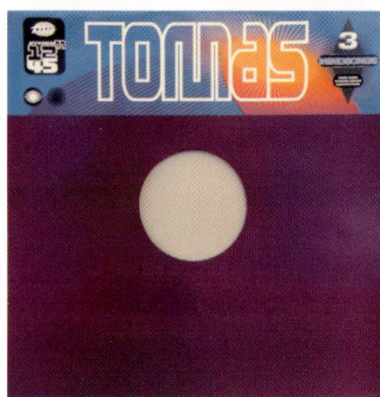

top: Clonk's coming: Sweet Exorcist's last single at the end of 1990 (WAP9) tried to coin a shortlived successor to the bleep. bottom: Tomas (Thomas Stewart) released one single, the progressive House track "Mindsongs" (WAP10), then promptly disappeared from music making altogether.

"Feel It", recorded during late night sessions in London, was intended as a distillation of the Coco Club's music policy. "It was quite messy and bassy and dubby, with a little tribal groove running through it. It was massive in Brighton, a real anthem." Mellor, who went on to become the editor of *DJ Magazine* during the mid 90s and eventually a DJ for BBC Radio 1, retains recollections that are typical for the time, a blur of good vibes and loved-up positive energy. But "Feel It" represented an era in dance music that Warp was soon to leave behind. Such positivist anthems became a staple of 90s club culture, but Warp's next move would take them further into the realm of the solitary artist. As it turned out, the music represented on *Evolution Of The Groove* would prove to be an evolutionary dead-end.

In September 1992, a local newspaper trumpeted Warp's continued growth: "A successful dance label with at least three major hit singles behind them and a worldwide mailing list which goes to 12,000 people. Add to that a turnover in the last financial year of £1.2 m (including Warp Records and shop, plus publishing company)... and you have a business which has established itself in no small way."[5]

Sweet Exorcist's "Clonk" laconically attempted to supersede the bleep, as Warp was tired of being pigeonholed. As an unidentified presenter on local TV culture show *PS* reported in 1991, "The nice people at Warp HATE the word bleep because they reckon it's going to kill off everything in the so-called Northern scene before it gets a chance to breathe." The clonk was described as having "a bass like the kind of noise a blue whale would make if it had been raised on a diet of 70s funk and sent swimming through a sea of soft

5. Quinn, John, "Music With Warp Factor", *Sheffield Star*, 21 November 1990.

toffee. The clonk – brought to you by the originators of the bleep, Sweet Exorcist – takes us further from the tune, but also fills in the middle bits that the bleep forgot."

By 1991 rave and breakbeat had swept through British clubs, and House was swiftly becoming entrenched as the mainstream dance music form. The run of hits in the early 90s had not been repeated, and the kind of tapes Warp was starting to receive did not look like being able to seduce a mass audience. For the first time, Warp felt the imperative to reassess, change with the times and keep moving forwards and away from the pack. Warp had brought a sense of self-analysis to House that left it in an unanticipated position, but by *Evolution Of The Groove* it was in danger of coming full circle and ending up as another bland purveyor of crowd-pleasing anthems. The compilation celebrates the peak and the demise of Warp's own House brand.

Chris Coco: "That's all you can do with a label: you get that moment, and you go with it, and the difficult bit is what you do after that. How you survive until the next moment comes along. But they have managed to do that."

Coco, Steel & Lovebomb's glam, neon-lit Ambient House shone briefly but didn't fit the emerging Warp attitude.

```
    WARP

Artificial Intelligence film (Motion)

@ Robin Rimbaud's Amazing Electronic Lounge
(9.02pm>1.02am)
Monday May 23 @ The ICA  The Mall London SW1
Admission: £1.50/£1.00 student/ub40
(Motion) performances: 10pm + 11pm


DJ Tony Morley plus drinking + talking
Scanner will be giving a talk entitled
(The Pros and Cons of the TX 434 Squelch Button)



23 fluxed giraffes
```

Flyer for the London premiere of *Motion*, the animated digital film accompanying Warp's *Artificial Intelligence II* CD, at the Electronic Lounge club at the Institute of Contemporary Arts. The success of this launch helped cement Warp as a force to be reckoned with in the London based media.

Artificial Intelligence

How electronic music moved from dancefloor to armchair

As 1992 got underway, Steve Beckett and Rob Mitchell were in a position to impose their own tastes and interests on Warp's output. In July, Warp released a various artists album called *Artificial Intelligence*. With a strong curatorial feel, it featured nine tracks by six artists new to Warp – The Dice Man, Musicology, Autechre, IAO, Speedy J and UP! – plus a closing version by The Orb's Dr Alex Paterson of the Ambient supergroup's "Loving You" live. Paterson aside, these artists represented a slightly younger generation of musicians than the first wave of Warp personnel. Most were born this side of 1970, which put them in their mid-teens during the mid 80s, growing up on a diet of electro and hiphop on compilations like the *Street Sounds* series, as well as video games and early home computers. Geographically they stemmed from all over the UK and abroad, rather than Warp's Pennines hot zone.

The Dice Man's "Polygon Window" track was by a young prodigy called Richard D James. He came from Cornwall, the furthest south west appendix of Britain, where various clubs around Penzance picked up on the burbly sound of Hardcore and Acid at the tail end of the 80s. Around 1990-1991, at venues like the Bowgie in Crantock, Grant Wilson-Claridge, Richard James and Luke Vibert would DJ old school hiphop and electro, laced with a frenzied dose of breakbeat at deafening volume to kids hopped up on cider and black. "Polygon Window", the track, advertised another of the many aliases James was already using by this time, but he was best known as AFX or The Aphex Twin. Other artists featured on *Artificial Intelligence* were Autechre's Sean Booth and Rob Brown, who had bonded in Manchester when they

listening

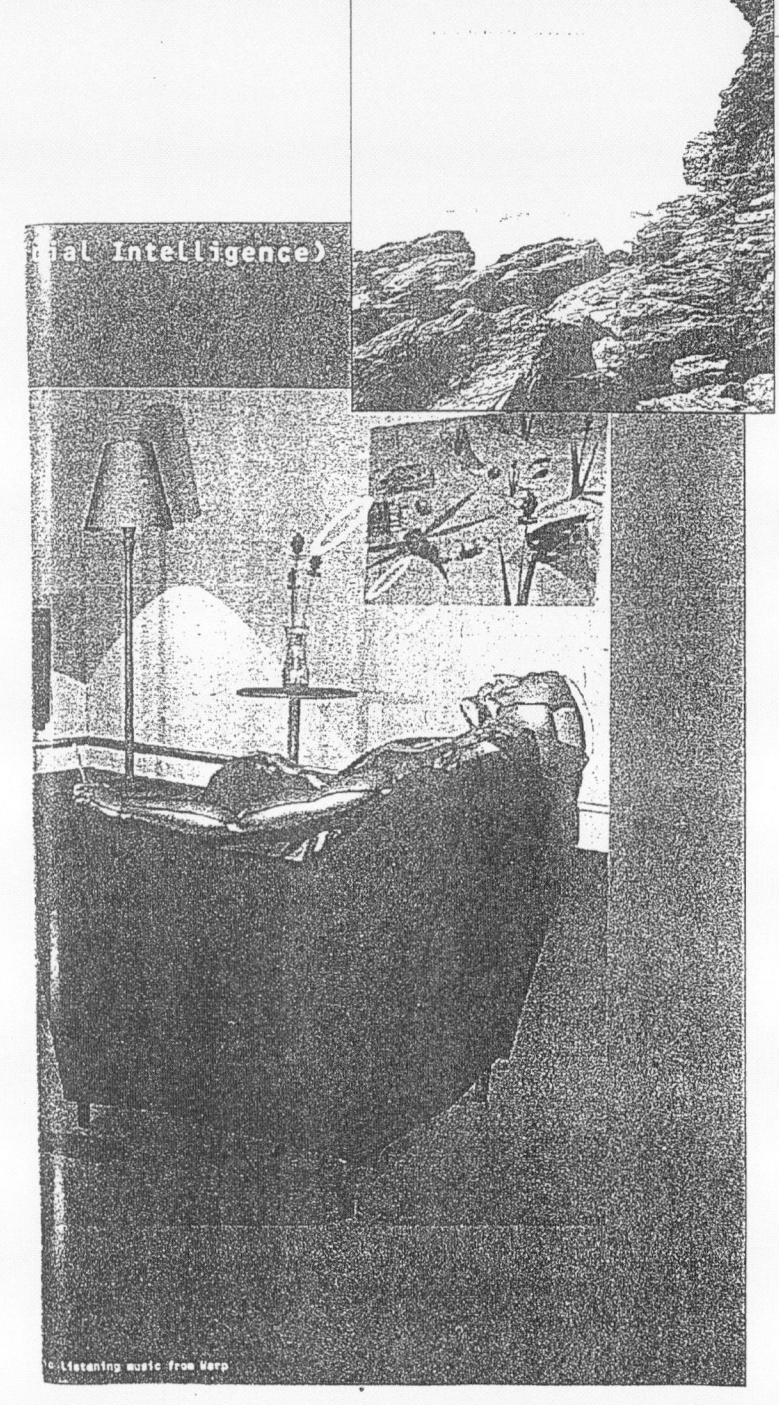

WARP RECORDS LTD

POLYGON WINDOW

RICHARD James, aka the Aphex Twin, Polygon Window, Caustic Window and a million other aliases, is, according to the Mixmag readership survey, your most popular artist, a joint tie along with Sasha and The Prodigy.

From the seminal 'Didgeridoo' - a 156bpm monster that kicked hardcore back into credibility - to the highly rated 'Selected Ambient Works' double LP for R&S to the deeply underground Caustic Window outings on his co-owned Rephlex, James is a master and a maverick of underground techno. Now the rock press have belatedly discovered him, it's been publicity overkill and he's somewhat sick of doing interviews. But he relented for us.

Indeed Aphex could be the first rock and roll techno star. Even getting a review in the Independent On Sunday for the recent Midi-Circus tour - where dedicated Aphex Twin fans could be found lining the front of the stage for his set clad in camouflage, boasting to each other about how many times they'd seen him.

LP - 'Surfing On Sine Waves': Edgy, nervy, accomplished stuff that at times carries a disturbing beauty, at others shatters the illusion with an intrusive squelch or a bass drum, as on 'Quixote'. 'Supremacy II' is minimal and schitzoid, 'Quoth', the single, a percussive clang.

Your first reaction to the 'Artificial Intelligence' concept?
"Well I was into albums and stuff because I was sick of doing 12"s. I wanted something to go further and I felt that was a bit of a void in techno."

Your reaction to the final result, 'Artificial Intelligence'?
"I didn't think it was amazing. I thought it was good, though. It showcased some people I hadn't heard of, that was the best thing."

Had you met any of the other artists before? Or since?
"I'm pretty good friends with Richie Hawtin. I don't really know the rest of them. I know Black Dog and B12 but we're not really friends. We're not the same kind of people."

Ever listen to 70s 'electronic' artists like Brian Eno or Kraftwerk?
"I didn't really listen to anything."

Feelings on Warp's category of 'electronic listening music'?
"Wicked. For me it's just shifting views. For me I hate the disposable techno attitude of the last few years. When the first house records came out people used to cherish them."

Do you make a living doing what you do?
"Yeah. I'm getting there. I've been working hard as anyone on deals." [With Sire for the USA and Warp for England.]

Previous employment?
"The best one I did was being a pimp. And before that I was a labourer, earning my equipment money."

What do people do when they're listening to your music?
"I don't care. Fuck knows."

'Artificial Intelligence'? 'Electronic listening music'? Isn't it all a bit pompous? Pretentious?
"A bit, I suppose. I really don't care. I just care about the music."

Most interesting quote the world deserves to hear.
"A maturing of the sound? I think it's too early yet. I don't think anyone's started yet. I haven't started yet and I've been doing it fucking years."

Directors: S.P. Beckett R.O. Mitchell. VAT Reg. No. 534 0349 67. Registered in England No. 2793717. Registered Office: 346 Glossop Road Sheffield S10 2HW

WARP RECORDS LTD

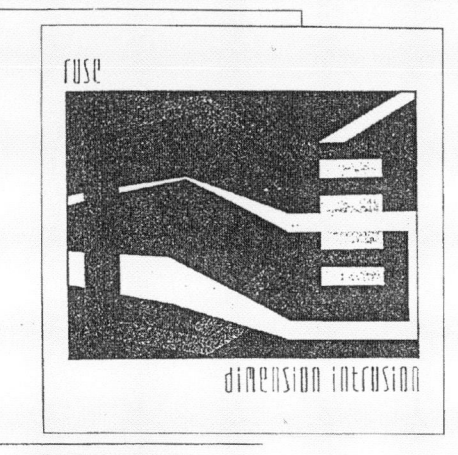

FUSE

RICHIE Hawtin, who is FUSE, amongst other things, was pioneering techno and acid with his own Plus 8 and Probe labels in Detroit long before the current craze for the sound of the 303. He stared off by DJing, and still does.

LP - 'Dimension Intrusion': It's perhaps the closest of these albums to traditional techno, particularly with tracks like the almost banging acid of 'A New Day' and 'Substance Abuse' and the slower trance of 'Mantrax'. Elsewhere tracks like 'Siac' and title track 'Dimension Intrusion' show FUSE can chill with the best of them.

Your first reaction to the 'Artificial Intelligence' concept?
"We had been talking to Rob [Mitchell, of Warp] before it had a name, about this concept thing. When we started [Plus 8] in late '89/'90, Warp was an influence. We liked the concept."

Were you pleased with the results?
"Definitely. The exposure was incredible. When it came out it had the spirit of what we talked about. With our first records, we caught a mood when techno was not a foul word. We were accepted. For the last year or so the trendy people gave techno a bad word and it's good to see everyone just getting into the music again."

Had you met any of the other artists before? Or since?
"I know Richard, B12, Black Dog. Speedy J was pretty much the first big person we signed. He wasn't known at all. He's been with us from the start."

Did you ever listen to 70s 'electronic' artists like Brian Eno or Kraftwerk?
"I was more into Tangerine Dream and Philip Glass."

Feelings on Warp's category of 'electronic listening' music?
"I would call it intelligent electronic music. It leans more towards easy listening. Chill out, trip out, meditation..."

Would you be upset if you heard 'Dimension Intrusion' in a club?
"Oh no. I'd be happy to hear it anywhere."

Do you make a living doing what you do?
"Yeah. I'm in a different position because me and my partner are running a label and DJing. I'm comfortable, but I still live at home. With my mother."

Previous employment?
"I was going to film school - I wanted to be a director of special effects or something. I dropped out of school in my third year."

What do people do when they're listening to your music?
"The last time I listened to it I was sitting in a cold warehouse at about 8 o'clock in the morning with my eyes closed with some friends."

'Artificial Intelligence'? 'Electronic listening music'? Isn't it all a bit pompous? Pretentious?
"I can't say 'no'. A lot of it is very pure. There's two ways of looking at it. In one way it's pretentious, in another it's just people putting out music without worrying about it."

Most interesting quote the world deserves to hear.
"There's enough people who've been into this music long enough that they don't want to just go to a club. It's matured. There has to be different types of music for different moods."

SPEEDY J

SPEEDY J, Jochem Paap to his mother, is the Dutch techno producer who shot to fame with the hardcore anthem 'Pullover' (originally on Plus 8's 'From Our Minds To Yours' LP). His 'Something For Your Mind' was another banging hardcore hit.

He'd also put out plenty of more cerebral techno releases and his contribution to 'Artificial Intelligence', 'De-Orbit' - perhaps one of the most emotionally effective and creative uses of a breakbeat ever - originally appeared on a Plus 8 EP called 'Rise'.

LP - 'Ginger': Paap named his album after the colour of his girlfriend's hair, and it is perhaps the most polished of the set. In the future, groovier shopping centres may well use sections of 'Ginger' in the background, which is not to downgrade the album in any way. Tracks like the wonderful 'Beam Me Up' are distinctly funky and hypnotic, 'Perfect Pitch' is a skeleton of a track, inspired in its simplicity. 'De-Orbit' is a modern classic.

Your first reaction to the 'Artificial Intelligence' concept?
"I had met Rob [from Warp] at Midem [the Cannes music business conference] two years ago and it kind of clicked. I had been interested in Warp's records and Rob had also been interested in Plus 8 and my records. It kind of appealed to me. There were some interesting names, people I really admire."

Had you met any of the other artists before? Or since?
"Just Richie."

Did you ever listen to 70s 'electronic' artists like Brian Eno or Kraftwerk?
"I was always interested in music with electronic sounds, more like the stuff from Trevor Horn and Arthur Baker. The early 12"s. Then it evolved, house music, hip hop. I'm not going to say 'Brain Eno and Kraftwerk are my heroes' - I knew the names. The style I'm going now evolved from dance music."

Feelings on Warp's category of 'electronic listening music'?
"It's a good phrase because it's better than ambient. Ambient, if you look at the phrase, means in the background. This focuses on that it has to be listened to."

Would you be upset if you heard a track from your album in a club?
"There are some tracks that I think would quite impress me if I heard them in a club. But I don't know a club where they would play it."

Do you make a living doing what you do?
"Yeah, quite a good living. I have a company. Everything I do - I do remixes, I do music for other people - everything I make I put in the company."

Previous employment?
"Basically, when I finished school I did this. To finance my equipment, I did some side jobs, stupid jobs, in a factory and stuff."

What do people do when they're listening to your music?
"I don't know. Maybe sit on the couch or drive in the car. Maybe when they come home after an evening clubbing. It's not an album with a purpose."

Most interesting quote the world deserves to hear.
"I like experimental things. I don't think it's too experimental, no more than the worst stuff. I think house and techno are standing still."

Directors: S.P. Beckett R.O. Mitchell. VAT Reg. No. 534 0349 67. Registered in England No. 2793717. Registered Office: 346 Glossop Road Sheffield S10 2HW

discovered the contents of their record bags were identical. They were both turned on by hiphop and electro, particularly Mantronix and Man Parrish, and by the increasingly wordless tracks emerging on pirate radio stations at the dawn of British Hardcore rave. Then there was the Musicology duo of Mike Golding and Steve Rutter, based in Romford, Essex, who had already established operations as B12 and Redcell, overtly influenced by the gleaming sci-fi and extruded surfaces of Detroit electronica. IAO was revealed to be an alias of The Black Dog, an initially reclusive trio who refused to locate themselves (on a map in the sleeve art, they position themselves on an atoll in the mid-Pacific Ocean). Speedy J was Holland based Jochem Paap, while UP! turned out to be a young Canadian named Richie Hawtin from Windsor, in a corner of Ontario just across the lake from Detroit, where he was making a name for himself for his uncompromisingly spartan minimalist 4/4 and Acid wrangling under the names FUSE and Plastikman.

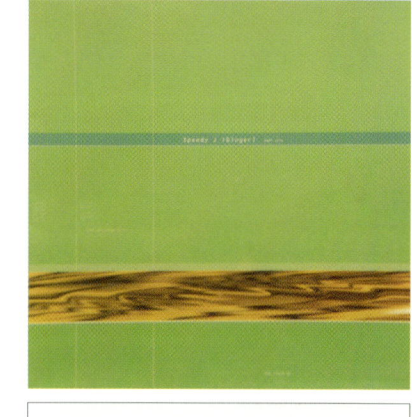

previous pages: Artists' profiles sent out with Warp's press releases for *Artificial Intelligence*, 1992 (WARP6).

Within the next 18 months all these artists would have released albums on Warp, under the banner *Artificial Intelligence*. While the blanket title would come to seem a millstone, at the time it placed the music under a sense of exotic futurity. There was something different about the music's production culture. Increasingly through the early milieu of New York electro and hiphop, and the electronic rave scenes of the late 80s, the gap between fan and artist was rapidly closing – listening to music, making it, engaging in rolling debate about it (on message boards) and releasing it were closely linked activities. And since this new music could be made and recorded in CD quality at home, in a domestic environment, recorded on a small hard disk recorder, the entire cumbersome process of

this page, above and left: The *Artificial Intelligence* series included albums by a new breed of self-reliant artist in 1993: Polygon Window's *Surfing On Sine Waves* (WARP7, Aphex Twin's Warp debut), Black Dog's *Bytes* (WARP8), B12's *Electro Soma* (WARP9), Speedy J's *Ginger* (WARP14) and FUSE's *Dimension Intrusion* (WARP12).

recording a demo, shopping it round record companies, then spending thousands on rerecording a perfect version of the music in studios, was becoming unnecessary.

The difference was, there would be no more chart successes like "LFO". It was less likely you'd ever hear the likes of Autechre, Black Dog or B12 on national radio. The music had wormed its way into a completely different network of listeners and fans, globally connected on internet message boards and discussion forums, which seemed to be its natural habitat. The stereotype of the 'bedroom songwriter' had evolved into the 'bedroom programmer'. Black Dog's early interviews were conducted by email only, to preserve their anonymous mystique. Aphex Twin had a net mailing list set up around his music called the Intelligent Dance Music (IDM) List, which survived long afterwards as the central totem pole around which the tribes of fans of the new electronica would pow-wow and swap stories.

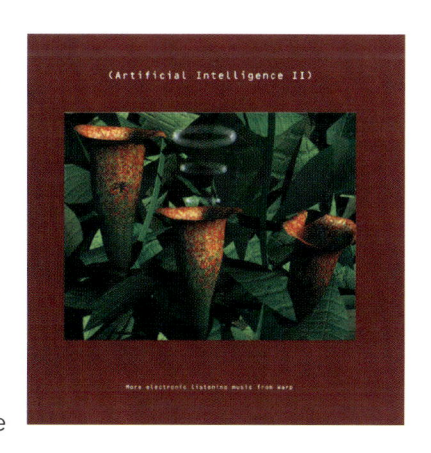

Virtual smoke rings on the hallucinogenic cover of the second *Artificial Intelligence* compilation, 1994 (WARP23).

"If anything really influenced me," Aphex Twin's Richard James told an interviewer in 2003, "it was playing computer games when I was in my early teens. It was realising that you could control things through computers – even the sounds of computer games and the fanfare they make when you're loading them in. I didn't see computers as connected with music making at first. I don't think many people did. Even Kraftwerk was electric keyboards, really."[1] Like many of his generation, James first encountered computers through the domestic units that hit the UK in the early 80s: the Sinclair ZX-81 and Spectrum, Commodore Vic 20 and 64, the BBC Micro. Software for these machines was input via cassette tapes. It was slow to load up and could often come precariously close to crashing these machines

1. James, Richard, quoted in David Stubbs, "Protection Racket", *The Wire*, no. 237, November 2003.

WARP RECORDS LTD

Studio 2 / 1 Brown Street
Sheffield S1 2BS
tel. 0742 757586 / 757505
fax. 0742 757589

ARTIFICIAL INTELLIGENCE

QUOTE:
"The ability of a machine, such as a robot or a computer, to initiate human actions or skills such as problem solving, decision making, perception learning, reasoning, self improvement.

One test for A.I. requires that performance improves with experience or operation; for example, the ability to play a chess game." (Encyclopaedia of Microcomputer Terminology by Linda Gail Christie & John Christie. Unwin paperbacks 1988.)

MISQUOTE 1:
Artificial Intelligence is not a term which was intended to be bastardised into the word Intelligent-Techno. The phrase was never intended to be aimed at "Intelligent" people (whatever *they* are) it was simply computer terminology which seemed appropriate to the style of music and was supposed to be a bit of a tongue-in-cheek dig at the people who said it was music made by computers that had no soul. We were trying to say that the computer was merely a tool to make music and that there was as much emotion in this music as in any other genre.

MISQUOTE 2:
This Album is simply a collection of some of the best artists making experimental or electronic music. This Album is not a collection of Ambient tracks. Ambient music sets a mood but is free from conventional structure.

Music which has a mellow feel or has no beats is often mistakenly called Ambient. Pure ambient music, as the name suggests, is music which sets an ambient feel to the room you are in. The music on this Album is structured and melodic and requires attentive listening. It is not an ambient album.

FUTURE QUOTE:
Where's the music heading? - Into intense, scary soundtracks for films about futuristic lunatic asylums?

Technology is one of the last frontiers where boundaries are being pushed back at an ever increasing rate only to reveal new and more exciting horizons. Technology is allowing people to express themselves by producing the final "product" without having to go through artistically restrictive filters they would have to have gone through 5 or 10 years ago.

It's not going to be long before an artist can make an album, film, CDI and CDO in his or her own bedroom for a few thousand pounds, advertise the "product" to hundreds of thousands of people directly via the computer networks and sell directly to them. This will completely cut out the the need for the usual trek around the major entertainment companies looking for finance, and could lead to things getting really interesting.

that had laughably tiny memory sizes (the Vic 20 shipped with a 'generous' 3.5K of RAM). Nevertheless, the games played on these machines, as well as dedicated Atari consoles, followed by early Playstations, were distinctive for their sound chips' lo-fi electronic blips. A sense of contingent, on-the-hoof inventiveness and market-unfriendly entrepreneurialism emanated from these small companies whose games were often sold on cassettes packaged in handmade photocopied sleeve art. Now, in 1992, a single machine – usually an Atari or Amiga – could be used to sequence music and even generate graphics. As The Black Dog's Andy Turner put it at the time, "Saturating the market's the only way: when everybody's got their little studio at home, with their multimedia set-up for 200 quid… That's when it'll be as it was in the beginning, somebody playing a bit of music to somebody else down the road."

above: A Cornish, pasty Richard D James circa 1992, on the cusp of fame and notoriety.
opposite: By the time of *Artificial Intelligence II*, Warp's press office is working overtime to tackle the growing debate, and misinterpretations, around 'intelligent Techno' (see page 60).

Artificial Intelligence's anonymously written sleevenotes attempted a manifesto: "Electronic music for the mind created by trans-global electronic innovators who prove music is the one true international language. Real people whose unity lies in a common sound + spirit and whose 'listening music' cannot be described as either soulless or machine driven. The atmosphere and emotion both come from the musicians, their machines are merely the means to a human end."[2]

The concept captured critics' imaginations. In the *NME*, Stuart Maconie called it "a welcome return to the Ice Age, to the cool, austere, irresistible grooves of Detroit, Cologne and, erm, Leeds. Techno with open spaces, skeletal structures, dreamlike hiatuses and cosmic melodies making endless journeys round the sun."

One contemporary review announced that the album "marks a watershed for electronic music", noting "a new discreet music: minimalism and

2. Warp press release, 1994.

Sean Booth (left) and Rob Brown of Autechre: veteran hiphop and electro DJs on Manchester's pirate radio circuit by their early 20s.

"'Intelligent Techno' was laughable enough for it not to bother us. It was almost like, How ridiculous is that? OK, well, we'll go with it, because no intelligent person would ever read anything into it anyway: self-defeating proposition."
Sean Booth, Autechre

restraint surfacing to conquer mindless techno clutter, the music seeking to provoke thought rather than to nullify it."[3]

For an audience conditioned to think of electronic music's sole province as the nightclub circuit, Warp's presentation reversed entrenched paradigms. The presence of The Orb gave an authority to the project, as Paterson had pioneered the chill out lounge at Heaven in London, revitalising exhausted ravers with washes of Ambient sound from Tangerine Dream to Brian Eno. London clubs Megatripolis, Telepathic Fish, the Ambient Club and the Big Chill, united E'd up ravers with a more sedentary crowd. And even the artists on *Artificial Intelligence* (average age 22), in short interviews, namechecked a range of formative sounds that ranged widely from Tangerine Dream and Popol Vuh via Coil, the Normal and Prince Far-I as well as the more expected recent innovators like Derrick May, Blake Baxter and Model 500.

Artificial Intelligence became a brand that extended over ten releases, including two compilations and eight single-artist albums, "to overcome the problem that a lot of brilliant music was being overlooked because it wasn't playable in the clubs." The series allowed Warp to develop its new strategy: separating singles (with their WAP-prefix catalogue numbers) and albums (prefixed with WARP) into distinct strands. As a press communiqué put it, the dance singles "serve three functions… they keep the label up to date with current trends, are a talent source for potential new album artists and make money, especially in the form of compilation albums."

3. Simpson, Dave, *Melody Maker*, 22 August 1992.

As a strategy, *Artificial Intelligence* was always fairly openended. Sean Booth of Autechre, whose *Incunabula* album is paradigmatic of the series, remembers the notion loosely appearing over a two year period.

"We sent stuff to Warp in about 91 originally, a load of Hardcore tracks, pretty mad ones, and they said, 'Oh, sorry, we ain't got any plans to sign any new artists for the time being'. We thought, 'OK, is that a polite no, then?' And then about a year later I rang them up first, I spoke to Steve, and I was going, 'Look, we've got all these tracks and you might like them because they're a bit like LFO but they've got better beats', and he was just laughing, going, 'Go on then, send them…'. So we sent them a tape full of tracks with random stuff really, a bit of everything. And then they rang us and said, 'Yeah, we want more stuff, and we've got stuff off a few more artists and we don't really know what to do with it.' So we met up and we were going, 'Who are the other artists?' and they're going, 'Well we've got Black Dog', who at the time we'd not heard of, 'and B12 and Aphex …' And we thought, 'Mmm, Aphex, this could be quite good actually', and that was it really, they started sending us tapes of tracks that they'd been sent, and we gave them two tracks and then kept sending them stuff, waited for ages, they weren't interested for like two years, and then suddenly turned round and said, 'Yeah, we'll do the album', and that was *Incunabula*. So we didn't really feel that it was much of an album because they'd picked out all their favourite tracks and then we put it together with them, and it was a bit more of a compilation of stuff that we'd done for pirate radio."

Transplanting the future sound of Detroit's inner city to the suburbs of northern Europe: B12 from Romford, Essex (above); Speedy J from Rotterdam, The Netherlands (below).

Date: Tue, 7 Dec 93 11:36:33 PST
From: Jon Drukman <jdrukman@us.oracle.com>
Subject: artificial intelligence & much more

Cim writes:
>All this discussion on AI is cool but criticising b12/FUSE for sounding
>too Detroitish is a bit stupid as this is where their interests lie; it's
>pretty obvious that they will end up sounding like the original techno.

Augh. is it too much to ask for a LITTLE reading comprehension around here? how many times do i have to say it: it's not the sounding like detroit that i object to, it's the constant shouts of "god this stuff is so innovative and original."

>As stated before, this is 'intelligent' techno, stuff to relax to but
>not becoming part of the background (like ambient).

I think it fails even on that point, and apparently i'm not alone - others have posted similar observations to this list in the past few days. (stephen hebditch i think said "too boring for listening music, not dancy enough for dance music" or something similar - i agree.)

>It is certainly not thump, thump nose-bleed techno.

I'm learning more and more about the british scene from reading all the articles on this list and it certainly sounds terribly pathetic compared to the range of diversity we have here in san francisco. is it really just a choice between AI and 180 BPM breakbeat? sad!

>And the Detroit derived sound is not merely copied; it is built upon
>to create #new ideas. You wouldn't get Derrick May/Juan Atkins doing
>something like b12's "Debris" would you?

Ha! I was waiting for that track to come up - that great intro is sampled from Brian Eno. And when the melodic element comes in, it 'definitely' reminds me of Derrick May. Not that I have anything against Eno or May, quite the contrary - but it just goes to prove that B12 are mindless copycats, not brilliant inventors.

>I've totally forgotten my point now but I think what I originally meant
>to say was that sounding Detroitish (sorry, my new word) is actually
>quite good and indicative of some intelligence and thought behind the
>music instead of the loop-a-breakbeat-with-a-909-over-it-at-180-bpm
>mentality, which is all good and well to dance to but not as good to
>listen to.

I feel sad for you guys if that's all you have to choose between.

Date: Wed, 08 Dec 93 01:42:11 EST
From: luber@aol.com
Subject: much ado about...

maybe i\we missed something jumping in mid-stream but why all this talk (too much talk?) about warp? does the AI stuff pay homage to the past? yes! but so what! would we be better off w\out warp? i shutter to imagine such a situation. granted, this greatfulness does not add quality to the music, but it seems that warp at the very least it is the cause of all this chatter. surely there must me something to be said about that, eh? anyway... with all this time spent on warp, etc there are loads of releases flying into the shoppes that deserve\command attention. how 'bout some chat on next year's warp? how 'bout some chat about how 5-10 yrs from now this net will be a distribution channel and labels, media hype will mean little when anyone with access will be able to buy - no matter where they are. ok. so this may be old hat but again the point i\we're trying to make is that the present is here.

why is so much effort being put into warp's (recent) past????

Date: Mon, 6 Dec 1993 14:25:26 GMT
From: steven@orbital.demon.co.uk (Stephen Hebditch)
Subject: Re: Artificial Intelligence

In article <9312021913.AA10151@dlsun87.us.oracle.com>,
Jon Drukman <jdrukman@us.oracle.com> wrote:
>well, i have to say that i'm pretty let down by most of it

Oh, so it's not just me then. :-)
Suffering from an excess of cynicism, I thought the AI series owed rather more to the quality of Warp's marketing than the quality of the music. The original concept was great, the packaging was wonderful, their pluggers managed to get loads of column space - not just in the usual dance mags too - and their distributors (helped by all the press acreage) got the albums into just about every outlet. Ker-ching!
The music though I found rather a disappointment. With the exception of FUSE there wasn't enough variety across each album. Mostly they weren't quite background enough for background music or interesting enough for listening to properly. There have been a couple of tracks on each that I've liked, but I don't think one gained much by having a whole double album's worth of music. Others seem to feel the same when I play them trance albums though...
I guess there must also now be a load of people now who've never heard the Detroit originals so it sounds fresher to them.
    Stephen Hebditch   TQM Communications   steveh@orbital.demon.co.uk

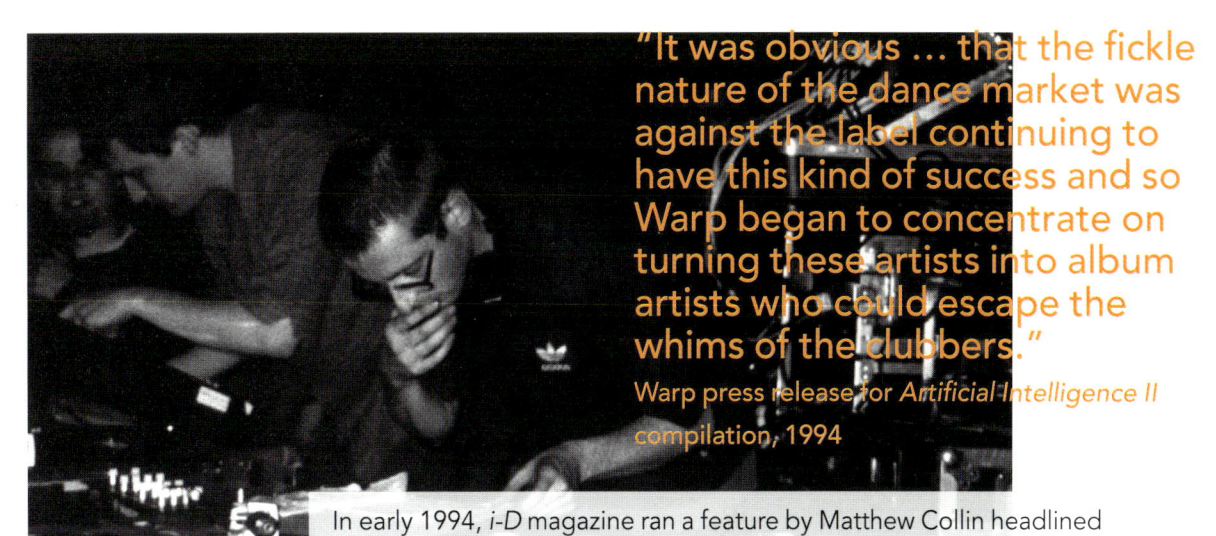

"It was obvious ... that the fickle nature of the dance market was against the label continuing to have this kind of success and so Warp began to concentrate on turning these artists into album artists who could escape the whims of the clubbers."
Warp press release for *Artificial Intelligence II* compilation, 1994

above: Walking like Egyptians: The Black Dog.
opposite: Rattling the cage of the IDM-List, 1993. This exchange of views was mailed out with Warp's press release accompanying *Artificial Intelligence II*.

In early 1994, *i-D* magazine ran a feature by Matthew Collin headlined "Life Beyond Dance". "Dance music is approaching crisis," Collin scrawled. "The week this article was written, the top four singles in the national charts were all dance tracks. They were also all rubbish." Complaining on the one hand about the ease of bedroom productions leading to a mountain of mediocrity, and on the other about a regression to funk and soulful tunes that took a parochial and safe exit to a past where "you didn't need drugs to have a good time", the article attempted to cut through the recent discourse about 'intelligent Techno', calling *Artificial Intelligence* "the first major league statement from our digital underground". It was clear that critical language was struggling to remould itself around some unfamiliar musical shapes. "The music has no name because nobody can agree on one – easy listening techno, chillcore, electronic dance music – none really fit; and is this even dance music any more anyway?"[4]

In another *i-D* billed as "The Future Issue", Tony Marcus breathlessly surveyed the contemporary electronica scene, noting the release of "a new computer package called Pro Tools 3 which contains something called a TDM bus.... It enables the musician to build an entire 'virtual' studio inside the computer."[5] The production of the abstract electronic music still had a quality of mystery to it; the digital production could leave a disorientating effect on the listener, with no spatial reference points, none of the 'ambient' sound of the space around the players. It seemed to emanate from a cold, mechanical place inside computers that were still barely in common use. That feeling nevertheless percolated through into an anticipation of a profoundly altered future for music.

Artificial Intelligence II was released on 30 May 1994, accompanied by a videotape release *Motion*, a computer-animated 40 minute film made by Phil Wolstenholme and Jess Scott-Hunter ("the film is an attempt to define an area of the consciousness that is normally inaccessible to the waking brain, known as the other"). The press release that came with this double-push felt the need to set the story straight on the 'intelligence' question.

4. Collin, Matthew, "Life Beyond Dance, *i-D*, no. 127, April 1994.
5. Marcus, Tony, "Future Sound of Music", *i-D*, no. 136, January 1995.

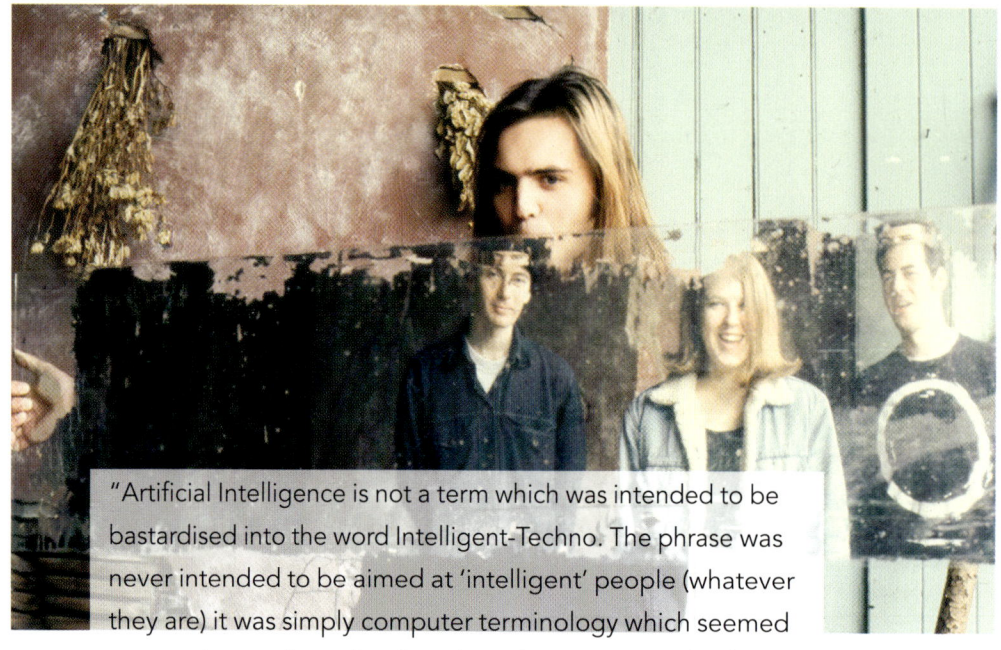

London guitar group Seefeel expanded the horizons of Warp's electronic music agenda. Left to right: Mark Clifford (aka Disjecta), Daren Seymour (holding mirror), Sarah Peacock, Justin Fletcher.

"Artificial Intelligence is not a term which was intended to be bastardised into the word Intelligent-Techno. The phrase was never intended to be aimed at 'intelligent' people (whatever they are) it was simply computer terminology which seemed appropriate to the style of music and was supposed to be a bit of a tongue-in-cheek dig at the people who said it was music made by computers that had no soul. We were trying to say that the computer was merely a tool to make music and that there was as much emotion in this music as in any other genre."

When the album was mailed out to journalists, it also came with four pages of online argument about Warp's new directions, copied from the IDM-List. 1994 was already a turning point in the popularisation of new technologies. Email and the internet were just starting to make an impact on the mass media. The sense of new frontiers opening up, and of potentially radical alterations to the way humans would communicate in the not too distant future, was palpable.

On *Artificial Intelligence II*, one eyebrow raising addition to the roster was Seefeel. A London based quartet who played guitars and were lumped in with what the music press dubbed the 'shoegazer' scene of effects-slathered ambient guitar rock, the group were desperate for reinvention. Their liberal use of effects pedals had drawn them further into using samplers and processed vocal microphones to amplify and distort singer Sarah Peacock's voice into a vaulting echo. Seefeel's three albums for Warp between 1993-1996, before the group finally crumbled apart, mark the move from shoegazing to screengazing. Guitarist Mark Clifford, who went on to release two albums for the label under the Samuel Beckett-inspired name Disjecta, said at the time:

"The ability of a machine, such as a robot or a computer, to initiate human actions or skills such as problem solving, decision making, perception learning, reasoning, self-improvement. One test for AI requires that performance improves with experience or operation; for example, the ability to play a chess game."
Linda Gail Christie and John Christie, *Encyclopaedia Of Microcomputer Terminology*, from 1994 Warp press release

"Warp aren't anti-guitars, they're not purists, and we can amaze them with guitar noises just as I can hear a synth noise and go wow! Three or four years ago, for Techno kids, guitars were like Satan. Now it feels like everyone's grown up: it's just music; it doesn't matter how you get there."
The presence of Seefeel in ths context was a powerful statement about a new eclecticism to the label and a vision of the state of music that went beyond the expected.

With these glimpses of a technological utopia very much in the mind's eye, art and music were not unaffected. In *The Wire*, David Toop published an article in which he imagined a "global campfire" at which far flung participants could make a networked music – a William Gibson-like vision of musical conversation via the ether or cyberspace. "The girl at all tomorrow's parties won't just be dancing to music," concluded Marcus's article in *i-D*'s Future Issue, "she'll be making music with her body, her hands, her breath and thoughts. And it won't just be music, as the machines generate both sound and pictures, rhythm and movies, into new shapes and textures. And these are revolutions, because the new technology makes music that is multi-dimensional, multi-media and multi-genre. And you'll know when the revolution happens, because at that instant everything you've ever known about music will change."

Warp had set themselves up for a degree of hubris with the *Artificial Intelligence* project. It allowed for so much interpretation and reading in meanings, as well as setting musicians and fans up for charges of elitism, that the term 'intelligent Techno' that sprang from it rather missed the point. But it set a standard which Warp constantly had to meet, and which created the preconception of the label as a cutting edge electronic operation – a view the label would spend much of the next decade trying to subvert, even as it expanded its horizons.

Intelligent Design Adrian Shaughnessy

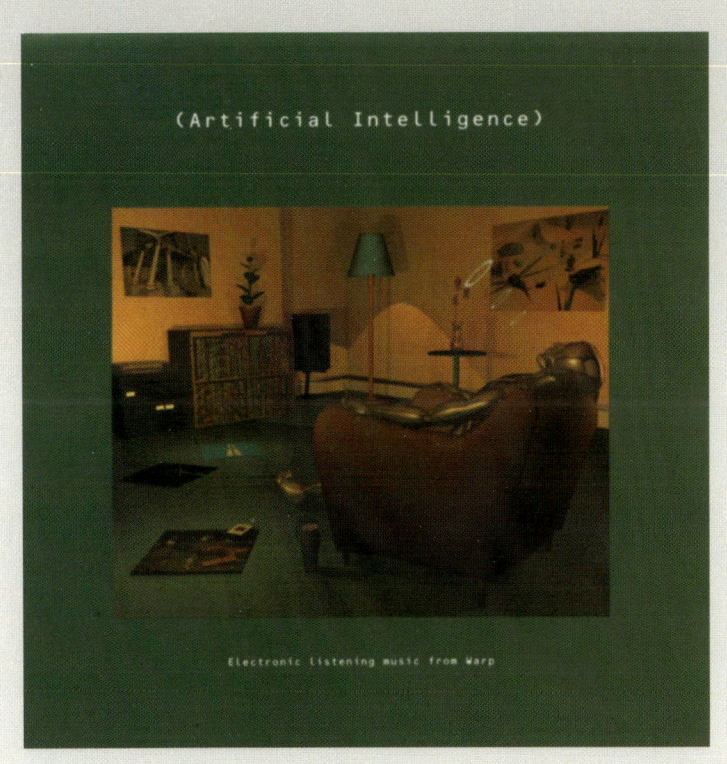

Reclining Warpbot on the sleeve of *Artificial Intelligence*, 1992 (WARP6).

Warp hit their stride in rave culture's first moment of introspection. The waning of the frenzied high of the dancefloor, the post-euphoric aftermath of the ecstasy rush, and the recognition that rave culture had gone mainstream, caused a reappraisal of the music and the lifestyle. Discerning ravers demanded something more thoughtful, and less blatantly exploitative: listening to music with the ears, rather than experiencing it through the solar plexus, became a desirable option. As Designers Republic's Ian Anderson notes: "I never related Warp to clubbing, I always related Warp music to the *Artificial Intelligence* records, or even, to me, a more academic interest."

The two *Artificial Intelligence* compilations of chilly electronic audioscapes were important signposts in the new direction dance music was to take in the afterburn of rave. The cover image for the first *Artificial Intelligence*, in 1992, was supplied by Sheffield based photographer, video artist and designer Phil Wolstenholme, and laid out by Designers Republic. Wolstenholme regularly attended local clubs in the late 80s and early 90s, and had already produced sleeve images for The Shamen's *Boss Drum* and The Orb's *UFOrb* LPs. In 1991 Warp invited him to contribute the image for the cover of The Step's "Yeah You!" single. In lieu of a fee, they offered to buy him a new Amiga computer system so that he could develop his digital artwork. Before the Artificial Intelligence LPs, he also created images for the compilations *Pioneers Of The Hypnotic Groove*, *Evolution Of The Groove* and *Tequila Slammers*.

In *Energy Flash*, in a chapter devoted to the rise of intelligent Techno, Simon Reynolds describes the cover artwork of *Artificial Intelligence I*: "It features a robot reclining in a comfy armchair, blowing perfect smoke rings in the air and chilling to the atmospheric sounds wafting from a sleek hi-fi unit. In his left hand, there's a fat spliff, at his feet, what looks like a can of Sapporo. Joint making materials – Silk Cut, extra-long Rizla papers – are strewn on top of an album sleeve on the carpet."[1] Two nod-out classics, Pink Floyd's *Dark Side Of The Moon* and Kraftwerk's *Autobahn*, are casually strewn over the robot's floor.

It is clear that this was music for listening to, and furthermore, it was music to listen to alone, preferably in the sepulchral, airtight space of headphones. As Beckett explains: "That's why we put those sleeves on the cover of *Artificial Intelligence* – to get into people's heads that you weren't supposed to dance to it".[2]

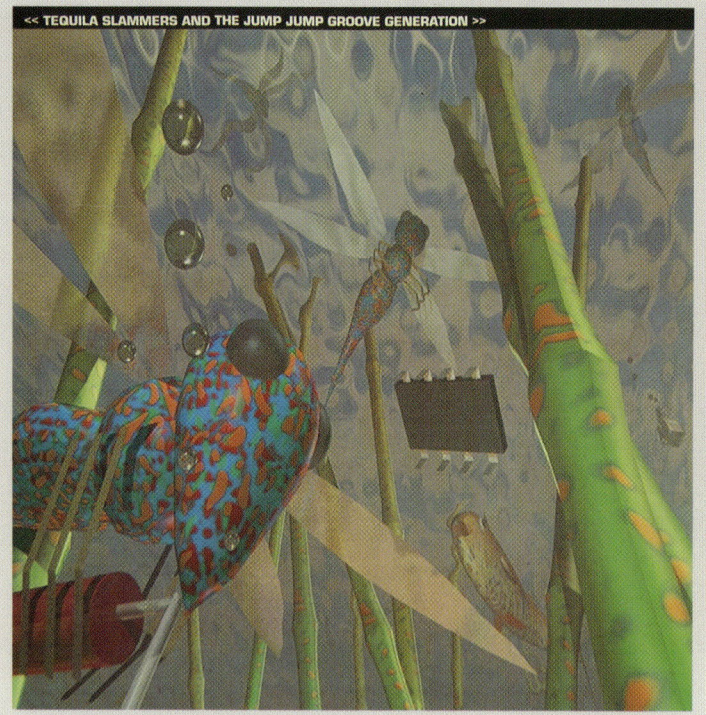

left: *Tequila Slammers And The Jump Jump Groove*, 1993 (WARP10).
right: *The Evolution Of The Groove*, 1992 (WARP5).

Wolstenholme's image, surrounded by Designers Republic's Optical read-out typography, is a quintessential graphic distillation of the period. It shows a slightly self-conscious use of early 1990s three-dimensional image-rendering applications. Just as contemporary music was being transformed by the new digital technology, so too was the contemporary image and graphic design in general. It was the opening up of what the writer Erik Davis has called "Silicone wizard worlds".

Prior to the advent of digital image making software such as Imagine, a complex illustration like Wolstenholme's could only have been created with an airbrush and a mind-boggling number of hand-cut masking overlays, not to mention prodigious levels of dexterity. But now it could be done sitting in front of a monitor and moving pixels around with a mouse. This is not to say that working with the new image generating software lessened the need for genuine aesthetic sensibility. On the contrary, it required an even more heightened sensibility. The 'buttons' allowed anyone to make complex imagery quickly and cheaply; no trick or effect was forbidden. But there was no guarantee of quality, and only those who brought old-fashioned rigour and genuine artistic self-control to this new graphic playground were likely to produce digitally-rendered work that could be favourably compared with the best traditional image making.

By 1994, when *Artificial Intelligence II* was released, a more confident aesthetic sensibility appears to be at work. The central image is less jocular than its predecessor. Fantastical tropical plant forms discharge *Artificial Intelligence*'s familiar 'brand-mark' of dreamy smoke rings. The claustrophobic, lost-in-the-jungle imagery finds a parallel in the fevered visions of digital illustrator Buggy G Riphead and his iconic work for Future Sound Of London. An even stronger evocation of the more overtly hallucinogenic style of Riphead can be found in Wolstenholme's cover for the Warp compilation *Tequila Slammers* And *The Jump Jump Groove Generation*, 1993.

Artist Phil Wolstenholme tells Rob Young about the process of creating his silicone wizard worlds

"I think I was probably the first person to try and do three-dimensional modelling in Sheffield. You can see the improvements because every image is vastly more detailed and textured than the one before, because more and more software was being developed and there was a point where we got a really weird kind of house style going with the sleeves. They were very arty compared to most of the Techno covers that were out at the time which were really obviously electronic. The kind of photography I did was all tangled foliage and organic matter, and it was the difficulty of reproducing that in a three-dimensional sense, because you have to build every object by hand. It was impossible to do an image that was full of intricate detail and so I spent two years trying to figure out ways of simulating that. The second *Artificial Intelligence* cover was the pinnacle of that.

"*Pioneers Of The Hypnotic Groove* was this kind of circuit board in a futurist desert; in *Evolution Of The Groove* this desert had slowly come to life, and there were plants growing out and all the [silicon] chips were now buried in sand dunes, and these weird insects were flying around, and it referenced a lost world. *Tequila Slammers* was even more bizarre because the desert had now filled with water and these insects were kind of flying underwater with the fish. There was a process of evolution in terms of the images as well: they all referenced the previous one, it was like a little story that was growing from nowhere, and none of us really knew what it meant, but it was so different to everything else that was being produced, that was the best bit for us.

"*Pioneers Of The Hypnotic Groove* had kingsize Rizlas on it, because everybody smoked dope, and it was nice to be able to put the whole family concept into the product – there were enough clues to let people know what was going on. Lots of people smoking dope and largely listening to music that Warp fans would be quite surprised to listen to. I remember we had one legendary night where we were all tripping, and I played Steve some of my farthest out Grateful Dead stuff because he'd never heard any of it. This stuff was so psychedelic, and we spent hours on our backs in the dark, and he said, "We've got to sign them… ", And I went, "Steve, they've already got their own label, they're really huge!" It was a sudden realisation that electronic music wasn't invented then [in the early 90s], it was invented in the late 50s – I've got albums now from 67, 68, really bizarre artists who were building their own synths and had no sequencing capability at all, but they were doing this amazing music, really heavy-handed.... We were listening to all that then, because it was more fun than a lot of the new stuff. The bleep thing did start to get a bit out of control really, because no one was listening to that at home – we all went clubbing in Sheffield and we were listening to House music, and then we'd get home and play stoner music, we very rarely played Hardcore Techno at all."

In 1994, Warp wheeled out their first film production. *Motion* was a 40-minute sequence comprising five separate short three-dimensional animated films accompanying some of the music on *Artificial Intelligence II*. David Slade supplied two of the five: *Nanotechnics.1* and *Corpus Porpoise Posthumous Non Polhemus*, with zebra-striped dolphins orbiting a gigantic planet. Jess Scott-Hunter created a nest of animated bugs to accompany Autechre's "Basscadet"; and Wolstenholme supplied *Mirage* and *Lifespan*, featuring the polished 'Artificial Intelligence' cyborg striding purposefully through an infinite desert, intercut with mechanical spermatozoa speeding through endless tunnels towards a digital ovum.

"Steve was definitely more interested than Rob in terms of the visuals," recalls Wolstenhome, "because I used to hang out a lot more with Steve anyway. He'd talk about it a lot before, but he very rarely said, 'this is what we want'. *Artificial Intelligence I* was the first one where they actively said, 'We'd like a guy sitting in an armchair', and that was about as concrete as it got, and then we gradually said, 'What about this weird robotic guy?' The favourite albums thing came up, and that was the first time we really got to play with this self-referential thing, because we had *Autobahn* and *Dark Side Of The Moon*. They were effectively saying, 'Look, this is where we're all from, we're all 70s/early 80s hippies…'

left: Cover of the domestic release of *Artificial Intelligence II*.
right: *Pioneers Of The Hypnotic Groove*, 1991 (WARP2).
opposite: Japanese box set special edition of *Artificial Intelligence II*.

"I spent about nine months producing all the bits of footage for my sections in *Motion*, I never turned the computer off for a year at all, it was on 24 hours a day. There were all these problems with compatibility: I was on an Amiga, Designers Republic worked on Macs, some output places worked on PCs, and everybody was going, 'Oh God, we can't talk to each other'. So I got a Mac emulator inside my Amiga so that I could output files for DR, and suddenly everything started clicking into place. It was all very Heath Robinson in that sense. The biggest difficulty was actually getting the footage off the computers and onto tape. I did three 30-hour sessions of just dumping frames one frame at a time onto Betacam tape, because it had to be editable. It took me a month just to get all my footage onto tape, and then we had two more continuous weekends of editing, no sleep at all from Thursday to Monday.

"David Slade edited it down to 40 minutes, and we did some amazing titles and credits – the 'fly through the cave' thing was just brilliant, the icing on the cake. Then we did a preview showing at [London's] ICA – it was quite nerve wracking because we didn't know what people would think, because Warp had made such an effort to be special, this was so quirky and weird that it could have fallen flat on its face. We played it and the place erupted in loud applause."

1. Reynolds, Simon, *Energy Flash*, London: Picador, 1998.
2. Reynolds, *Energy Flash*.

During the course of the 1990s, Warp's core artists descended like 'ultravisitors' from an unknown musical planet, developing unique sonic approaches and presenting it in ways that broke new ground while continuing to entertain. Left: One of Aphex Twin's bears baits the crowd at The Clink, South London, November 1996.

ultravisitors

Fed with weird things: Aphex Twin, Autechre, Squarepusher

1996: an autumn night on the south bank of the River Thames. The begrimed Victorian warehouse called The Clink used to house a prison but has just been converted a museum celebrating its own gruesome past. Its interior décor – costumier's dummies tricked out in leather masks and bondage apparel, and wax figures of peasants in stocks and gibbets, display its other function as an S&M club. But on this particular night it has been taken over by Aphex Twin and hundreds of revellers, at a release party for his album *Richard D James*. All that can be seen through a barred window at the rear of a tiny makeshift 'stage' is James's flame haired head, concentrating on something out of sight. After he has softened up the crowd with several minutes of breakbeats and distended snare rolls that develop stretchmarks, a platoon of giant orange and yellow teddybears suddenly materialises in the midst of the crowd. Their hollowed-out faces are filled with identical masks of a gurning Richard James, with a village idiot grin and a demented stare through saucer-like sockets. The bears frug and tussle with each other, bending double and almost kneeing themselves in the face, then without warning they are down amongst the suffocating crowd, shoving and knocking people down as they become increasingly manic. Throughout the lengthy set, James hardly even looks up from his concealed equipment. The dancefloor descends into a chaotic maelstrom as the bears slug it out with the crowd.

The *Artificial Intelligence* series introduced a new cast of strong characters to Warp's drama, but after delivering an album each, the label became the theatre in which they could pursue their own distinctive styles. The technological 'cool' of the early 90s began, slowly, to be disrupted through sheer force of sonic personality. Iconoclastic albums followed: Nightmares On Wax produced *Smokers' Delight*, a classic of downbeat chilled out funk;

The Aphex Twin will be playing other peoples records tonight.
Hear them.

and Andrew Weatherall's Two Lone Swordsmen duo with Keith Tenniswood picked up where his dancehall Techno group, Sabres Of Paradise, left off, continuing with a string of records through the 1990s. But the three central artists in Warp's emerging roster, who honed and pursued relentlessly individual approaches during the mid 90s, were Autechre, Aphex Twin and Squarepusher. And together these alien, sonic 'ultravisitors' have left a body of work that testifies to the worth of Warp's policy of 'hands-free' artist development.

Reproduced By Kind Permission of Warp Records Ltd™

No room for misunderstanding: Warp slogan postcard by Designers Republic.

LFO may have had Warp's first big chart hit, but Aphex Twin was Warp's first proper star. Having grown up near the tip of Cornwall, and due to the fact that he made most of his music in the unglamorous confines of his own bedroom, Richard James might have seemed an unlikely public figure. Although a peep into his press files reveals an enormous amount of contact with the media over the years, most of those encounters appear uncomfortable, strained; interviews taking place on park benches, grubby cafes, art galleries; James often dashing off the moment the stop button was pressed. But the legends of the tank, the submarine, the homebuilt 'magic boxes', the lucid dreaming, the tracks released under unknown aliases, the collaboration with Philip Glass, the DJing exploits with a sanding machine and liquidiser: all these made him an irresistible character.

His close friend Luke Vibert, aka Wagon Christ and Plug, used to attend club nights at the Bowgie in Cornwall where James was DJing:

"Acid House hit Cornwall later than everywhere else, it was really 1990 when it kicked off. I just went up to him in March 1990 – we'd just had a couple of tapes passed around before, 89 or something, and we thought, who the fuck's this weird guy? He had managed to get loads of records that no one else could get in Cornwall, so I just went up to him and did the usual, 'Nice one mate…'. We just started chatting that night, and then the next time I'd seen him, we were already acting like good mates… I think we just liked the same things, and being in Cornwall, there weren't that many people into it – there was me, him, Grant [Wilson-Claridge, co-founder of James's Rephlex label], Tom Middleton [of Global Communication, and one of the partnership behind Warp's *Theory Of Evolution* compilation of 1995], my mate Jeremy [Simmons, aka Voafose] – not that many others, really. Then there were loads of kids who were happy to be punters and take drugs and weren't so bothered about DJing and finding the tunes. The Bowgie had a really nice sound system. It was really clean, dry and close, and tons of fucking bass. And you could sit on the bass cabs, over in this big line by the window."

Richard James in the slammer at The Clink, London, 1996.

The clubs would usually shut by 1am, but there was a lively after-club scene. "They were the best thing," recalls Vibert:

"Rich would DJ at a couple of them. We were probably lucky, being in Cornwall, because the police were really slow to catch on to it, and there were loads of empty buildings around – barns and warehouses – so you'd just go and get the speakers off someone and set up mini-raves, which got bigger and bigger really, and loads of police started coming in summer 91. But it was wicked for a while – we got away with 'in the middle of nowhere raving'."

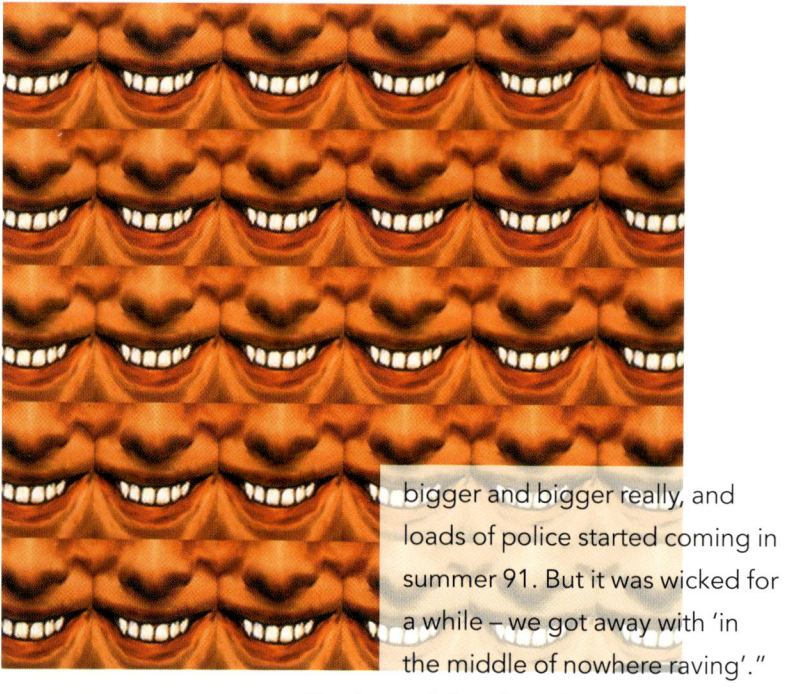

"In the middle of nowhere" aptly describes the mood of Aphex Twin's 1994 double album, *Selected Ambient Works II*. Sprawling across two CDs or four sides of vinyl, its 21 untitled, almost entirely beatless tracks went to the opposite end of the scale from the 'bonkers' dance tunes of Warp's early years. It was also closer in spirit to Brian Eno's original notion of Ambient as peripheral, evocative sound than Aphex's earlier debut for the Belgian R&S label, *Selected Ambient Works 1985-92*, which used the Ambient buzzword to pull together a random clutch of bouncy post-Acid tunes he'd been recording since his teenage years. *SAW II*'s peculiarly lonely, occasionally desolate quality perhaps comes from its use of enormously long reverberation on most of the synth lines. Plangent, faintly choral sounds drift in forests of digital delay and, while the apparent mood is calm and reflective, repeated listening reveals a fundamental instability: tones waver and wobble, recording levels nudge into the red of distortion, rhythmic traces never quite assert themselves.

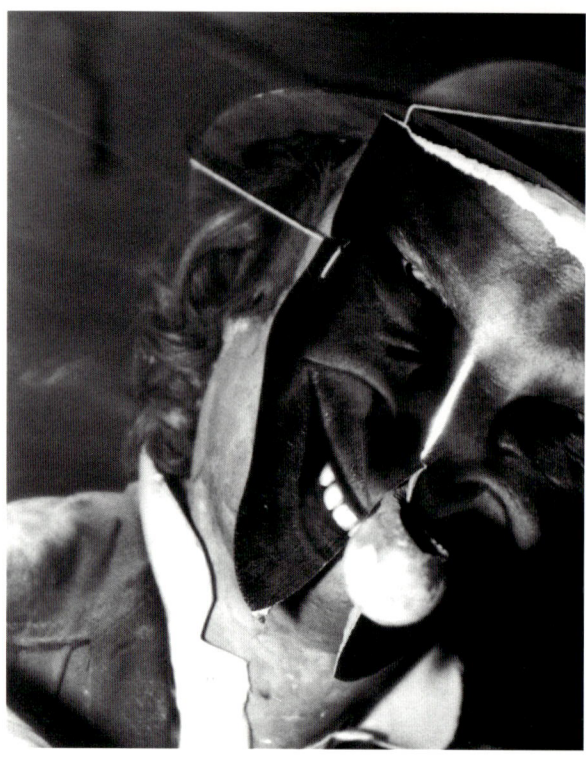

top: Aphex Twin's *Donkey Rhubarb* EP, 1995 (WAP63), included his collaboration with minimalist composer Philip Glass, "Icct Hedral". bottom: The mask starts to slip...

> "There's something magical about having all your equipment in the same room as your bed, and you just get out of bed and like do a track and go back to sleep and then get up and do some more and do tracks in your pants and stuff."
> Aphex Twin interviewed on www.disquiet.com

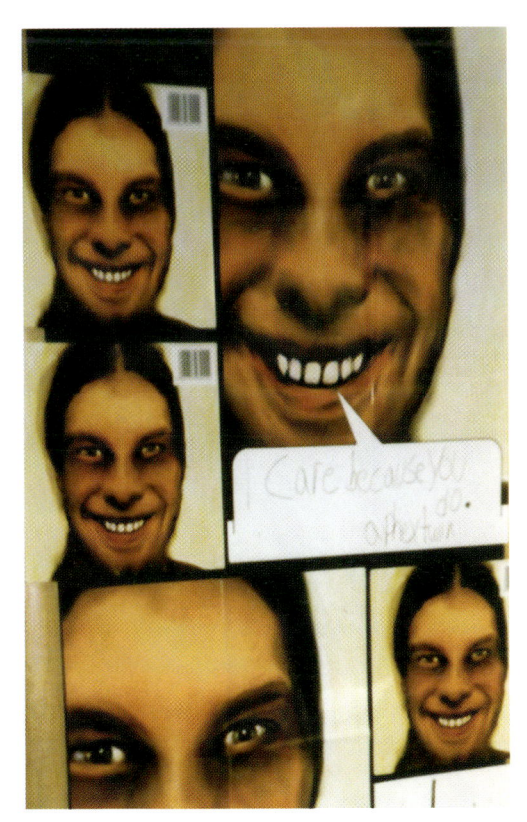

Once he had begun the rumours about building and customising his own equipment, Richard James soon clammed up in later interviews about his secret methods. But there was a brief window where he let his guard down in early interviews, especially with musicians' magazines. In mid 1993, in the period when he was presumably working on the tracks that became *Selected Ambient Works II*, he mentioned he had just bought a Roland 100M modular synthesizer system.

"I've been buying a lot of synths, but not because I'm interested in the electronics side of it. I've bought ARPs and things like that, but I've taken them all apart straightaway. With the 100M, I started taking some screws out before I got sidetracked into something else, but I'll get back to it. Everything just comes apart straight away, because I really like to see how people put these things together. I don't use them as instruments, I want to see the electronics….

"I use bits of other keyboards all the time – or the sliders, the case, the keys. But I don't use the actual sounds. Although I have made a box about the size of a packet of fags which has got everything from a TB303 in it except the sequencer.

"There's not a lot you can do to digital keyboards… I'm very interested in digital noise, but it's not as apparent as analogue customising, so I've only scratched the surface. I mean, I will record onto DAT and then fuck the tape up in different ways – like put a hair dryer on the tape, or sprinkle stuff onto it, or crease and fold the tape. You can get really mad sounds doing that."

The face that launched a thousand microchips: Instore display for Aphex Twin's *I Care Because You Do*, 1995 (WARP30).

above: Stills from the promo clip for "Windowlicker", 1999 (WAP105), directed by Chris Cunningham and shot in Los Angeles. Aphex Twin's stunning cartwheels around Garage rhythms were complemented by a video that upset the conventions of R&B stereotypes.
opposite: Aphex Twin overloads the system, late 90s.

1. James, Richard, quoted in Phil Ward, "Cagey, Canny & Krafty", *Music Technology*, July 1993.
2. James, quoted in Ward, "Cagey, Canny & Krafty".

For his live work at this time, James also talked of "four homemade sequencers, with different things going from each one, and I can compare things as I'm going along. But I've made something that I couldn't imagine gigging without as well, because I can control everything from it: it's a sequencer, which can store samples, trigger filters, trigger bits of equipment, turn filters on and off." And what is Richard's name for this wonder device? "Dunno… er, master control box".[1]

What does seem beyond doubt, though, is James's sheer productivity. The reason he can be so unsentimental about his own output is that his music is excreted in a practically unceasing stream of tracks, mixes, loops and fragments. Even in 1993 his workload called for complicated data management:

"I have a library of stuff, but it's stuff I haven't used yet. Once I've used it, I wipe it so I don't use it again. For instance, if I have a DAT with 500 clonks on it, and I use 20 of them, erasing those 20 means I've whittled that backlog down to just 480. Just as when you're DJ-ing, you'll put the records you've already played to one side, so you don't have to look through them again."[2]

Richard James continually seemed uncomfortable with the role he was cast in: as electronica's paladin saviour, worshipped, plastered with fan mail, fêted with praise, money and fame like few 23 year olds. Between *Selected Ambient Works II* and the 1995 follow up, *I Care Because You Do*, he appears to have taken a conscious decision to fight back by shredding his image, chopping into

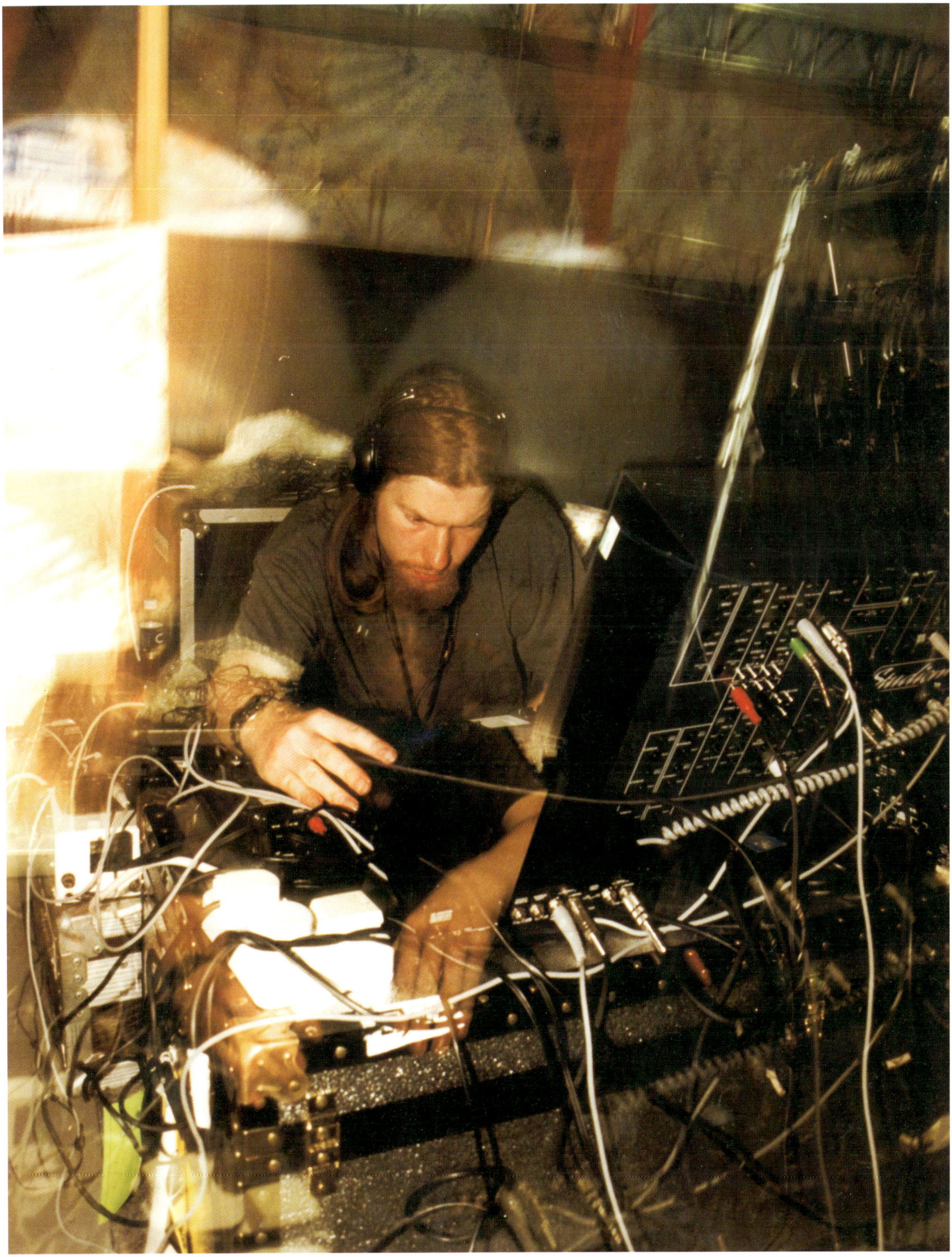

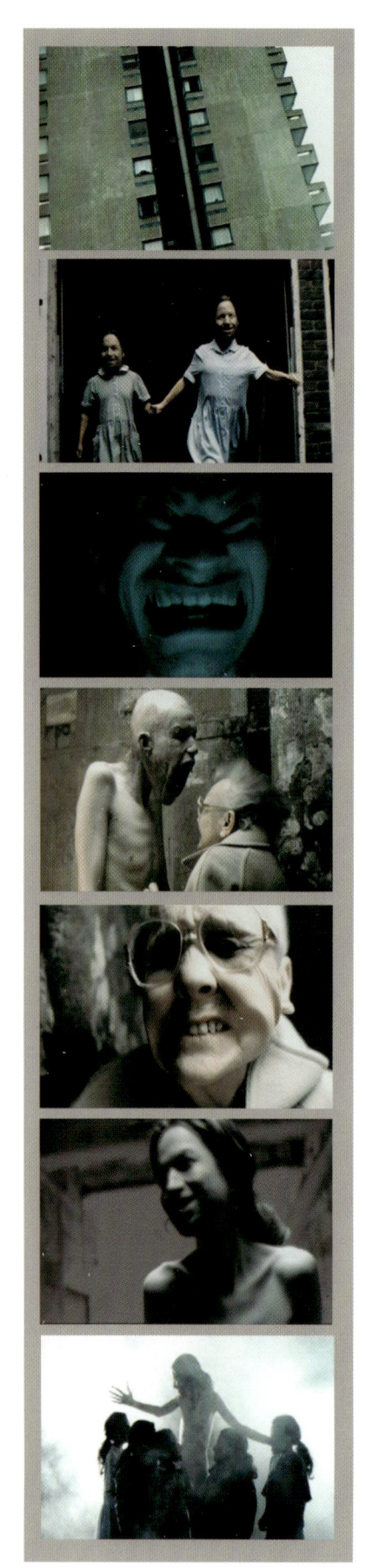

Urban Gothic: Stills from Chris Cunningham's video for "Come To Daddy", 1997 (WAP94). Both children and dwarves, masked to resemble Aphex Twin, were used on the shoot, which took place on a housing estate at Thamesmead, East London.

digital images of his own face, making himself appear like a smudged, grinning loon (perhaps the 'Smojphace' he sometimes uses as a DJ alias); as a gurning demonic mannekin on *Richard D James*, 1996, and with the help of video director Chris Cunningham, replicating his face, à la *Being John Malkovich*, onto the midget children of horror-Jungle piece "Come To Daddy" and the busty LA models of 1999's perverted Garage tune "Windowlicker". Criticism that this signals a cynical detachment of the man from the music misses the overriding point: that all of this music is about himself, is a replicant form of himself set free to mutate and spread virally across the musical landscape. The clue is in the multiple anagrams he began to use for his track titles on *I Care…*: The Aphex Twin becomes "The Waxen Pith", "Wax The Nip", "Wet Tip Hen Ax", "Next Heap With"; Richard D James becomes "Acrid Avid Jam Shred". Then there are the several references to his Cornish home county, from the cover shot of *Polygon Window* to titles such as "Cornish Acid", "Redruthmix", "Logon Rock Witch" (Logans Rock is a prominent feature of Cornwall's coastline), "Mt Saint Michel + Saint Michaels Mount". Scattered autobiographical gestures include the cover of the *Girl/Boy* EP, depicting the Canadian grave of James's late brother, also called Richard James, who died in 1968, three years before he was born; and on 2001's *Drukqs*, glimpses of his parents: "Lornaderek" has an ancient tape recording of his mother and father singing him "Happy Birthday",

> "I'm really obsessive about control; being in a band never excited me at all."
> Richard James, 1993.

I want your soul: The Analord himself, Richard D James.

while "54 Cymru Beats" alludes to their current home in Wales. And although he's often thought of as a purely electronic musician, there are plenty of instances where the digital veneer is torn apart for a split second and a voice, or a snatch of room ambience and movement, or an acoustic instrument, is suddenly revealed in the stereo space. Since *Drukqs*, he has concentrated his musical efforts through his own label Rephlex, and it's not clear whether he will remain under contract with Warp in the future. But it is with Warp that his reputation was cemented, and the personal eccentricities and contradictions coupled with the endless conundrums of his music add up to Warp's most endearing and enduring artist.

Spray-on smiles:
Aphex Twins
Adrian Shaughnessy

left to right: Aphex Twin's *Drukqs*, 2001 (WARP92), *Come To Daddy* EP, 1997 (WAP94), *Richard D James*, 1996 (WARP43), *Windowlicker*, 1999 (WAP105).

Aphex Twin, the cosmic joker of electronic music, allows a river of dark humour to run through his cover art as with his music and videos. Admittedly, it's a mildly threatening humour – the serio-comic gallows humour of a sonic assassin – especially in the way he uses his own face and body in a bludgeoning attack on the over-cosmeticised imagery of contemporary pop. James is not afraid to distort his own features into a simulacrum of ugliness. He grafts his head onto the bodies of LA super-babes and turns himself into a one-man digital dadaist gag, sitting in sharp contrast to his emotive, sophisticated and profoundly serious music. The sleeve for the single "Windowlicker", 1999, and the album cover for *Richard D James*, 1996, demonstrate James at his most disturbingly playful. Both sleeves (the former is designed by Designers Republic) owe a great debt to film maker Chris Cunningham. James's relationship with Cunningham goes some way towards explaining his adoption of weird imagery. Cunningham is the *eminence grise* of the music video. He is the contemporary master of the futuristic grotesque, and in Richard James he has a willing accomplice – an artist ready and able to subvert his own image in the name of bravura image making. In Warp, both James and Cunningham have a willing and enlightened patron.

> "The idea isn't to throw as much at the listener that they can't handle it. That's just something that might happen."
> Tom Jenkinson (Squarepusher) 1998

Tom Jenkinson, the Squarepusher, quietly abusing his beloved bass guitar.

During his time in London Richard James has always lived surrounded by friends, mainly the people associated with the Rephlex label. In the mid 90s his rhythms were souped up at precisely the moment he made the acquaintance of Tom Jenkinson, aka Squarepusher. The sawtooth, rasping drum 'n' bass snares of *Richard D James*, "Come To Daddy" and many subsequent tracks was the mirror image of the manic, flailing breakbeats of Squarepusher, who began releasing tracks on the Brighton Spymania label in 1994, and London's Worm Interface imprint, then put out his first album, *Feed Me Wierd Things* (sic) in 1995 on Rephlex. A virtuoso bass player with a penchant for the hyperactive jazz funk fusion of Weather Report and Stanley Clarke, Jenkinson started making breakbeat tunes in 1992-1993, after dropping out of Chelsea Art College where he had been studying combined media as part of fine art degree, but focused on sonic art. The crunch came when he exhibited himself, doing a music performance with bass and mixer at a degree show, and was criticised by the staff.

As well as short stints in various groups, Jenkinson developed his own methods of compacting together recycled Jungle breakbeats, sped up and kaleidoscoped into hyperkinetic, dazzling flights, peppered with his real time funk bass playing. "I didn't get into House music, or 4/4 with regular electronic sounds, until 1990," he explained, "so I missed the Acid thing. I was hearing the earliest breakbeat manifestations, pretty much from Hip House [a fusion of hiphop and House]. Again, the transatlantic jumping around thing. I think the Hip House thing kickstarted the breakbeat scene over here. And then suddenly got infused with all these… it was like a race. And the bpms started getting faster and faster year by year. It did seem like a kind of – Shit, everything's been torn to pieces, everything's falling apart completely. It's mad. And at the time I related to it because it was using drum breaks, and that was the bit where I really came in.

"It was a bit mad. In 92 I was 17, and I was just beginning to get a wider consciousness about stuff, about the world, i.e. realising that there was a world as opposed to just me and my mates, and I thought, this seemed fucked up. Going to raves, and seeing people... I still associate that sound with seeing people up against walls – I'd never seen people like this before – shivering, and hardly being able to move. I'd always seen the heroin stuff on TV in the 80s, but this was so twisted, so perverted, with hard beats – the only way I can say it is end of the world music."

In a short sleevenote on *Feed Me Wierd Things*, James explained how he met Jenkinson on a memorable night outside the George Robey pub in North London. In 1998 I asked Jenkinson to specify what qualities captivated him about Aphex's music.

He replied: "[It's] the thing which fires me off on most music which I love, which is a way of making anger and happiness meaningful: capturing it and communicating it. Maybe because I'm English, I like the sound of controlled rage."

Squarepusher at that time seemed hell bent on taking revenge on all that had cheapened the social landscape during the 1980s, encapsulated in the title "Freeman Hardy & Willis Acid", referring to a chain of shops selling cheap shoes, and that cynicism clearly chimed in with Richard James's compulsion to debunk his own fame.

Appropriately, his musical gear consisted of a fake Fender Jazz bass and an Akai S950 sampler he admitted was "totally outdated".

"I just have things for total object value," he said. "The value of them is the value of what they can do. People surround themselves with goods, not just in music, but surround their lives with ornaments and decoration, and items more because of the symbols of wealth that it entails. I just like having the bare minimum. So it's constantly pushing me."

Squarepusher's Warp releases such as *Port Rhombus*, 1996, *Hard Normal Daddy* and *Big Loada*, both 1997, pushed his frenetic breakbeat style close to breaking point ("Big Loada" achieved speeds of a monstrous 190 beats per minute): a garbage crusher for recycled musical detritus. "Picking up really crap samples, sampling things with really bad samplers as a reaction to how clean everything sounds," he said, "it's really exciting to have a really dirty, grungy sound: it's a bit more earthy." He was locked in a musical game of 'chicken' with the Aphex Twin drum 'n' bass material of the same period. "It was extremely hectic," Jenkinson said about their relations at the time, "and when we first met, the race I was talking about was intensified, doubled three times over, you know. It was like a conversation, actually. Going between us, from 95-97, was really like a conversation. It wasn't like we were trying to better each other; or at least if it was we never came out in the open about it. We were just like, 'Oh yeah, man, that's wicked', and then turn up the next week with a DAT: 'Check this out'. But it was brilliant."

From 1998's *Music Is Rotted One Note* onwards, the Squarepusher sound diversified, and subsequent releases

Squarepusher's ferocious Jungle rhythms and precocious bass playing made for jawdropping, unpredictable live performances. Photo (top): Iris Garrelfs.

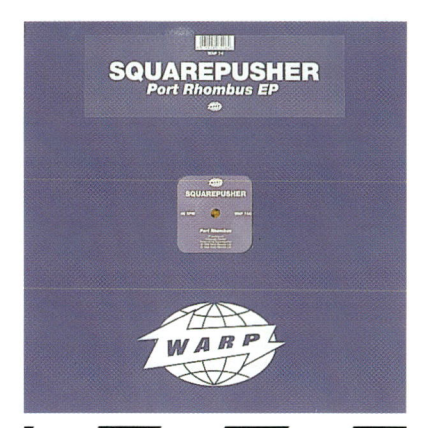

After fulfilling a dream to appear in a 'classic' Warp purple sleeve with *Port Rhombus*, 1996 (WAP74), Squarepusher's *Big Loada*, 1997 (WAP92), reprised the very first Warp logo from 1989. *Hard Normal Daddy*, 1997 (WARP50) and *Vic Acid*, 1997 (WAP90), melded lo-fi graphics with mundane scenes of contemporary British life.

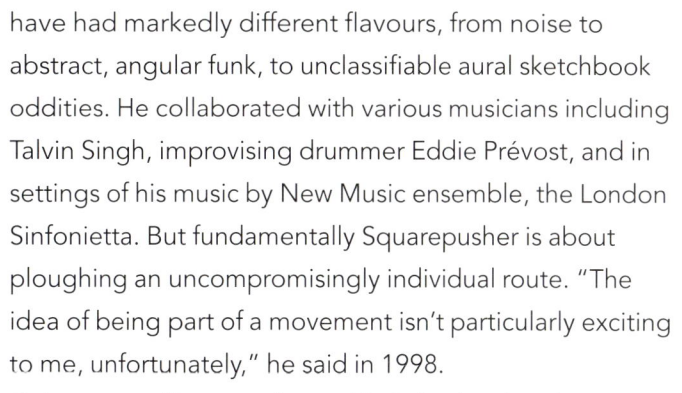

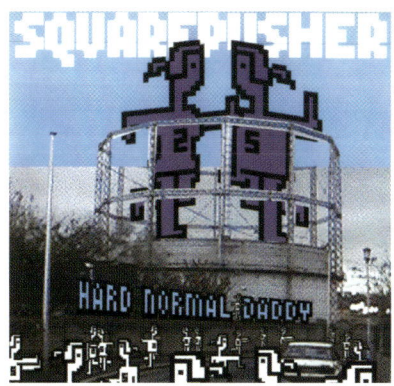

have had markedly different flavours, from noise to abstract, angular funk, to unclassifiable aural sketchbook oddities. He collaborated with various musicians including Talvin Singh, improvising drummer Eddie Prévost, and in settings of his music by New Music ensemble, the London Sinfonietta. But fundamentally Squarepusher is about ploughing an uncompromisingly individual route. "The idea of being part of a movement isn't particularly exciting to me, unfortunately," he said in 1998.

"It just seems like part of some kind of cultural regime, that doesn't mean shit to me. It's probably because apart from anything else I was brought up a 'Thatcher's Child'. You follow your individual path: that's totally the thing of Thatcher's politics, and you get back what you put in. And as much as I despise the Tory party and Mrs Thatcher.... It just gets in your brain and makes the way you are.

"It's actually an idea which was stated most eloquently by Carl Jung in *Man And His Symbols*, which is basically saying, 'Yes, we have gone past the point of accessing political [dimensions]; we are beyond God – God is dead, so where do we look? And we don't know where to look. Basically what he says is, we have to look back inside, and reacquaint ourselves with the primitive mind and so forth. Basically, he argues that in the twentieth century, we're just obsessed with 1+1=2, rationality, we attack the problem like this. [Jung's] saying, Look back inside and reacquaint ourselves with the primitive, instinctive, the old mind, if you like. That will itself reveal where we've got to go – as in, not just trying to work it out rationally, because logic and rationale are not providing the answers any more.... With what I do, I'm attempting to reacquaint myself with a part of me which can almost be autopilot."

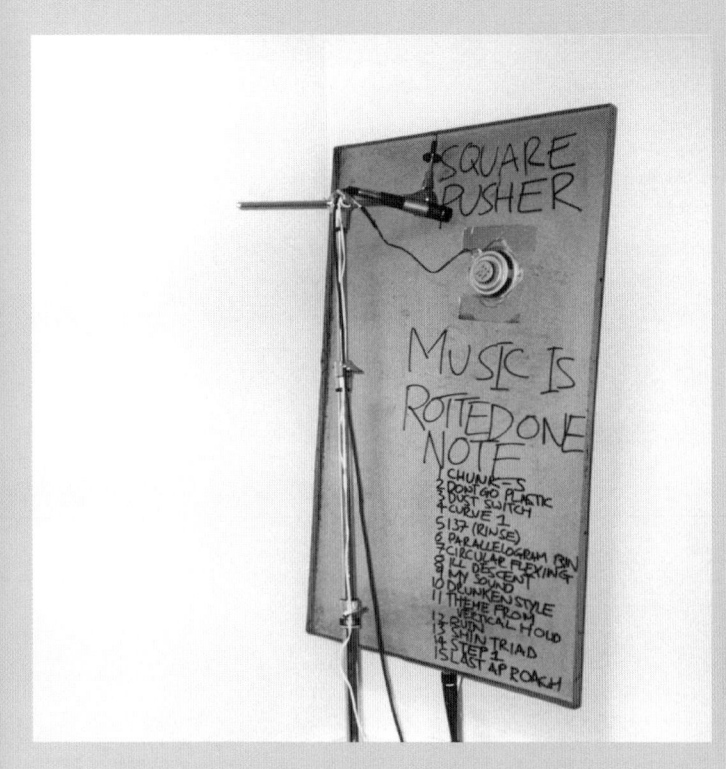

Grit hits the fan: Squarepusher

Adrian Shaughnessy

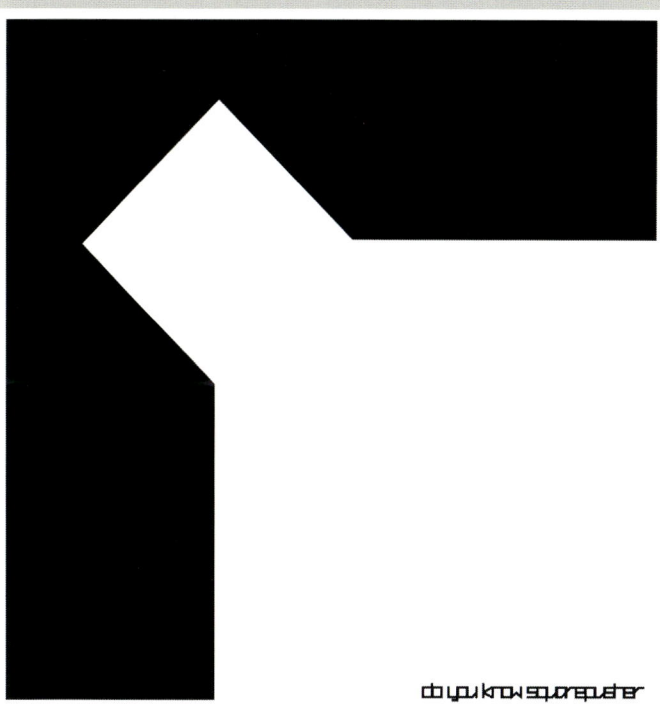

left to right: Squarepusher's *Music Is Rotted One Note*, 1998 (WARP57), *Budakhan Mindphone*, 1999 (WARP62), *Ultravisitor*, 2004 (WARP117), *Do You Know Squarepusher*, 2002 (WARP97).

Squarepusher covers exhibit enough stylistic diversity for an entire label. For the most part, Squarepusher (using his real name Tom Jenkinson) co-designs his sleeves in partnerships with professional graphic designers. The results are mixed: not all Squarepusher sleeves cut it. Too many fail to encapsulate Jenkinson's idiosyncratic, jazz-injected, bass-riveted music. To the casual observer, it is almost as if every time Jenkinson designs/commissions a sleeve, he takes a decision to do the mirror opposite of what he did on the previous occasion. The art-installation cover for *Music Is Rotted One Note*, 1998 – design is credited to Jenkinson and Kleber, a well-regarded web design company – has a handmade Fluxus-like beauty, as does the scruffy audiophile homage of *Budakhan Mindphone*, 1999, also credited to Jenkinson and Kleber. Jenkinson, however, plays no part in the most successful Squarepusher sleeve: *Do You Know Squarepusher?*, 2002, which is designed by Alexander Rutterford. This sleeve has a haiku-like graphic purity that makes it a minor classic of contemporary sleeve design.

Autechre during the second All Tomorrows Parties festival at Camber Sands, West Sussex, 2001. Photo: Eva Vermandel.

"There's a joke in the office", says Ian Anderson of the Designers Republic about the Autechre duo, "they always say the next album's going to be 'much more hiphop'." Fiercely protective of their reputation and possessors of a fearsomely rigorous digital sound, Autechre shied away from their *Incunabula* debut to produce a string of increasingly abstract, endlessly fascinating releases. Sean Booth and Rob Brown have always insisted on maintaining contact with their roots in early electro and hiphop, and much of their practice still involves real-time manipulation of sound modules, effects and loops, as a result of being seduced by prototype Acid House. "You can actually hear us messing about with some of the sounds in the track," Booth said in 1994, "and that's something we always like to hear in other people's stuff. That's just from the days of Acid. You used to hear just the one sound all the way through the track, and you'd focus on the one sound…" "… be guided, constantly," added Brown. "But you knew it was just a guy twiddling a knob," Booth finished. While their methods may remain fixated on hands-on beat and sound processing, each successive album marks a new breakthrough as they twist their tracks into ever more perplexing and complex sonic alloys and plastics, as if the molecular structure of music has been broken down and reconfigured. Despite the frequent hyperbole and critical flights their music continues to inspire, Sean Booth tries to keep his feet on the ground.

"What happens is, you put it out into the world and everyone tells you what a genius you are… some of the things are a bit different, you know, but… intrinsically we've never really valued originality that much. I think it's just the people that write about us that value it, and they seem to see it in what we do… maybe because we're taking more chances or something, I don't know."

Another perception they're at pains to debunk is that their music is the sole product of computer processing.

"When we did [1997's] *Chiastic Slide* people thought it had all been done on a Mac, but probably 90 per cent of it [wasn't], it was just mixed on a Mac, you know? It's just because people assume… like, people now are all going, 'Oh, you use Max/MSP [software], you build your own [virtual] instruments'. I'm going, 'No, I've never built an instrument in MSP in my fucking life' – I used it for sequencers to do that five years ago; I haven't even used Max/MSP for the last three years. I think a lot of the time it's people just projecting their idea of what we get up to in our studio onto us. I mean, basically we still sit in there arsing around with drum machines and keyboards, we're not doing anything technically amazing and flashy. We're just really into it."

Autechre in a press shot circa 1994.

Whatever the mundanities of their actions in the privacy of their studio, the result has been a sequence of highly iconoclastic releases. Architectural metaphors seem to work well in articulating the complexities of the Autechre sound. Like the French composers of the GRM school such as Bernard Parmegiani, whom they admire (and unlike Aphex Twin's frequent injections of room ambience and human voices), Autechre are purely, occasionally airlessly electronic and digital. With the sequence of *Tri Repetae*, 1995, *Chiastic Slide*, 1997, *LP5*, 1998 and *Confield*, 2001, they manipulated more and more microscopic detail and the amount of activity in any given duration of their music increased dramatically. Rob Brown is a former architecture student, and the organisation of their sound into

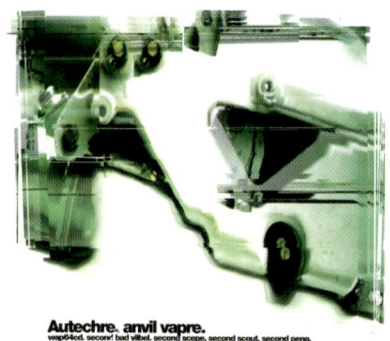

top: Autechre's *Amber*, 1994 (WARP25).
bottom: *Anvil Vapre* EP, 1995 (WAP64).

lines and curves, convergences and chaotic splinterings, suggests the impossible structures of architect Zaha Hadid, or the thrusting, paraboloid bridges of Santiago Calatrava. Of the few clues the pair have given to their working methods, Sean Booth has spoken of a state of mind they try to achieve that deals with spatialities. "We're quite into graphics that are simultaneously two- and three-dimensional", he told an interviewer in 1997. "We're… into more sort of fluid structures that are simultaneously the most efficient, the most beautiful, and the most engineered… It's kind of like trying to make straight lines from curves, but involving shapes that sort of dictate what the curves are, if you like, and the difference between two separate pieces creates a third transitional piece. It doesn't really exist; it's just basically lots of different stages between the two pieces, and you end up with a third shape that doesn't exist but is suggested to you by the image. That's what we're trying to do. It's similar to what we've been doing with our tracks… to take two completely separate elements and come up with a third in some way."[3]

Over the years Autechre have produced Warp's most consistently challenging body of work. Having set initially high standards, the relationship they have built with the label is built on confidence that they will continue to surpass themselves. Explaining the logistics of the relationship between label and artist, Booth explains:

3. Booth, Sean, interviewed on www.disquiet.com.

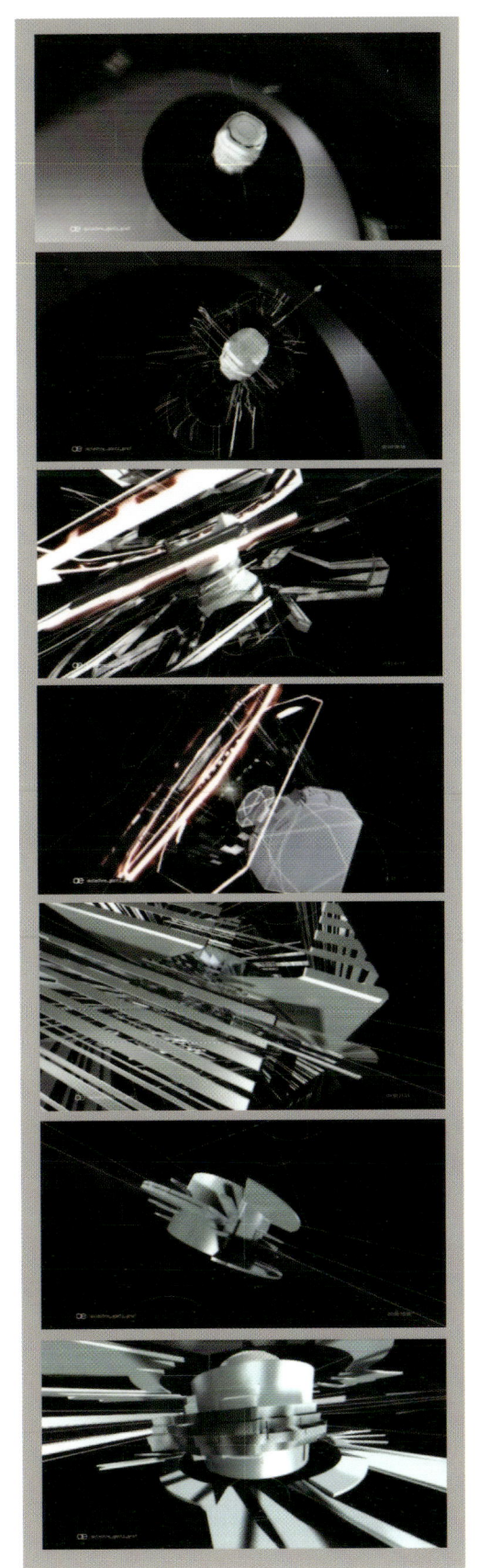

Stills from video for Autechre's *Gantz Graf*, 2002 (WAP256). Film maker Alex Rutterford's computer-generated graphics were, he claimed, inspired by an LSD trip.

"With us it's more like we send the CD to Warp thinking this is done, and we really hope that they're happy to go with it, because there has been a couple of times when they've said, 'change something', but most of the time they're just totally with us, and they'll just deal with it, and they'll say, 'OK, we think we can sell this, we've got to keep the production costs at this', and we work it like that, rather than it being like, 'Oh, you've got to make your album saleable so that we can all make a profit because this is how much we aim to sell of everything'. [It's a] completely different way of working, with them. We can say to them, 'OK, well, [how many] would you shift of this if we did a tour, and we did some press and x, y and z?', and then get a rough figure in terms of what we can afford to spend on actually making the thing. We get an advance and then we have to live on that; if you don't get the album done in that amount of time then we have to find some money from somewhere, but usually we work it out. I mean, we used to put out one album every 14, 15 months, now it's gone to about one every 18, 20 months… but that's purely because we've got back catalogue out there, and we can afford to spend a bit more time doing the records now because we usually get a royalty on top of the advance. We haven't been through any periods where we've not recouped with Warp, thankfully."

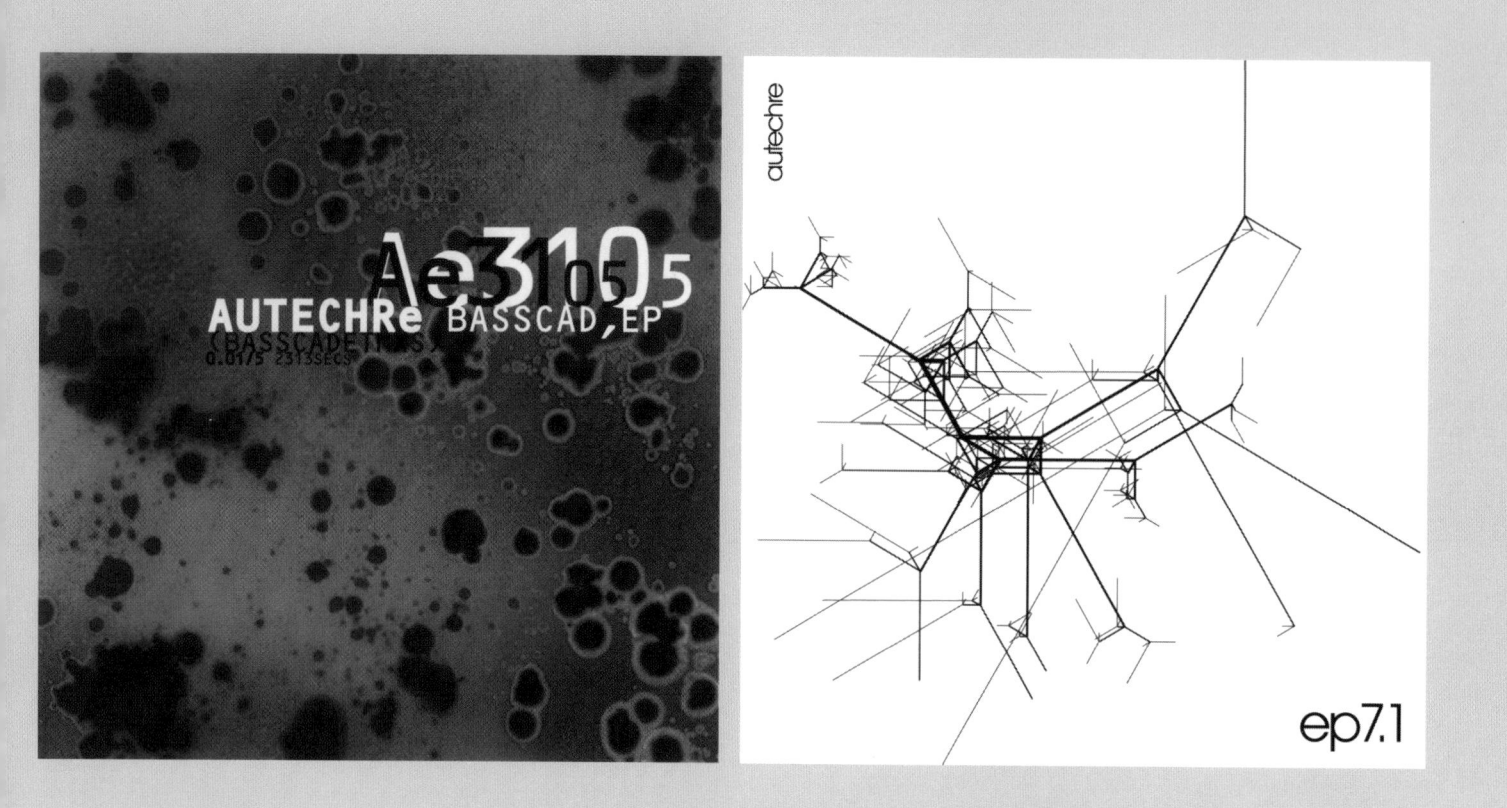

The art of Autechre
Adrian Shaughnessy

left to right: Autechre's *Basscadet*, 1994 (WAP44), *EP7.1*, 1999 (WAPEP7.1), *Chiastic Slide*, 1997 (WARP49), *Confield*, 2001 (WARP128).

It isn't every musician who knows how to commission worthwhile design, and some execrable design is perpetrated by musicians, not to mention weak designers trying to satisfy the untutored whims of these same musicians. However, it is unthinkable that independent labels like Warp would dictate to an artist how his or her sleeve should look. In the case of Autechre – musicians who control their sleeve design with auteurist conviction – it has resulted in perhaps the finest body of sleeves on the Warp label. The visual austerity of the best Autechre covers matches the aural austerity of the duo's digital music. Their sleeves feature a panoply of fractured typography, shards of half-envisioned architecture and cortex-disturbing illustration – the cover for *Chiastic Slide* (especially in its resplendent 12" vinyl format) by Designers Republic, is a magnificent example of a genuinely iconoclastic and utterly modern record sleeve. Designers Republic has not designed all Autechre sleeves, and yet when they work for the Lancastrian duo, they produce work of great finesse.

Other Autechre sleeves are self-designed, most notably *LP5*, 1998, and *Confield*, 2001. These sleeves have a maverick charm, but they look understated and tentative when compared to the work of Designers Republic, or the designer of later Autechre sleeves, Alex Rutterford. Rutterford's imagistic sleeves, *Draft 7.30*, 2003, and *Untilted*, 2005, have a splintered beauty that neatly demonstrates the evolution of computer-generated imagery: it has evolved into a sophisticated abstract visual syntax, unrecognisable from its early roots in 3D hyperrealism.

"The Autechre stuff that we did is probably my favourite," notes Ian Anderson of Designers Republic. "If I had to name my all-time favourite Warp artist it would probably be Autechre. Rob and Sean are really nice blokes. We'd seen them grow in stature from being two lads who turned up from Rochdale with carrier bags full of really cheap pop and crisps... we used to say 'the pop and crisp lads are coming in'. They were just young lads, but they were really good, and it was interesting to see how they developed."

Anderson's favourite Autechre sleeve (and the duo's favourite, too) is *Incunabula*, 1993. "I thought *Incunabula*

left to right: *Draft 7.30*, 2003 (WARP111), *LP5*, 1998 (WARP66), *Incunabula*, 1993 (WARP17), *Untilted*, 2005 (WARP180).

was a really great cover," notes Anderson. "What we always try to do at DR, especially with music, is create something that has equal value visually to the value of the sound, and so you've got two pieces of art, if you like, coming from the same inspirational source. This means they exist in parallel, and they complement each other, and are sympathetic to each other. But it's not like, here's a piece of artwork inspired by the music. For me, I never think that works. So *Incunabula* really set the tone. From a punter's point of view, I think if you listen to the music you should be able to look at the cover and they should have some sort of relation. A good example of this is *Unknown Pleasures* by Joy Division: there's nothing really to look at, but you could listen to that album and stare at that image, and there's something about it that's right. I think that works for *Incunabula*. *Amber* was a nice cover too, but it's a bit of a one-liner. It's a great image, and I think it was the right image – we wanted a polar opposite of *Incunabula*, but still sort of keep this idea of these weird landscapes. But there's actually a real image here, as opposed to an overlaid thing, and I think that suited the music as well."

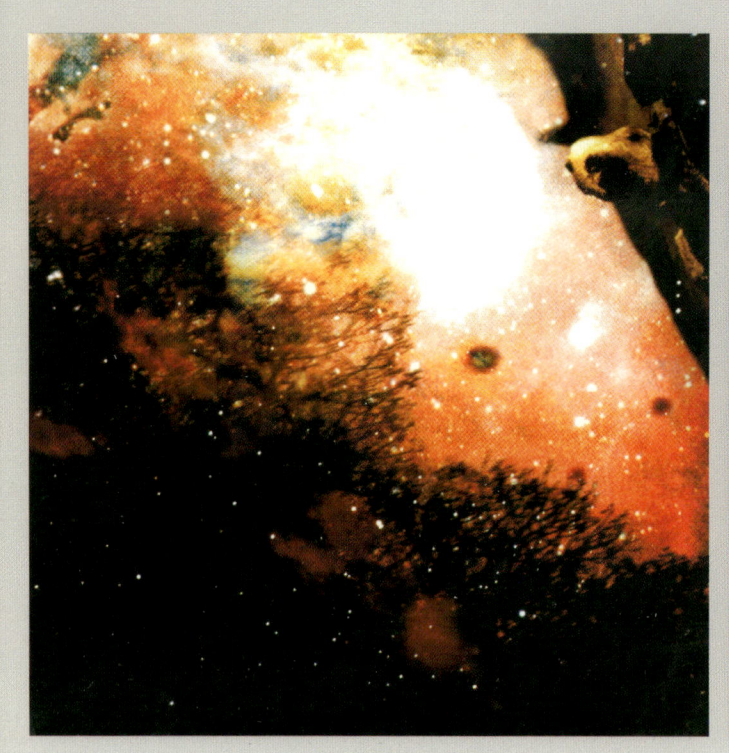

Mind elevation:
Nightmares On Wax
Adrian Shaughnessy

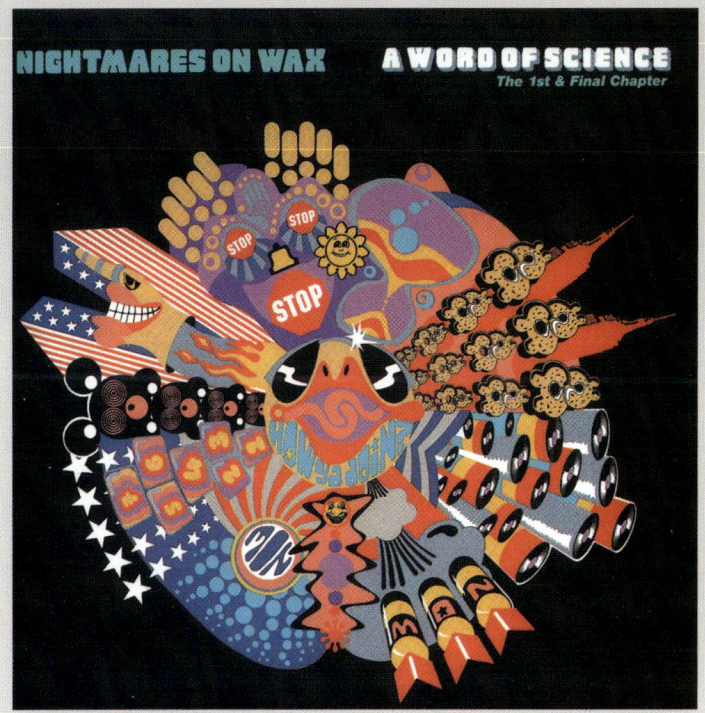

left to right: Nightmares On Wax's *Mind Elevation*, 2002 (WARP95), *A Word Of Science*, 1991 (WARP4), *Smokers' Delight*, 1995 (WARP36).

Hallucinatory imagery suggesting the soporific high of the marijuana puff, rather than the beatific high of the ecstasy rush, characterised certain releases on Warp in their fledgling years. The early sleeves of smokers' favourites Nightmares On Wax constitute a mini subgenre of 1990s reefer-chic. The cover for *A Word Of Science*, 1991 (by Designers Republic), is a seductive attempt to evoke the great, doped-up, Mandela-festooned covers of the 60s – but with a sharp smack of modernity. The style reaches a befuddled nadir in 1995's *Smokers' Delight*. Designed by Leigh Kenney, Lee McMillan and Sweet Design, it's a cartoon vision of a hash smoker's nirvana, entirely lacking Designers Republic's graphic poise. It's doubtful, however, if the intended audience would have noticed. The Sabres Of Paradise and Red Snapper, both favourites amongst music fans who enjoy a recreational puff while listening to music, maintained this strand of graphic rawness.

Die-cut flyer for Blech, the small Sheffield listening club set up by Warp in 1996. Ian Anderson of Designers Republic developed his variations on the 'Sissy' character after an inspirational trip to Tokyo, where he was entranced by commercial packaging and Manga graphics. Blech's cartoon characters ushered in a new phase for the label, projecting a more human, humorous face to the world.

Children at play

Brand new retro, nostalgia for the future: Blech, Mira Calix, Broadcast, Boards Of Canada

"Blech was really sort of my baby in a way", says Chantal Passamonte, who became Warp's in house press officer in 1995, then later moved sideways to become the artist known as Mira Calix. She was still working at the label in 1996 when Warp moved into a bigger, more spacious office in the Ballroom, the former Constance Grant Cavendish School of Ballroom Dancing, on West Street, and launched a new club space, Blech. Launched on 20 September 1996, and billed as "the cutest, cosiest club in Sheffield", the music policy and the design of Blech's flyers featured a character called 'Sissy', taking off from Designers Republic's Ian Anderson's obsession with Japanese cartoon graphics which he had devoured on a recent trip to Tokyo. After the solemnity of the *Artificial Intelligence* phase, Blech offered a draught of fresh air. "It was actually to inject some fun into it," confirms Passamonte. "Because the thing that kept coming across was people taking it all very seriously, and not actually the music, but the image of Warp, this image of serious geeky kids, and so Blech was definitely a counteract to all that – to recontextualise and to listen to it in a different way." Sheffield's club scene had fizzled out by the mid 1990s, and Blech took place in a back room next to Old Skool at the Music Factory, in line with the rise in 'listening clubs'.

On the day of the club launch, the *Sheffield Telegraph* published a lengthy article marking Warp's seventh anniversary and assessing its current status in a city whose music scene had substantially changed since the Jive Turkey days, and had repositioned itself around the growing student population. In the same article, there are hints that Warp are outgrowing their native city. "It's getting harder and harder", Steve Beckett is quoted as saying; "we spend two or three days a week in London and we end up sitting on a train and the tube for hours and then trekking from office to office." Revealing that the

factor 7

POP: Warp Records are celebrating their seventh anniversary in style. **Martin Lilleker** reports

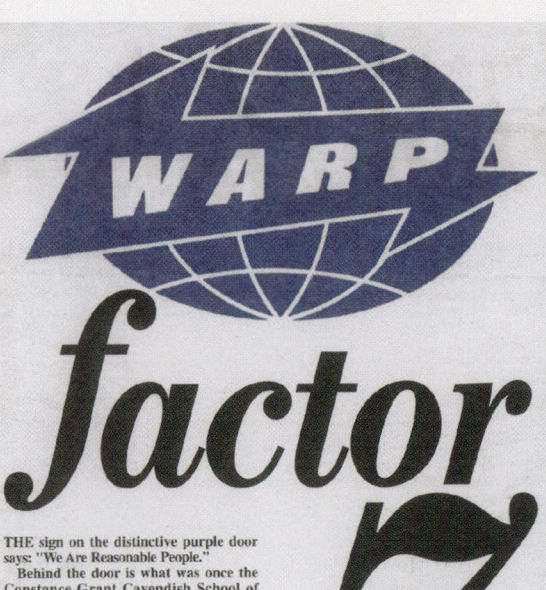

THE sign on the distinctive purple door says: "We Are Reasonable People."

Behind the door is what was once the Constance Grant Cavendish School of Ballroom Dancing, complete with stage which once accommodated a four-piece band on Saturday nights and a booth from where the records would be played on a wind-up gramophone for fox-trotters, cha-cha-chaists and military two-stepists of old to strut their stuff.

Now the premises on West Street, which were still in use in the Eighties, resound to a style of music which the late Miss Grant, doyenne of the dancefloor in Sheffield for more than 50 years, would probably be simply confused by.

Techno, ambient, house and other modern styles were most likely alien to Miss Grant who died in 1989, the same year that the new residents of the ballroom, those most reasonable people, Warp Records, came into existence.

The internationally-acclaimed label made the move earlier this year, seven years after starting out from the back of the Warp record shop on Division Street.

But it is only recently that they decided that Warp would stand for "We Are Reasonable People".

"It sounds really nice and sort of sinister at the same time," says Rob Mitchell who, along with Steve Beckett, started the company.

Not that there is anything sinister about Warp, apart from the occasional piece of music, particularly by biggest-selling act, Aphex Twin, which would put the willies up any ghosts - of the ballroom dancing kind or otherwise - that may inhabit their new HQ.

Indeed, tonight Warp re-launches what it calls "the cutest, cosiest club in Sheffield", Blech, which is designed to be "fun and have a relaxing atmosphere".

Or, as Steve puts it: "Just an expensive way of ensuring there is somewhere good for us to go on a Friday night."

Blech is being held in the intimate atmosphere of the backroom upstairs, next to the Old Skool, at the Music Factory.

"To a degree it is part of a national move kicking against the stadium DJ mentality and 4/4 beats of the likes of Cream and Back To Basics, the popularised and formularised standard product that people have become happy with," says Rob.

"Since Waxlyrical closed down at Kiki's there has been nowhere that plays new music, that doesn't replicate rather than originate."

The latter phrase neatly sums up the Warp approach over the years, something which is encapsulated on the first Blech CD, released this weekend.

The 23-track budget-priced CD - dubbed "the electronic equivalent of Gucci," this week by influential Muzik magazine - is the pick of some of the finest music released by Warp over the last seven years, from 1989's Dextrous by Nightmares On Wax and Autechre's Flutter from '94 to today's The Last One by Red Snapper and the yet-to-be-released Downtown by latest signing Jimi Tenor.

It has all been remixed by DJ Food, who will also be behind the decks at the opening Blech night.

"The CD is a history and a kind of future of Warp," says Rob. "We also hope it will help break people's conception of it as a techno or ambient label."

Warp have also remained fiercely independent despite offers of patronage from various major labels. "They know better now and don't bother anymore."

Which is perhaps why another of their favourite slogans is "100% Independent".

"It's a bit of a reaction to all those so-called independent labels which are funded by major labels. We just wanted to make a bit of a point really," says Rob.

As owners of the Warp record shop on Division Street, Rob and Steve have seen from both sides how the industry operates.

"There are always ways and means of getting round the rules for records qualifying for the charts.

"For instance a major label will come in with a single - and put another 20 free on the counter. We can then sell them cheap - 99p rather than £4.49 full price. Then there's all the merchandising. All stuff that an independent label couldn't do. If you were torn between two records with that price difference, which one would you buy?"

But Warp has managed to survive the various minefields the industry has to offer and is now thriving to the point where it has an annual turnover of £3m-plus, employ nine people on the label, another nine at a small distribution business, Ideal, which Warp has set up in Birmingham to handle house and techno imports from the States, and another five at the record shop.

But they are by no means complacent.

"It's a completely risky business," says Rob. "The bigger you get the more money you spend. All the money goes on the bands. We are signing house-sized cheques every week.

"You are gambling on your own taste all the time and nobody has absolutely perfect taste.

"Sometimes you sign bands because you see something there but you have absolutely no idea whether they are going to be massive, middling or completely non-existent.

"The main thing is that we are not going for that big pop thing which involves loads of money. Ours is more underground with sales of 10,000 to 50,000 per album.

"There is no manual for this industry. You have to learn the ropes as you go along. We have never been afraid to look stupid to find out how things work. We looked at people who had already done it, such as Daniel Miller at Mute Records, and we'd phone them up and ask. Now we get people phoning us up and asking for guidance.

"We've learned the hard way and we know from bitter experience not to work with just one company. We handle everything from hearing the first demo tape through to getting it in the shops: the manufacturing, marketing, visuals, distribution, computer software, copyright, publishing… you name it.

"We have always tried to be down to earth and realistic all the time. We always try to the best of our ability to get the best in that area of music although there has been the minor aberration…"

Indeed there have been questions about the two acts in which Warp are currently investing their future - solo performers Jimi Tenor and Squarepusher, described respectively as "Gary Glitter meets Elvis on acid" and "Weather Report on 78".

"Jimmy Tenor will be huge," says Steve, who claims to have discovered the Finn playing his keyboards, caressing a large and particularly smelly salami, in a bar in Vienna.

"He's already massive in Germany. We have had people screaming down the phone to licence his stuff for the German market."

But nothing should be a surprise coming from a label which has always been an innovator: pioneering the infamous "bleep" movement; hypnotic groove; having huge success with almost wholly instrumental music; selling ambient music to the mass market with its Artificial Intelligence series.

Music by Aphex Twin has been featured on a Pirelli TV advert while another of the label's acts, Sabres Of Paradise, has had pieces featured on adverts for Baccardi and The Times.

The only down side of the Warp success story is that they may have to eventually uproot for London.

"It's getting harder and harder," says Steve. "We spend two or three days a week in London and we end up sitting on a train and the tube for hours and then trekking from office to office."

They are now in the process of buying an office and a flat in London to ease things. "We've only just moved so it's certainly not going to be in the near future. We'd rather stay up here but we are still waiting for Sheffield to be dragged into the 20th Century when it comes to being a 24-hour city."

Warp have played their part in attempts to achieve this, trying to turn the Hallamshire Hotel on West Street into the decent mid-sized venue the city so badly needs. The brewery were not interested. They have also appeared before magistrates to help plead the case for entertainment licences for the likes of The Republic. Ironically the last time they had to do this was when they applied to change the licence of their new premises from entertainment to office use.

Last week there was also the irony of seeing Pulp win the Mercury Award. Warp helped them get out of a previous "terrible" record deal by setting up the indie label, Gift. That led to the deal with present record company Island but, as Steve says: "If we were the size we are now we would have been able to keep them."

Surely even dear old Constance Grant would have liked Pulp?

label has already acquired a flat and an office in London, he adds, "We'd rather stay up here but we are still waiting for Sheffield to be dragged into the twentieth century when it comes to being a 24 hour city."[1]

By now Warp had achieved global status, a recognisable worldwide brand. An Aphex Twin tune had been used in an advert for Pirelli tyres, Sabres Of Paradise tracks had been used to advertise *The Times* newspaper and Bacardi Rum. In addition, their worldwide fanbase was bordering on obsessive. "A lot of poor students who had come from Japan or whatever," says Passamonte, "thinking they were coming to some great scene, would turn up at the office with carrier bags – poor bastards. They had nowhere to go until we started the club thing. There were kids like that, and then I think for the actual Sheffielders, it was probably a combination of a bit of respect, sort of favour-pulling, and a bit of sniping. The usual thing you get in your home town."

Warp was clearly growing, and the six full time staff found themselves running out of space in the Brown Street office. "We just couldn't cope with the amount of work and there was no space so we were literally just sitting on top of each other. At that point a move was pretty crucial." The Ballroom was a huge, much needed improvement.

Although Warp and its artists have generated a phenomenal amount of press coverage over the years, the job of being its press officer – liaising between artists and journalists – is a thankless one. Many of its musicians are reluctant heroes, far more inured to creating tracks in privacy than holding forth about the state of the world, or analysing their intentions into a mic. The reputation of Warp itself

above: Cover of *Blech* cassette, 1996 (WARP40), and another club flyer.
opposite: Rob Mitchell and Steve Beckett appear in the *Sheffield Telegraph*, 1996, celebrating seven years of Warped trading.

1. Beckett, Steve, quoted in Martin Lilleker, "Warp Factor 7", *Sheffield Telegraph*, 20 September, 1996.

Cavendish Buildings, 210-218 West Street, Sheffield, as it looked in 2005. Warp's office in a former ballroom dancing school was situated here between 1996 and the move to London four years later. Photo: Rob Young.

helped Passamonte sell features and reviews, even though dealing with the artists could be unorthodox. "I don't think it's that people wanted to be 'faceless Techno bollocks', but on the other hand they didn't want to push themselves forward. That's not what any of it was about: everybody wanted to make really brilliant music, and I think wanted it to be noticed, but not in the way of having to sell themselves. That suited me fine – that wasn't something I had to battle with. The only big battles were actually getting people to show up."

One of her abiding memories involves an attempt by a French journalist to interview The Aphex Twin.

"I was waiting at Patisserie Valerie for Richard to turn up, and of course he didn't, and I actually saw someone on the street that looked quite like him, who I attempted to bribe to come and do the interview. The guy was kind of keen, and then obviously thought better of it, and so didn't actually do it. I was there pacing the streets of Soho trying to find a Richard lookalike.

"It wasn't like working at other labels where people had managers and they turned up on time. None of the artists at that point had managers, that I was dealing with. That came later. I did a lot of calling people's parents, in order to move my artists around or find them when they disappeared.

"Rob and Steve wanted as much press as they could get, so that people knew the record was out and so distributors would be happy. But they always really wanted their artists to be individual, so although the ethos of the label was quite strong, they knew, even back then, that for the label to succeed the artists had to make it in their own right – that the Warp logo would look great on the record but it shouldn't be just the thing that sells it. It should open the door but not keep it open."

> "I was waiting at Patisserie Valerie for Richard to turn up, and of course he didn't, and I actually saw someone on the street that looked quite like him, who I attempted to bribe to come and do the interview"
> Chantal Passamonte

The second half of the 90s was an era of rapid burn-out for many electronic music microgenres: Jungle had mutated in many pertinent ways, moving from hardcore underground to adoption by the likes of Everything But The Girl, David Bowie and adverts for household air fresheners within a couple of years. As the internet penetrated public life and became another shop window, familiar to all, electronic music was on its own course of subsumation into a wider consciousness. Festival-friendly groups such as Chemical Brothers, Leftfield, Daft Punk, Underworld and Fatboy Slim enjoyed mainstream hits and MTV exposure. The question for Warp was whether to take some steps towards emulating this sort of popular success, and if so, how to rationalise it with their uncompromising attitude to independence. There was also the dream of Warp Vision, which was becoming more of a priority for Beckett and Mitchell. Film production needed far greater capital than the average indie label could muster, especially one with such generous concessions to its artists.

Blech also ushered in a new phase of the label's music character as the music floated further from its 'intelligent Techno' roots. In 1996 Warp found itself with a new wave of artists whose music dealt in various ways with nostalgia, a childlike sense of play on a private and intimate scale, instead of being aimed at the dancefloor. This emerging trend could be located, at one extreme, in the faux-naif electronica of Mira Calix and at the other, the Benny Hill-style infantilism of Aphex Twin's "Milk Man" (from 1996's *Girl/Boy* EP), in which Richard James' earnest falsetto expresses a longing to "drink milk/From the milkman's wife's tits". It was not that the futuristic energy of the *Artificial Intelligence* period had run out of steam, but 'electronic culture' was now a mainstream concern, and the use of electronic and digital music was in itself no guarantee of sounding at the bleeding edge.

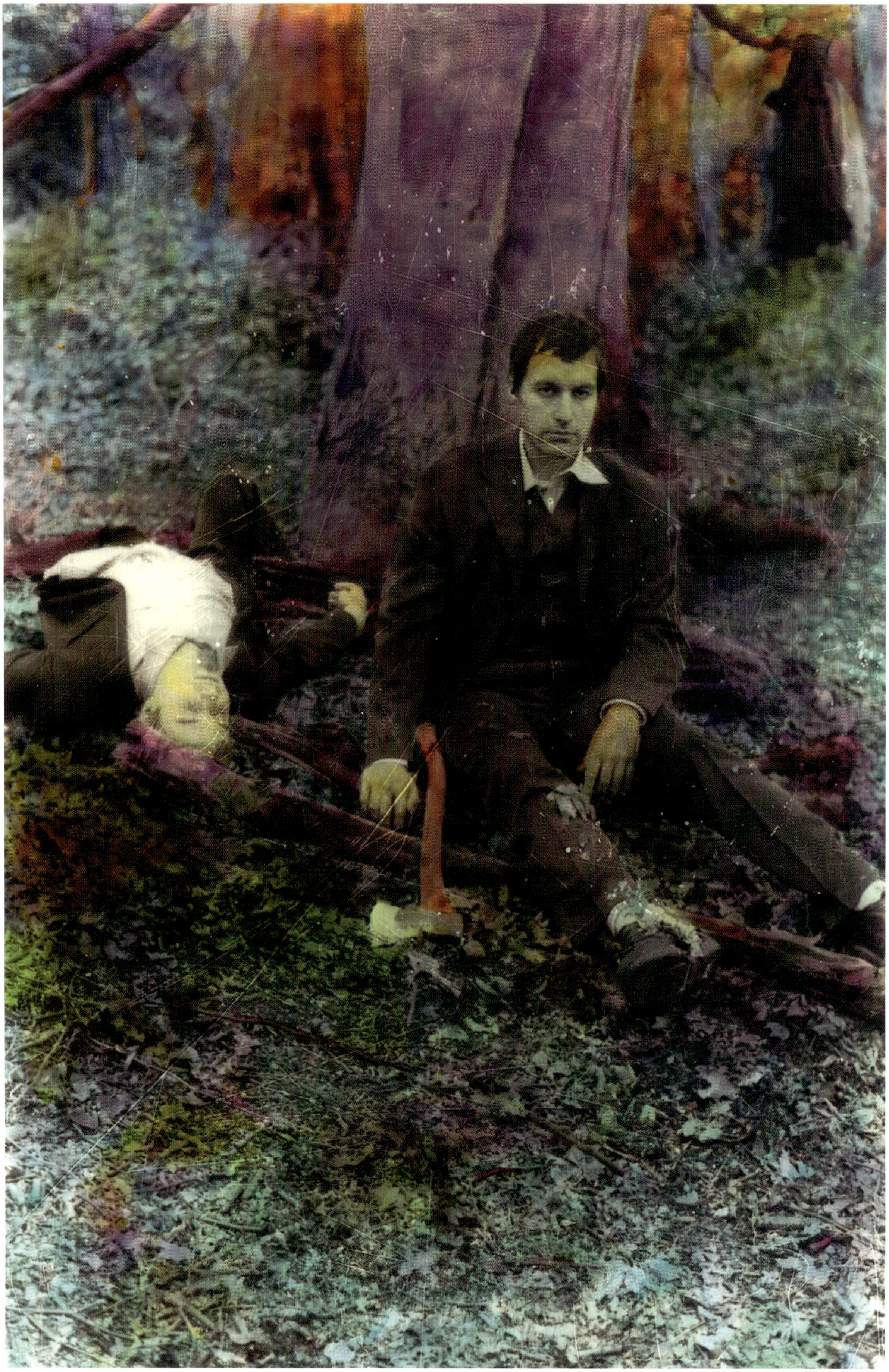

In the UK and the US, especially, a boom in independent labels was in full swing, many modelled on Warp itself. Clear Records, for instance, with its graphic style blatantly based on the graffiti tags of early 1980s New York, was an outlet for several Warp artists to produce more electro-influenced music under different aliases: Plaid (Ed Handley and Andy Turner, formerly of The Black Dog), Tusken Raiders and Jake Slazenger (both aliases of Mike Paradinas), Jedi Knights (Link/Global Communication), and Gescom, a loose collective linked to the Manchester based Skam label that included the two members of Autechre. Through this alternative channel this generation of artists, mostly in their 20s, exercised an innocent sense of fun and nostalgia for the music they must have been bodypopping to in their early teens – summed up in the title of the Gescom EP, *The Sound Of Machines Our Parents Used* and the later Max Tundra single, *Children At Play*. The *Star Wars* references in Tusken Raiders and Jedi Knights was a reminder of the influence of the rich array of sound effects the George Lucas movie had introduced to the musical galaxy: the bursts, bleeps and pings of laser bolts and comically humanised droids.

And something of *Star Wars*'s marriage of fairy tale and science fiction lay behind the invigorating new music that was coming out on Warp. Mira Calix's *Ilanga* EP, the two Disjecta records by Seefeel's Mark Clifford, Freeform's *Prowl* 12" and Plaid's *Not For Threes* LP all had a sense of conscientious play with machines; complex constructions in digital Playdoh, Meccano, Lego and Sticklebricks. Simon Pyke, aka Freeform, describes his music making as like delving into a toy box: "'Playing' was and still is a central part of composing – it has to be fun. I just got excited at the possibilities of things you could do with samplers and synths. I rarely started a track with the result in mind, so the process was very much producing a kind of box of nice sound objects, then building a structure with those objects. The process was basically, play lots, then chip away and sculpt a track."

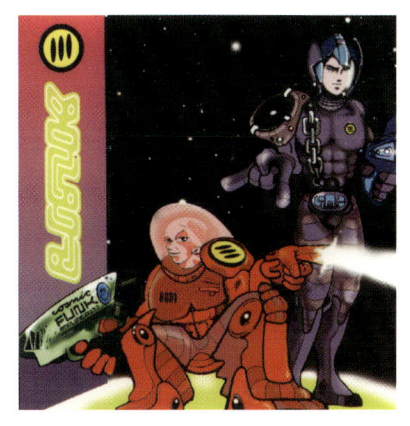

top: Freeform's Simon Pyke, and (middle) his *Prowl* EP, 1996 (WAP73).
bottom: George Lucas meets future funk with Link (aka The Jedi Knights) on *Antacid*, 1995 (WAP59).
opposite: Plaid bury the hatchet.

above: Birmingham post-rock outfit Broadcast running aerodynamic tests. The group's visual identity (below, video for "Papercuts", 2000) displays an obsession with post-war avant garde cinema and psychedelic 1960s electronica.

Other acts overtly referenced and reinvented sounds of a lost analogue age. Broadcast, a group from Birmingham influenced by Stereolab (who themselves released a lone LP on Warp in 1998, *Aluminum Tunes*), were more of an indie pop group than an electronic act, influenced by United States Of America's experimental analogue synth work, The Velvet Underground's art rock snarl, and the spooky, spatial arrangements of Ennio Morricone. Lovers of uncanny atmospherics, they also cited such subtle chiller movies as Milos Forman's *Love Of A Blonde*, Hans Richter's surrealist *Dreams That Money Can Buy*, and Czech horror flick *Valerie And Her Week Of Wonders*. Albums such as *Work And Non-Work*, 1997, *The Noise Made By People*, 2000, and *Haha Sound*, 2003, are loaded with reverberant kettle drums, ancient echo chambers, *Forbidden Planet* electronics from vintage keyboards, and adorned with cover art by long time friend Julian House that playfully references the typewriter experiments of Lettrist poet Henri Chopin. Vocalist Trish Keenan had the abstracted, vacant quality of lost female vocalists such as Brigitte Fontaine, Vashti Bunyan and Linda Perhacs. Their near neighbours Plone, a vocoder/analogue synth trio, similarly fetishised proto-electronic pop, but failed to transcend their influences with the same panache as Broadcast.

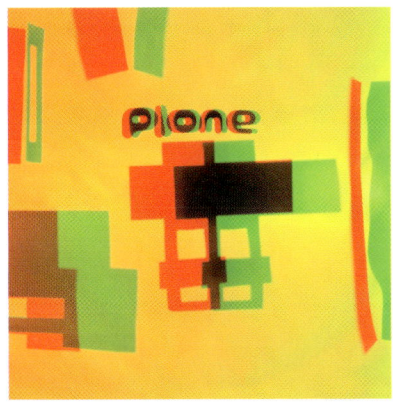

Under the name Jake Slazenger, Mike Paradinas' obsession with sampling keyboards from Herbie Hancock led to the dayglo funk of *Das Ist Ein Groovy Beat, Ja?*, 1996. His fat, puffy basslines resembled the theme tune of children's TV series *Grange Hill*, while he would 'solo' over the top making liberal use of the synthesizer's pitchbending toggle. In 1996 he described his concentrated working methods:

"I use something that sounds like it's almost in tune – the tune's right but there's one note in the sequence that sounds slightly off, or using chords that sound slightly off, and it sounds really nice. It's the same with old analogue that goes out of tune. That's what makes me like old Human League records and stuff done on analogue. Depeche Mode were slightly out of tune: it goes in and out. That's what I like about sound. I really like detuning, and Jungle. And I've sort of combined them."

The Black Dog split, none too amicably, in 1995. Ken Downie continued using the name; Ed Handley and Andy Turner made Plaid their main focus, resulting in one of Warp's most enduring acts. Infused with elements of Latin percussion, fizzy electro, a hydraulic dynamism and a lightness of touch in the programming, they have always taken a relaxed view of their position in the scheme of things. "It's tempting to search for originality", Turner said in 1997, "but I think that search actually detracts from the music itself. There's not a lot of pleasure in searching for something original. I don't always think it's that sincere. Originality comes from relaxing or stopping the search."

Retro-fitted artwork (top to bottom): Jake Slazenger's *Nautilus* EP, 1996 (WAP75) and *Das Ist Ein Groovy Beat, Ja?*, 1996 (WARP42), Plone's *Plock* EP, 1998 (WAP107) and *For Beginner Piano*, 1999 (WARP64).

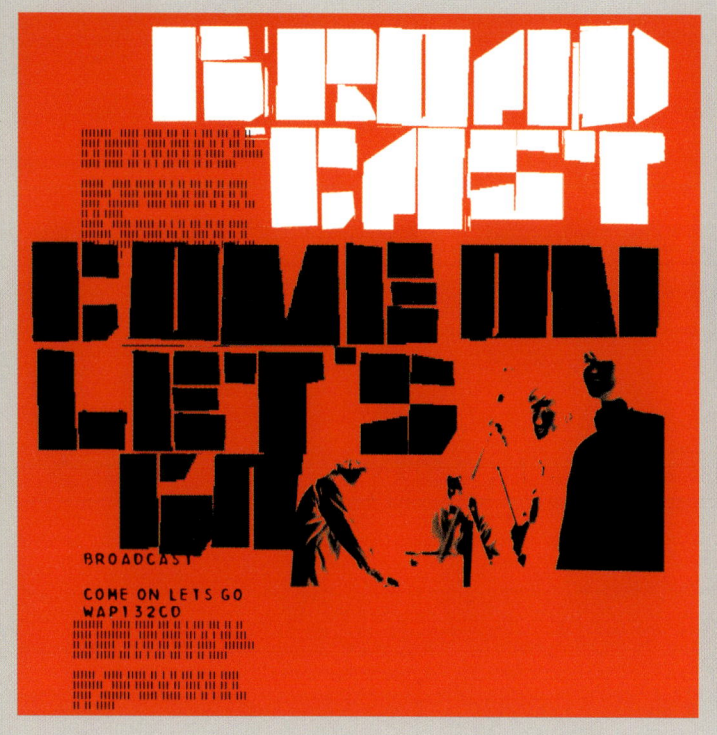

Electronic woodblocks: Broadcast
Adrian Shaughnessy

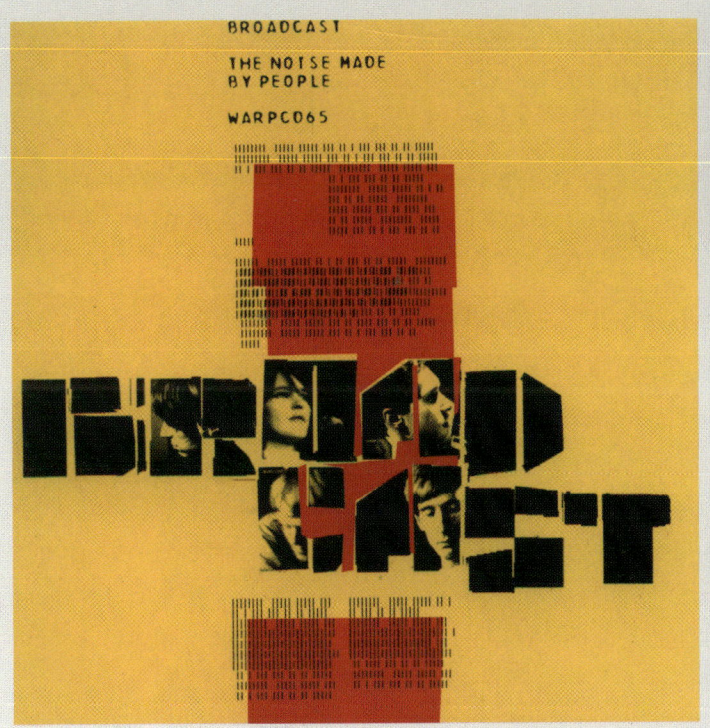

left to right: Broadcast's *Come On, Let's Go* EP, 2000 (WAP132), *Work And Non Work*, 1997 (WARP52), *The Noise Made By People*, 2000 (WARP65), *Haha Sound*, 2003 (WARP106).

The Birmingham based group Broadcast represents a turning point in Warp's musical policy. Along with Jimi Tenor, Vincent Gallo and Prefuse 73 – amongst others – Broadcast are an example of a Warp act that doesn't fit the tag 'Warp electronica'. Using a welter of subterranean influences, Broadcast have a hybrid style that could be described as 'futuristic retro'. They use a vast array of influences from pop's storehouse of weirdness – but the context in which they place their findings from pop's dressing up box is hardly 'retro'. Elephants Memory, Morricone, United States Of America, Raymond Scott, Krzysztof Komeda, and a dozen other arcane sources, all of whom are characterised by a disarming modernity, are melded together by Broadcast to form a smorgasbord of sharp-brained musical nowness. In Julian House, Broadcast found a graphic designer capable of rendering an external formulation that captures the fundamental intelligence and space-beatnik eclecticism of their music. House's style reached its apotheosis in *Haha Sound*, 2003, a magnificent piece of graphic fabulism that failed to gain the recognition that House's earlier work for Primal Scream was accorded, but which in nearly all respects surpasses that body of work.

> "*Not For Threes* is a nursing term… basically, if they have a patient admitted into hospital, they sign a consent that if they were to have a heart attack or collapse, do they want to be resuscitated or do they want to be left. And if a patient's designated 'not for threes', it's 'don't call the crash team'."
>
> Andy Turner, Plaid

As electronica became more abstract, it also existed in a vacuum of social and political discourse. Many of the artists held distinctive political opinions, but there was little desire to embed explicit ideas within musical structure or content. Plaid's music exemplifies a sense of spirited, liberated play and inventiveness from within an apolitical bubble.

"A social revolution is made up of lots of little personal revolutions," said Andy Turner around the time of the appearance of their *Not For Threes* album: "Maybe the music can make that happen, but then every generation goes through this discovery period. Maybe because of the media now, it seems to be a big thing. But essentially not a lot's changed really, freedom-wise. We seem to be less free. If the question is, Do we have any political motivation?, I think it's no. But I'm not sure. Maybe you're part of a great thing, but you're influenced by your environment, so you take it in, then spew it out in whatever form you express yourself, and that then influences someone else to do something."

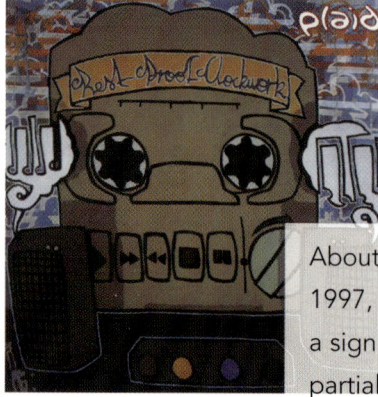

"Without lyrics," added Handley, "it's all very vague anyway. You can say 'this is an aggressive piece of music or a melancholic piece of music', but you couldn't say 'this is a piece of music encouraging personal freedom' – you can't be that specific."

About the significance of the title of *Not For Threes*, 1997, Andy Turner has commented: "I think 333 has been a significant number for quite a long time, so that was partially the attraction of it. It's cropped up a lot. I think it's supposed to represent the abyss or something." Handley added, "It's not a very specialist album. It's not delving into repetition too heavily, or minimalism, or orchestral grandeur or anything. It is pretty middle of the road in a way. But then not really. It's middle of the road, but not a road that we know."

above: Plaid's *Not For Threes*, 1997 (WARP54), and *Rest Proof Clockwork*, 1999 (WARP63).
opposite: Andy Turner and Ed Handley, slaves to the rhythm.

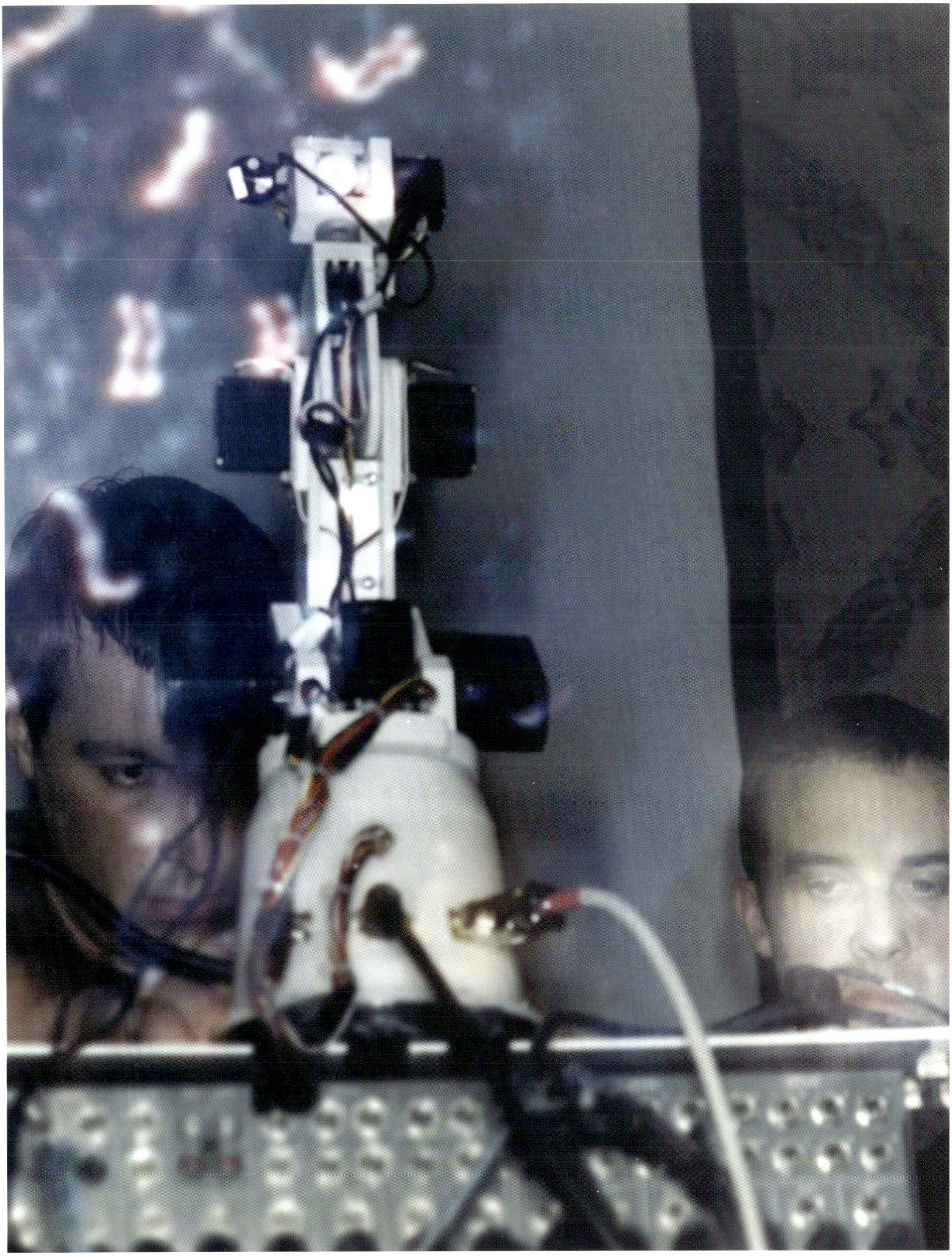

Chantal Passamonte worked as Warp's press officer before assuming the identity of Mira Calix.

Chantal Passamonte had been DJing for several years since arriving in London from Durban, South Africa. Originally working as a photographer, she discovered her flatmates were musicians and DJs and became drawn into London's early 90s post-rave scene, eventually hosting Ambient parties under the Telepathic Fish banner. Occasionally she would borrow her flatmates' equipment and dabble with some musical experiments of her own, gradually buying the components she liked using. Several years later, she made the transition to being an artist almost on a whim. While she was employed as Warp's press officer, she recalls:

"Steve came round for dinner and I just played him the tracks, and he really liked them, and said, 'Oh, can we put them out?' And I was like, God, that's a bit weird, and we sat and chatted about it, and straight away I thought, 'It's got to be silver, because I just love mirror board and silver, and so we just had a laugh, and then, 'It's going to be a 10", perfect', and I didn't give it too much thought, other than I didn't want to put my name on the record because I was dealing with all the press. But Steve and Rob kept pressuring me and eventually said, 'Look, we'll give you a deal, just go, get out of the office'. So I went part time for about six or seven months."

clockwise from top left: Mira Calix's *Pin Skeeling*, 1998 (WAP97), *Prickle*, 2001 (WAP145), *One On One*, 2000 (WARP73).

The 10" was the two-track *Ilanga* EP, but the new arrangement was not entirely satisfactory, as she was having to fill three days with five days' worth of office work, added to her expanding DJ career. Beckett and Mitchell recognised that this wasn't a practical option, and offered her a record deal which would allow her to write music. She left her desk at the Warp office, taking her Apple Mac computer as a leaving present. (She was also given a unique piece of Designers Republic artwork representing herself as the 'Sissy' character. This bore the catalogue number WAP99, but has never been seen in public.) She gave birth to her first album *One On One*, 2000, on that computer. "It wasn't a

right: A childhood idyll pictured on *Skimskitta's* back cover.
below: Mira Calix's *Skimskitta*, 2003 (WARP104).

very strong machine," she recalls, "but it saw me through. The funniest thing about it was, I was doing a remix and I'd just got the mix correct and pressed record on the DAT machine, and it blew up! I was totally distraught, there was smoke coming out of it and everything. But it was great, because I had the recording of the explosion." The sound of the Mac's demise can be heard on her remix for Austrian artist Pomassl "Goodbye To The Golden Goose" (on *Retrial Error*, Laton Records).

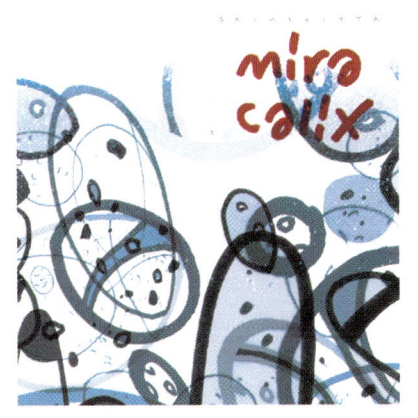

"I am a great procrastinator," she admits, "I waffle around a lot". If that makes her sound like a bored kid finally forced to finish its homework, the results are deeply introspective, and as much as electronica can be a 'first person' narrative, there is a conspiratorial intimacy, and a sense of secrets imparted, a child leading you to a hidden cache of treasures. An array of tactile sounds and noise scuttle around the tracks, among a forest of delay, digital noise, interruptions of music box melody, and short loops and beats that sound like cheap toy drum machines.

"I'd always been a person that made things since I was a child. I made clothes, I made sculptures, I made paintings. I find doing music incredibly honest. I'm going on instinct, I want to record what I'm feeling, which is awkward because sometimes you don't know what you're feeling, and you almost don't know it until you're halfway through it."

The sleeve of 2003's *Skimskitta* features an old family photograph of herself as a toddler, pulling a toy tortoise through a neatly manicured garden. Likewise, an atmosphere of conscientious exploration and childlike wonder permeates the tracks. She adds vocals in a barely audible gurgle ("Pin Skeeling", "Woody", "Paarl") and sources some of her sounds from objects she finds in nature (with her husband, Autechre's Sean Booth, she now lives in the rural county of Suffolk). That delicacy transferred to Passamonte's later project, *Nunu*, based around digital transformations of insect sounds. Originally commissioned by a New Music festival in Geneva, Switzerland, in 2002, she has also played it with the London Sinfonietta, accompanying their orchestral arrangements of her music with contact-miked live insects on stage.

Shadows and fog: Boards Of Canada on the Scottish coast, 2002. Photo: Peter Iain Campbell.

Faux-naif, ambiguous 'innocence' traits fuse with mathematical intricacy in the music of Scottish duo Boards Of Canada. Autechre's Sean Booth hipped Warp to their sound after hearing a cassette. The duo of Marcus Eoin and Mike Sandison lived for a while at a remote spot in the Pentland Hills, a few miles south of Edinburgh in Scotland. It's a wild zone within reach of the capital city, a mixture of ancient monuments, forests and winter ski lodges. In their base in a small group of houses, they formed part of a free ranging collective of friends who have been involved with music, graphic design, photography and video since the late 1980s.

Both the duo's parents had decamped to Canada soon after they were born, and their name hints at that experience, as well as the nature and public information films of the state-run National Film Board of Canada. After they returned to Scotland, by the mid 80s Sandison had begun recording music at professional studios, and the pair – together with a floating collective of around 20 artists, film makers, photographers, teachers of art, and enthusiastic friends – embarked on increasingly ambitious projects involving live instruments, minimal electronic music, photographic projections and films. In the early 90s, they had day jobs (they have hinted they worked at a university for a time, and Eoin studied artificial intelligence). The collective, named Hexagon Sun, held outdoor music and art events, where proto-Boards Of Canada music would be played with children's song records and tapes mixed and reversed over the top, while kaleidoscopic images swirled around the trees. By 2002, the friends had dwindled away to four or five, but the isolation was still crucial to the production of their sound. "It's the only way to do it", Sandison has said. "Cut yourself off, pull the shutters down." Eoin added, "I'm really paranoid about security. We've got all these tapes and discs going back 15 years or so. I've got this really complicated solar alarm on my house so that it's impossible to switch it off without cutting five different wires in different places simultaneously."[2]

In classic psychedelia, tiny details become massive; similarly, Boards Of Canada's *Music Has The Right To Children*, 1998, and *Geogaddi*, 2002, are littered with buried, foxed vocal samples and curious rhythmic tics; distorted as if heard through a hallucinogenic prism. They favour reversed samples and tapes (including aural palindromes – sentences that sound the same read both ways), references to pagan rituals ("You Could Feel The Sky" contains the words "a god with hooves"), and musical structures arranged, tuned and spaced at root level according to mathematical equations such as the Fibonacci sequence and Golden Ratio ("A Is To B As B Is To C", "Music Is Math", "The Smallest Weird Number"). Hidden references are meat and drink to Boards Of Canada's fans, who regularly observe that the total playing time of *Geogaddi* is 66:06, its total hard drive space when ripped to MP3 is 666 megabytes, etc. For Boards Of Canada themselves, numerology is "the grown up face of our work, the pessimistic side". There are simple, almost naively deployed elements: many of the voices they spin backwards or forwards into their music are taken from their own friends, others are pulled from ten year old videotapes. "A lot of the synthetic-sounding things you hear are actually recordings of us playing other instruments", said Eoin, "pianos, flutes or twanging guitar strings or

top: Mike Sandison (left) and Marcus Eoin.
bottom: Here come the Cold War jets – artwork by Hexagon Sun.

2. Quoted in Richard Southern, "Boards Of The Underground", *Jockey Slut*, December 2000.

"We grew up in the 70s, a time of great paranoia about science, a paranoia which comes across in the science fiction of that era, in books as well as films. It's this paranoia, this pessimism, this fear of science, which can be found in our music along with other influences. When we were growing up in the 70s, the view of the future shown in TV and films was very dark, very powerful."

Boards of Canada, quoted in Ariel Kyrou and Jean-Yves Leloup, "Two Aesthetes Of Electronic Music", *Virgin Megaweb*, June 1998.

field sounds we get from walking around with portable tape recorders, like electronic beeps in shops, or vehicles, then they are mangled beyond all recognition. We have an arsenal of old hi-fi tricks up our sleeve and we basically destroy the sounds until they're really lovely and fucked up."[3] On "Rue The Whirl" they heard birds outside their studio during playback, so recorded them and folded the sound into the finished track. But the sinister is ever present. The *In A Beautiful Place Out In The Country* EP references David Koresh – a close up of the cult leader's eye adorns the cover; "Amo Bishop Roden" refers to a Branch Davidian cult member who used the phrase that became the EP title.

They've talked about their ideas being disguised with melodies, like a juicy worm with a hook inside it. Their tones are often bent and wobbly, suggesting a record with an off-centre hole or the Doppler effect of music heard on fairground rides. Their beats are often weighted as if with lead or toffee, the music's edges seem dulled and blunted, and the slightly muffled acoustics suggest a baby's undeveloped ears perceiving the world from inside the womb. One of the many rumours around this group that they have a 'secret weapon' instrument that gives their unique sound quality. "We don't have lots of synths," they once said; "we use hi-fi gear and other tricks to achieve our sound… we take such long, individual paths to get where we go,

Kaleidoscopic artwork accompanying *Geogaddi*, 2002, by Hexagon Sun.

3. Eoin, Marcus, quoted in Mark Pytlik, "The Colour And The Fire", *HMV Magazine*, 2002.

paths that nobody else could ever follow…. Where some people will work on a track solidly for four days, we'll spend that long just on a hi-hat sound."[4]

Above all, Boards Of Canada's uncanny, uncomfortable mix of rustic, youthful innocence and subliminal menace comes from two friends who grew up during the end of the Cold War era, who have never quite forgotten the ever present potential for annihilation, as if an angel of destruction is hovering over their pastoral idyll. "For us," Sandison said in 2002, "the whole point of writing music is to get something infectious into the back of a listener's mind, something that feels so personal to you that you couldn't even possibly convey it in words to a close friend… there's a sort of knowing connection there between the listener and the musician that ordinary language would never be able to achieve. In a way it's like the closest you'll ever get to being psychic."[5]

The great outdoors: Boards Of Canada's disorientating sound was influenced by outdoor parties held in woodland close to their home. Photos: Peter Iain Campbell.

4. Quoted in Southern, "Boards Of The Underground".
5. Sandison, quoted in Pytlik, "The Colour And The Fire".

Flipping hexagons:
Boards Of Canada Adrian Shaughnessy

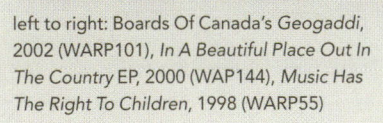

left to right: Boards Of Canada's *Geogaddi*, 2002 (WARP101), *In A Beautiful Place Out In The Country* EP, 2000 (WAP144), *Music Has The Right To Children*, 1998 (WARP55)

Boards Of Canada design their own sleeves. In comparison to the anarcho-visual assault of Aphex Twin, Boards Of Canada sleeves are tranquil moments of off-kilter oddness. The results lack any hint of graphic design formalism, yet they retain a touching naivety and delicacy – qualities found in abundance in the Scottish duo's music. Easily categorised as 'pastoral electronica', Boards of Canada's music sits alongside early Pink Floyd, The Incredible String Band and a handful of other lysergic 60s visionaries, as a near perfect sonic encapsulation of a dreamy antediluvian Eden. The cover for *Music Has The Right To Children*, 1998, is credited to Boards Of Canada; *Geogaddi*, 2002, is credited to Hexagon Sun (the name of the group's recording studio). It's doubtful if any professional designer could muster the necessary otherworldly innocence to design sleeves to match these self-designed covers – even 4AD's Vaughan Oliver, the most mystical and tactile of graphic designers, seems to offer too much formalism and structure to match the wan beauty of Boards Of Canada at their ethereal best. Both these sleeves fail as examples of technically accomplished graphic design, but as constituent parts of the group's aesthetic vision, they are mini-triumphs of the art of 'band designed' sleeve design.

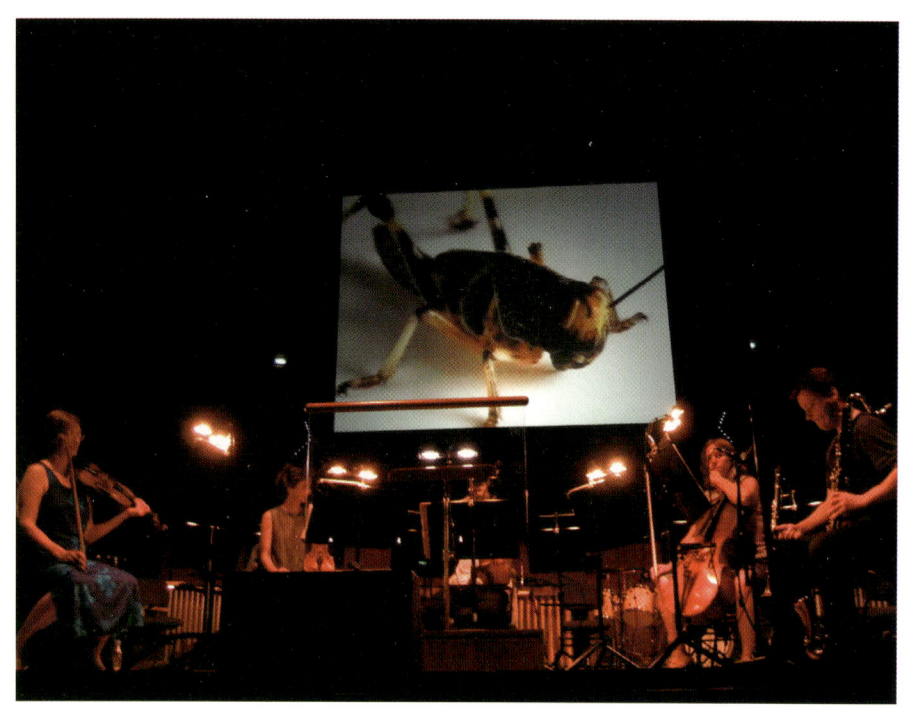

London Sinfonietta perform Mira Calix's *NuNu* with live insect accompaniment at Rome's Parco della Musica, July 2004. Warp's tenth anniversary in 1999 ushered in a phase of profound changes for the label, with the loss of one of its founders, relocation to London, and increasing diversity of musical styles with an internationalist outlook.

A second decade

Warp goes global. Tenth anniversary and beyond. Lex Records: the hiphop connection

Despite the closure of the Warp record shop in 1997, Warp's label roster ticked over nicely during 1997 and 1998, with releases almost exclusively coming from the family of artists it had nurtured so far. The only notable new addition was Jimi Tenor, the flamboyant, iconoclastic Finnish performer who had captured Steve Beckett's imagination during a gig in Vienna when Tenor stroked a lump of meat that was perched on top of his Moog synthesizer. Allied with the Helsinki Sähkö collective that originally included the duo Pan Sonic, renowned for their minimal, austere electronic throbs and drones, Tenor had lived for a while in Manhattan, soaking up the outgoing nightclub life and fashions, and people-watching while working as a lift attendant in the Empire State Building. For the recording sessions that led to his first Warp album *Intervision*, 1997, he lived temporarily with Steve Beckett in Sheffield. "I guess a lot of old school Warp fans would see me as the start of downhill," says Tenor, "because they didn't have that kind of uniform sound any more." His musical persona was a semi-comical glitter-lounge star, equal parts schlocky Vegas sleazeball (on one memorable occasion, at the massive Sonar Festival in Barcelona, he made an entrance riding through the crowd on a white horse) and Suicide-style vintage synth abuse. Tenor released a handful of albums and singles, including licensed back catalogue, up to 2000, when Warp bankrolled the hugely ambitious *Out Of Nowhere*. Utterly unlike anything else in the Warp catalogue before or since, it's the kind of record Curtis Mayfield might have made if he'd been a fan of Tarkovsky, Ligeti and cyberpunk. It featured an enormous international cast recorded in a variety of locations: Tenor travelled to Warsaw to record the Orchestra of the Great Theatre Lodz at Radio Polskie;

Finland's Jimi Tenor, in character – as usual.

added vocals by the Pro Canto Choir in Helsinki; and laid down the rest in London with a hired band of musicians including a sitar player, harmonium and various guitarists and drummers, plus his wife, Nicole Willis, on vocals. Switching styles between spectral orchestral abstractions and Prince-like falsetto pop, as a bravura work of folly, it's a magnificence addition to Warp's canon. However, the scale of the project took its toll on Tenor and on the label. "Maybe it moved a little bit too fast. I was about to go mad," he confesses, "I had a nightmare writing the scores. I hired an orchestrator and we started working and the results were really slow. All of a sudden, a couple of weeks before going to the studio, I realised that this guy wasn't good enough to do it. So I had to let him go and sort of learn myself how to do that hard part. Then I hired another guy, Mike Kearsy – that worked out really well."

Despite the heroic efforts of all concerned, his relationship with Warp terminated almost immediately after the release of the album, and Tenor moved to Barcelona and dramatically scaled down his output. "I would have continued, but they kicked me out because I think *Out Of Nowhere* was so expensive and maybe it didn't work out as planned. I think they were hoping to be signing people like John Barry. Because of the money situation it was clear that I had to do the smallest possible record, budget-wise, at home, electronic based – so that was what I did."

Out Of Nowhere, 2000 (WARP76), was Tenor's masterpiece, but its huge orchestral budget nearly broke the bank.

The backbone of the catalogue has always been British, but Warp's international outlook dates back to around 1992, when they released one-off singles by DSR, a gospel-influenced House act from Miami, THK (German Thomas Kukula), and Eternal (Australian producer Mark

Scott Herren, aka sampladelic shaman Prefuse 73 and Savath + Savalas. Photo: Grace Villamil, 2005.

James). Links were forged with the influential music scene in Detroit when Richie Hawtin aka FUSE was signed in 1993, and the Michigan connection continued with releases by Kenny Larkin, whose *Azimuth* was an early installment in the *Artificial Intelligence* series in February 1994, and later singles by Kelli 'K' Hand, Joey Beltram (a New Yorker linked with legendary Detroit label Transmat), the eternally enigmatic outfit Drexciya, and much later, by Detroit born Jimmy Edgar. European Techno was represented in the mid 90s by Speedy J (Dutchman Jochem Paap), Mike Ink (Cologne's Wolfgang Voigt, founder of the Studio 1 and Kompakt labels), and Move D (an alter ego of Heidelberg's David Moufang, owner of Source Records). A later branch of intricate Miami electronica, inspired by Autechre and Boards Of Canada, was represented by Phoenecia and Richard Devine.

Chicago's Tortoise brought a dash of experimental post-rock to Warp's roster with the release of *Standards* (WARP81) in 2001.

The signing of Chicago experimental rock group Tortoise's *Standards* album in early 2001 sent clear signals that the label would henceforth be more actively acquiring a stable of acclaimed international underground acts. Fellow Chicagoan Scott Herren, signed to Warp in both his aliases Prefuse 73 and Savath + Savalas, brought in yet another dimension to Warp's sound: the quirky and shapeshifting hiphop of Prefuse's *Vocal Studies And Uprock Narratives*, 2001. !!!'s "Me And Giuliani Down By The School Yard (A True Story)" 12", 2003, and *Louden Up Now* LP, 2004, have brought a whiff of revivalist No

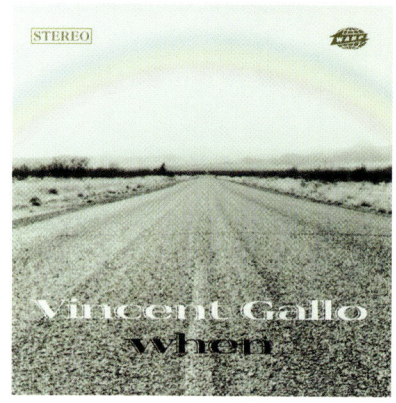

Maverick film maker Vincent Gallo's self-written music for films such as *Buffalo 66* received their first record release on *Recordings Of Music For Film*, 2002 (WARP96), following the folksy song collection *When*, 2001 (WARP87).

Wave funk vitality from downtown New York. But the real scoop was winkling two albums out of reclusive and controversial film director Vincent Gallo. *When*, 2001, and *Recordings Of Music For Film*, 2002, showed a hitherto unheard side of the *Buffalo 66* director: a wispy voice and a clutch of folky songs sung with intimacy and a delicate, fragile touch.

Hitting their tenth anniversary in 1999, Warp decided to go big. There was plenty to celebrate: not only had they survived ten years during which time many other independents struggled to make ends meet, they had adapted, avoided being led up generic dead-ends or following musical fashions, and ended up with a spread of artists they could reasonably claim to have nurtured singlehanded. That year they also announced the arrival of Warp Films, a linked but separately funded company that would be producing independent films and developing film projects with a selection of young directors.

The ten year mark was also a time to look back and reflect on the label's path to date. Three mammoth box set compilations – *Influences*, *Classics* and *Remixes* – commemorated prehistory, early days and present trends. *Influences* collected two CDs' worth of the House, Techno and breakbeat tracks that inspired Warp's foundation, and was a tribute to the Detroit and Chicago innovators such as Mr Fingers, Reese & Santonio, Phuture, K Alexi Shelby and Farley Jackmaster Funk, as well as prototype UK bleep tunes such as Nitro Deluxe's "Let's Get Brutal", Unique 3's "The Theme" and 808 State's "Let Yourself Go". *Classics* offered a primer on Warp's first three years, with a selection of tracks from the early, out of print singles including The Forgemasters, Nightmares On Wax, The Step, Sweet Exorcist, Tuff Little Unit, and LFO – perhaps as a much needed history lesson to younger fans who still retained the image of Warp as the inventors of intelligent Techno. *Remixes* was panoramic and carefully curated: 26 tracks from Warp's back catalogue were handed out to 26 current artists to remodel in their own image. And the remixers were not necessarily Warp artists: they included sympathetic outsiders such as Underdog, Rephlex label's Bogdan Raczynski, Mogwai, Labradford, Oval, Andy Votel, Jim O'Rourke and Spiritualized. Some of the results – Pram's melange of two tracks by LFO and Aphex Twin – are among the best work to appear on the label, and there was an encouraging inclusiveness and awareness demonstrated in the judicious choice of guests.

Car Boot Soul: George Evelyn of Nightmares On Wax is Warp's longest serving artist, with releases dating right back to 1989.

The ten year consolidation was followed in 2000 by the most drastic move of all: Warp's relocation from Sheffield to London. The concentration of the music industry, and the film business, in the UK capital made the position in Yorkshire increasingly isolated, and Mitchell and Beckett were spending less and less time in the office as they were on the road attending meetings elsewhere. By 2000, a very small proportion of their artists were Sheffield based. Only Autechre, Mira Calix and, temporarily, Tom Jenkinson of Squarepusher. But with the departure, the family nature of the label was unravelled for ever and from now on, Warp would more explicitly act as a virtual hub connected to a widely dispersed network of disparate musicians.

Another defining event happened after the move. Rob Mitchell was diagnosed with cancer, unfortunately too late for life saving treatment. He died, aged 38, on 8 October 2001.

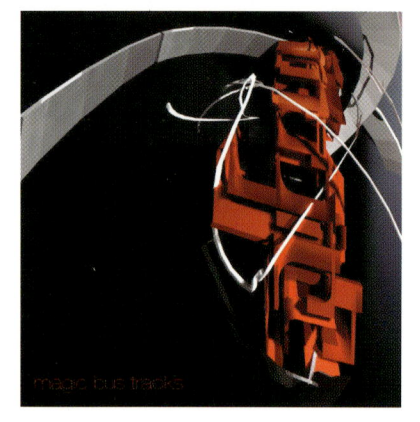

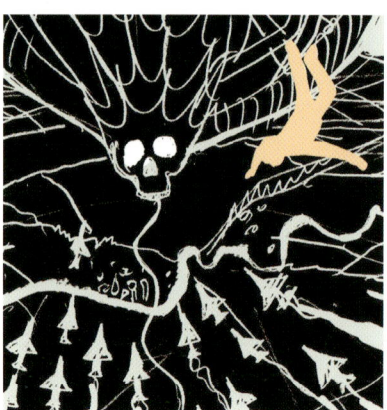

After 11 years as an effective and complementary partnership, the entire weight of the company fell onto Steve Beckett's shoulders – just at the moment when Warp was finding its feet in a new city and gearing up for further expansion. With 11 albums released during 2001 (including *Drukqs*, the first Aphex Twin appearance for several years), the company was at full stretch. 2002 saw no let-up, as a large Warp contingent – including Plaid, Mira Calix, Chris Clark, Richard Devine, Phoenecia, Russell Haswell and various invited guests – took to the road on the Magic Bus Tour around the UK and mainland Europe. Increased curatorial involvement with a variety of live events helped Warp to connect with their substantial audiences, from their new Nesh club nights in London and elsewhere, to their now annual Warp Festival at the spectacular Fondation Vasarely in the south of France, an appropriately futuristic memorial to architect and artist Victor Vasarely. At 2003's Ether Festival at London's South Bank Centre, another ongoing partnership was set in motion with the contemporary music ensemble, London Sinfonietta, performing orchestrated versions of Warp tracks by Aphex Twin, Squarepusher, Boards Of Canada, Mira Calix and Jamie Lidell.

top: Adventurous contemporary music ensemble London Sinfonietta have forged a strong relationship with Warp, adapting and performing music by Squarepusher, Aphex Twin, Boards Of Canada and others. Photo: Kai Bienert.
middle: *Magic Tracks*, 2002 (WARP100), a compilation released in tandem with the label's Magic Bus Tour of Europe and the USA.
bottom: *Empty The Bones Of You*, 2003 (WARP107), by recent Warp signing Chris Clark.

As of 2005, Warp could go anywhere: the artists most recently added to the roster include New York based clipped electronic funksters Home Video, the passionate Britpop/Smiths-inspired Tynesiders Maxïmo Park, the blackheart folk rock of Bristol's Gravenhurst, flamboyant young French producer Jackson, and the one-man soulsonic force of Jamie Lidell. The state of Warp reflects the reality that, by the middle of the twenty-first century's first decade, purely electronic music could no longer remain privileged as the only forward looking, experimental or creative sector of contemporary music. As a label with a substantial and influential history behind it, expectations continue to run high around its output – with the consequent problem that it is continually judged by reference to its past achievements. Anyone still expecting a predominantly electronic music label will inevitably be surprised and confused by the presence of groups like Broadcast, Maxïmo Park, !!! and Gravenhurst, but in fact Warp has perpetually reshaped itself since 1989, absorbing changing trends in music but never becoming sidetracked into any single genre, or stuck in a groove. The slide towards mainstream dance acceptance was halted with the *Artificial Intelligence* 'listening' phase; when Jungle, drum 'n' bass and Speed Garage saturated the market, Warp offered Squarepusher and Aphex Twin's extreme take on Hardcore rhythms, which were never acceptable in mainstream Jungle circles. In the beginning, Warp set out aims that, 16 years

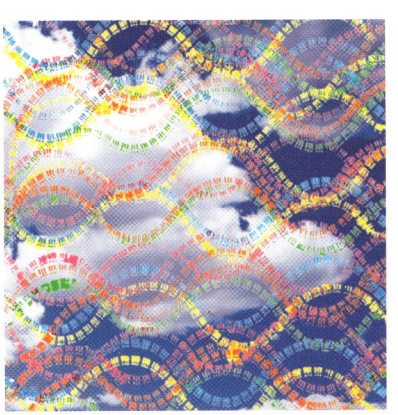

Three releases signalling Warp's ever more divergent music taste.
top. Gateshead's Maxïmo Park: their angsty, angular post-punk placed them among the front runners in the 2005 Mercury Music Prize. Photo: Deidre O'Callaghan.
middle: New York art funksters !!!'s *Louden Up Now*, 2004 (WARP121).
bottom: Gravenhurst's *Flashlight Seasons*, 2004 (WARP120): brooding, pastoral folk rock.

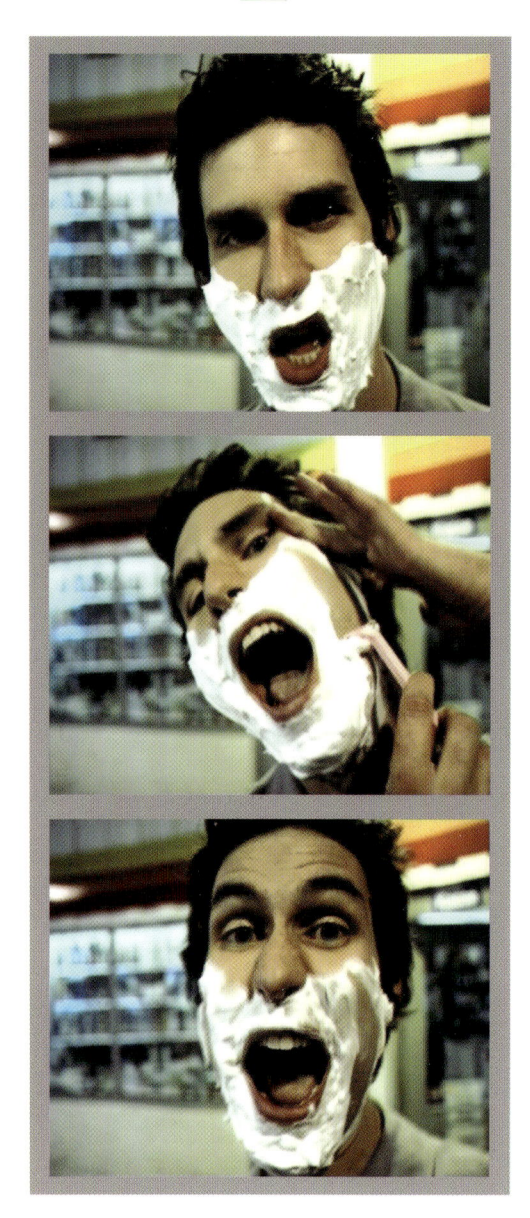

Jamie Liddell, stills from the video for "The City", 2004.

later, appear relatively humble: to give a platform to certain, very specific, aspects of dance music. If they had restricted themselves to that approach, it's unlikely the company would have ended up celebrating a decade and half of existence, let alone have had the resources and persuasive power to set up its own film production company and cutting edge music download service. Diversity and mobility have been the label's key strengths, as well as an ability both to jump on new trends and to cultivate longer-term artistic careers – two approaches that are often mutually exclusive to major label operations. There is no longer a 'Warp sound', but there is perhaps a 'Warp attitude' that holds true for the majority of the 100 or so artists that have been associated with the company over the years. What links many of them is a seriousness, a conscientious approach to music making and an impatience with the machinery of promotion and marketing illusionism that can sometimes come across as aloofness. When Warp's Reasonable People have fun, they do it without airheaded frivolity; when they experiment, they invent something substantial with the results rather than simply releasing the dry process; when they innovate, it appears to have occurred by accident rather than by smug design. Warp has always been fuelled by enthusiasm and run on intuition rather than sharp, calculated business logic, which is the secret of its success. It may have begun by gambling on its own taste, as Rob Mitchell once put it, but over 16 years it has also managed to raise the stakes.

Warp enters the digital download domain with Bleep.com, set up in 2004.

Building blocks: *Warp 10* Adrian Shaughnessy

WARP10+3. REMIXES

left to right: *Warp 10+1 Influences* (WARP67), *Warp 10+2 Classics* (WARP68), *Warp 10+3 Remixes*, all from 1999.

Few sleeves better epitomise the dual sound and vision aesthetic of Warp than the label's celebratory tenth anniversary compilations – *10+1 Influences*, *10+2 Classics* and *10+3 Remixes*, all 1999. These architecturally derived visuals are striking explorations of a northern English urban dystopia: alien environments invaded by quasi-architectural shapes that seem to colonise, virus-like, the grey unforgiving geometry of municipal architecture. The sleeves are credited to Designers Republic; they are unmistakable DR artefacts. They are the work of designer Michael Place, who worked at Designers Republic for almost nine years. He now functions on his own (under the craft-alluding name Build). During his time at DR, Place designed numerous Warp covers and his distinctive signature can be detected in them, none more so that in this milestone series.

"Because it was their anniversary," explains Place; "we wanted to play up the famous 'Warp purple' colour, and so we came up with the idea of the colour creeping into our everyday lives. We originally thought it would be good to actually paint objects – cars, bridges, carparks – in purple and photograph them for the covers. This wasn't really practical since we wouldn't be able to fully control the outcome, so I decided to do it digitally. I went out for about three days photographing Sheffield and Leeds. Both these cities played an integral part in Warp's history – Sheffield being the label's then home, plus the home of acts Sweet Exorcist and The Forgemasters, and Leeds was home to LFO and Nightmares On Wax. I wandered in and out of private buildings, tower blocks, uni versity corridors, carparks, overpasses and underpasses. I was really into architecture at that time and wanted to document the urban environment that reflected the electronic music Warp released over the years. I wanted the photography to be the main focus, with minimal typographic interference – all tracklistings and credits were arranged on a single side of the inlay – with semi-abstract swathes of purple sometimes interacting with the image, sometimes deliberately working against the image."

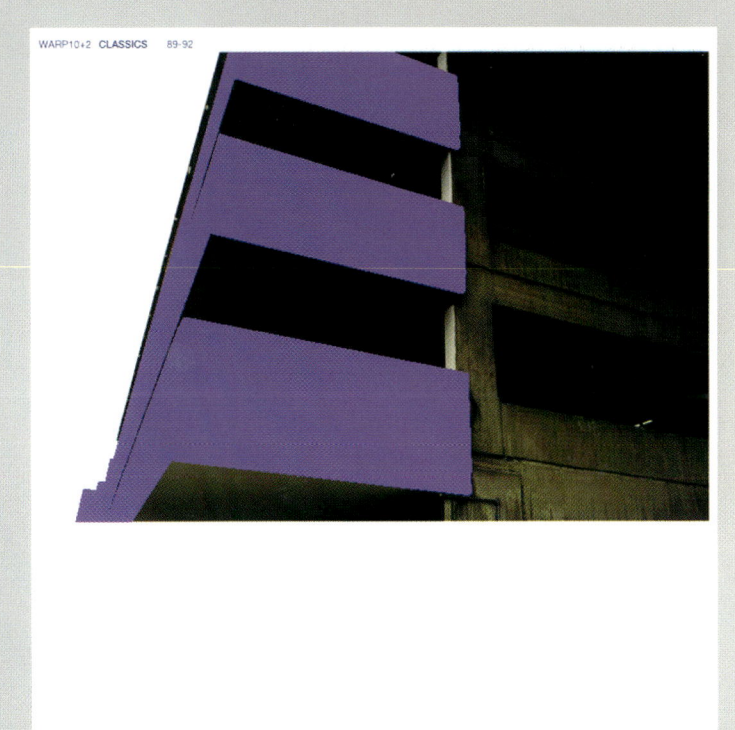

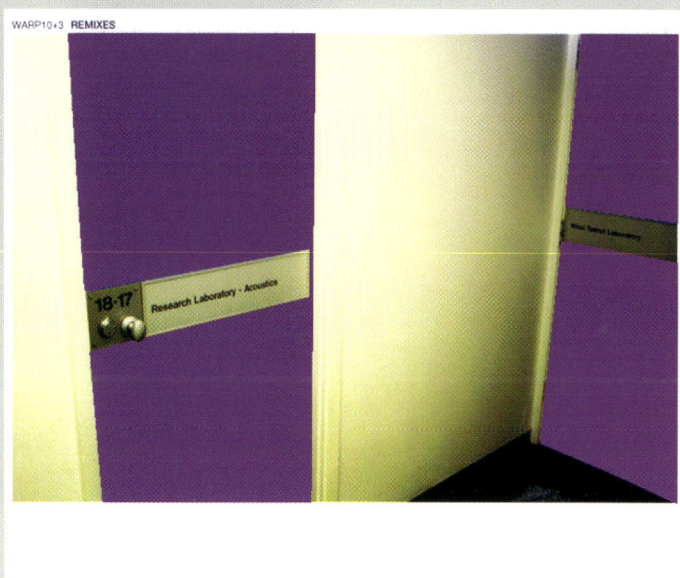

The task was to prove demanding. After shooting all the locations, Place worked "three days straight" designing the graphic overlays. The series encompassed three 12 page CD booklets, three gatefold 12" sleeves and one limited edition 12" box set. Roughly 56 different images were used in total, and every page on every format had a different photograph, with accompanying graphic overlay. Place maintains that the finished set made all the long hours worthwhile. "But I couldn't stand the colour purple for a long time afterwards," he notes ruefully.

For Place, the benefits of working for Warp are easily stated: "Designing covers for artists that I had personally liked was a real buzz, especially at the time when the whole Sheffield electronic scene was huge. It was a nice label to design for because the music – mostly – was really good. And it's always easier to design a sleeve for someone whose music you like!"

DR's Ian Anderson adds a more acerbic note: "What I like about Warp is that decisions are made on principle. Some of the results piss me off, and some of the decisions they make are wrong. In terms of artwork, they said that to have longevity you need to develop the artists and not the label, because if the label goes then the artists have no sort of base or grounding, so I think that was good."

Both Place and Anderson independently describe the pleasure of working as graphic designers for a label with the vision and intent that Warp regularly displays. At a time when graphic design has largely become yet another corporate plaything, a mere tool of the impersonal black arts of marketing, branding and consumer persuasion, it is heartening to find maverick organisations like Warp willing to take risks and – most impressively, in our risk-averse culture – to occasionally fail.

Lex Records

In the late 90s, changes were afoot in the state of hiphop. At grassroots level, a mine of leftfield reinventions of the hiphop tradition were opening up across the United States. Andre 3000 of OutKast has frequently alluded to a love of Squarepusher and electronic music; Antipop Consortium's Beans, Priest and M Sayyid, coming from NYC's poetry slam scene, spat dense alliterative verbal assaults over homemade minimalist beats and sub-bass tones, with none of hiphop's common self-referential sampling of rare grooves or old school breaks. Prefuse 73's Scott Herren, in his various guises including Savath + Savalas and Delarosa And Asora, took cut-up sampling and turntablism to new limits of virtuosity. In Oakland, California, a small community of itinerant musicians, MCs, DJs and producers had formed the Anticon collective, surgically filleting hiphop's braggadocio backbone. The astonishing barrages of text from rappers Doseone, Sage Francis and Yoni Wolf (aka Why?), more akin to experimental poetry and self-therapy than street-style rap vernacular, fused with fractured and fragmented backing tracks frequently using live instrumentation, documentary recordings and found sounds. Renewed interest in dynamic turntable showmanship, and crossover moves between hiphop and post-rock by such artists as Fog and Boom Bip, added up to a sea change in the sector which Warp was primed to exploit.

A new frequency was added to Warp's sonic range in 2001, with the signing of Brooklyn rap group Antipop Consortium and Chicago based experimental producer Prefuse 73. At the same time, Warp employee Tom Brown promoted a night called Dropping Science in Sheffield before instigating the Lex Records imprint in 2001. His first signings were Rhode Island's Non-Prophets (Joe Beats & Sage Francis), and Boom Bip from Cincinnati. Lex has also been responsible for the first solo albums by DJ Signify (turntablist with Mr Dibbs, Buck 65 and Ego in the group 1200 Hobos), the duo of Danger Mouse + Jemini, and Prince Po (Prince Poetry, onetime partner of Pharoahe Monch in Organized Konfusion), and Tes. The series kicked off with the *Lexoleum* series of 12" compilations featuring exclusive tracks; since then Lex's distinctive and lavish packaging (by design company EH?) has graced records by Boom Bip, Fog, Danger Mouse & Jemini and Hymie's Basement (a duo of Fog's Andrew Broder and Why?).

Lex has fairly loose boundaries: the first *Lexoleum* compilation included tracks by Peaches and Jamie Lidell, and the label's acts have engaged in some interesting stylistic interplay, with Boards Of Canada remixing Boom Bip's "Last Walk Around Mirror Lake", as well as Boom Bip working with Super Furry Animals singer Gruff Rhys. Brown bought back the company in summer 2005.

Left to right: Tes, *X2*, 2003; compilation album *Lexoleum*, 2003; Boom Bip, *Seed to Son*, 2002.

Rob Young: What's the background to the setting up of Lex – how did you come to be associated with Warp?

Tom Brown: I answered an advert for a job in the Job Centre on West Street, Sheffield. It read something like, "Must love music and not be afraid of computers." The job was running WarpMart, which was tiny at the time. I think the pay was £3.25 per hour. When they asked me if I had any more questions at the end, I said, "Yeah, have I got the job?" They didn't tell me, though.

I ran WarpMart through the move to London and the dotcom boom. By 2001 I was bored of doing the same job and I was planning on releasing some 12" singles. Steve and Rob asked me if I wanted to keep inside the company. I said yes and set about setting up a 12"-only imprint.

Because it was only going to release 12"s, I commissioned a super-nice house bag. I wanted one as good as the Designers Republic-designed Schematic house sleeve, but I didn't want to use DR. I got given a magazine called *Hold No Hostage*. The layout was amazing so I sent them an email and asked them if they'd do the house bag. They became EH?. I asked them to keep the sleeve free from big graffiti burners – they totally ignored what I asked for, but it looked amazing. That set the tone for the whole relationship.

The first artists I asked to give me music for 12"s were Non-Prophets, Boom Bip, Tes, Disflex6, Kid Acne and Mummy Fortuna's [Sketch and Mr Cooper, associates of Req in Brighton]. I just wanted to put out a cool series of EPs. Most of the artists offered me full albums, so after a couple of 12"s I abandoned the idea and moved on to releasing full albums and working full time on the label.

Can you describe the Dropping Science nights in Sheffield?

I grew up in Bradford. Which is 30 odd miles away. But in the mid 90s it was culturally thousands of miles away. I went to university in Sheffield and I couldn't believe all the cool stuff going on in that city – people wearing nice clothes, listening to cool music and smiling. I started Dropping Science the summer I finished at Sheffield University. The guys who ran The Old School and later NY Sushi in Sheffield made me want to put on events. They were much more into drum 'n' bass and big beat. I was really into New York hiphop that *The Source* magazine covered, and the weirder major label leftfield stuff from the early 1990s – New Kingdom, Justin Warfield, A Tribe Called Quest, De La Soul, Beastie Boys, etc. I wanted to have a night that was based around that kind of music.

Shortly after I started Dropping Science, I began working at Warp. Tom Panton and Tom Mitchell began to help with the nights. Squarepusher, Broadcast and Boards Of Canada were probably the first albums I loved, but I worked my way through the catalogue quickly. Dropping Science ended up having people like Luke Vibert, Gescom, Strictly Kev, Andy Votel and Squarepusher DJing and playing live, but also The Automator, People Under The Stairs, Blackalicious, Latyrx, Ko-Wreck Technique and other hiphop artists too.

We always had lavish, way-too-expensive flyers. Often there'd be more than one flyer for a show – they fitted together in sets. People like Kid Acne and Req and James Burton from Warp did the designs.

Most of the nights lost money but they were fun. It was stressful for me and the other two Toms (Mitchell and Panton) because we couldn't afford to lose money and we had day jobs that didn't really give us much free time, but we got a lot out of it or we wouldn't have carried on. The shows themselves were always about 200 capacity. If the line-up was good, they'd be full. A lot of cool Sheffield people would come down: [RAC's] Chris Duckenfield, Autechre, Seb from Sumo, Designers Republic and lots of kids who liked hiphop and the odd bit of spastic Techno.

When Warp moved to London, I started the Nesh nights with Ned Beckett, so in some ways Nesh and Lex are the successors of Dropping Science.

What exactly is the relationship now between Lex and Warp, do you get totally free rein in A&R?

Lex is totally me and there is absolutely no creative input from Warp, but Steve is really supportive. He seems to particularly like Tes, Prince Po, Boom Bip and Danger Mouse.

The only time when Warp have any influence on A&R is when they won't pay for something. At one point Danger Mouse was going to knock out an album with [Wu-Tang Clan's] Raekwon but Warp wouldn't front the cash for the project. They were probably right.

What kind of discussions take place between yourself, artists and your designers EH? in dealing with the sleeve designs? Is it all EH? ideas and is there any conflict if artists don't want to be 'branded' with the label's house look?

To be honest, everybody normally falls out. The EH? guys are definitely artists and they don't like being told what to do. Sometimes it works out, like with Signify or Danger Mouse + Jemini, but most of the time there's friction. I don't mind who does the artwork so long as it's good. EH? are brilliant and most people agree, so they end up starting most projects with the musicians' support. They just often end up feeling less enthusiastic. I don't think there's much of a house look. I think the sleeves are all quite distinct.

What's your favourite of all the sleeves so far and why?

I think that both Boom Bip albums, Tes, Danger Mouse + Jemini and DJ Signify all have sleeves exactly the way EH? wanted them and they are all great in their own way. Maybe the Tes sleeve is my favourite.

How did you tune in to the artists that ended up on the first Lex releases – Boom Bip, Non-Prophets, Danger Mouse & Jemini, etc.?

I came across each artist in a different way. With Boom Bip I bought an import copy of *Circle* [his collaboration with cLOUDDEAD/Subtle MC Doseone] when it came out [on Mush, 2000]. I just loved the record. I knew Doseone was working with Prefuse 73 on an album under the name Communication Project, and so I asked him to put me in touch with Boom Bip. Before that, I was in touch with [Non-Prophets'] Sage Francis. I had seen Sage involved in some diss-fest on a messageboard and I thought, Who is this belligerent guy? I followed a link to his site and heard the tracks from the first Non-Prophets 12", which was the only thing he had out at the time. I really wanted to sign him and we started talking about a record. I actually tried to sign him to a multiple album deal back then, but Warp only allowed me $1000 and it was very embarassing to ask, but I did anyway. In 2001 I flew out to Cincinnati to [hiphop festival] Scribble Jam and stayed with Boom Bip and caught up with Sage and lots of other people in the scene – Edan, the Anticon guys – and it was really good to see them face to face.

By the time I met Danger Mouse, all I was getting in the way of demos was really weedy indie hiphop. I wanted Lex to be an eclectic label and I didn't want all the hiphop I released to be similar. Danger Mouse called by one day and left four mixtapes on my desk. They were really funny. Partly mashed up indie rock staples and hiphop classics and partly just good tunes. When he called back, I'd been listening to the mixtapes for a couple of weeks. We met up and he played me demo beats and filled me in on this MC he wanted to track down in New York. The MC was Jemini The Gifted One. I talked Steve into giving me $3000 to fly Danger Mouse out there and get a song or two recorded. He did, and that was the first EP. I signed him straight after that.

Did any artists take much persuasion to be on Lex?

I think Sage Francis is the only artist who has released an album on Lex that I really had to persuade. He's very assertive and he knows what he wants. Everyone else was very enthusiastic about it.

What is the appeal for you of the Anticon 'school' of production and rap, and to what extent do you think it represents a new phase in hiphop's development?

I like the Anticon guys as people and I like the way they make largely non-macho music that's low on bullshit. I think – although maybe *they* don't – that they are all making quite different music. Doseone sounds more like Cee Lo than Sole.

Recent releases by Hymie's Basement, Boom Bip and Fog have pretty much pushed the music outside anything that sounds like hiphop in a recognisable form – more like experimental songwriting. How flexible, stylistically, is Lex designed to be? Is there a quality that will always define it as different from Warp? Why, for example, aren't Beans or Prefuse 73 'transferred' to Lex?

That is definitely a Frequently Asked Question. Warp is Steve Beckett and Rob Mitchell's label. Lex is my label. It's all personal taste. At the start Rob said that there was no point in me releasing projects by Luke Vibert and Push Button Objects because it was too close to Warp stuff. Rob was actually really keen on signing Boom Bip. But like most labels, they just have a bunch of bands they think are great. There's stuff on Warp that could fit on Domino or Ninja Tune.

I was the person who first brought Antipop Consortium to Steve's attention and I was a big fan of Prefuse 73 from the start and helped with his first album campaign, but Lex didn't exist at that time. I was involved in getting Req on board too. Lex was never set up as a hiphop annex for Warp. It's a common misconception and one that neither Warp or Lex has ever tried to foster.
I want Lex to have a reputation for design like Factory. I want the roster to be diverse. It's small right now – just Fog, Subtle, Boom Bip and Danger Mouse are on long term contracts.

Warp Vision

Warp has had a close relationship with film since its early days. The likes of Jarvis Cocker, David Slade and Phil Wolstenhome were commissioned to make Warp related promotional films back in the early 90s, and later ongoing collaborations with Chris Cunningham and Alex Rutterford, working with Aphex Twin, Squarepusher and Autechre, have produced some of the most striking and memorable music videos of the last ten years. Largely instrumental and highly textured, much of the music of Warp lends itself naturally to soundtrack usage, and sounds by Warp artists have been used in film, TV and even advertising. Some of Aphex Twin's woozy soundscapes from *Selected Ambient Works II* cropped up in Chris Morris's queasy radio and TV comedies, *Blue Jam* and *Jam* – and Warp eventually released a double soundtrack CD of sketches and music from Morris's fiendish, wonky comedy. The imaginative soundtrack of Lynne Ramsay's *Morvern Callar*, 2002, included Aphex Twin, Boards Of Canada and Broadcast, and the original soundtrack appeared as a Warp album. In 1999 Warp Films was inaugurated as a separate but linked company with an award from NESTA (National Endowment for the Sciences, Technology and the Arts). The first release featured Chris Morris's debut as film director, *My Wrongs #8245-8249 & 117*, which appeared in 2003. The 12 minute film stars a dog called Rothko, and Paddy Considine as a man who has ceased using a name. It notched up around 23,000 sales on DVD, well above average for unconventional short film work. *Dead Man's Shoes*, directed by Shane Meadows, appeared in 2004. Meadows followed his 'Midlands Trilogy' (*Twentyfourseven*, *A Room For Romeo Brass* and *Once Upon A Time In The Midlands*) with this modern day revenge tragedy made in a two week shoot, with a low budget and no fixed script. Like the bedroom studio approach that gave Warp Records so many of its core music releases in the early 90s, the world of film was now taking advantage of cheap technology and production techniques which allowed theatrical film releases (such as *Blair Witch Project*, *Tarnation*, etc.) to be made for tiny fractions of typical movie budgets.

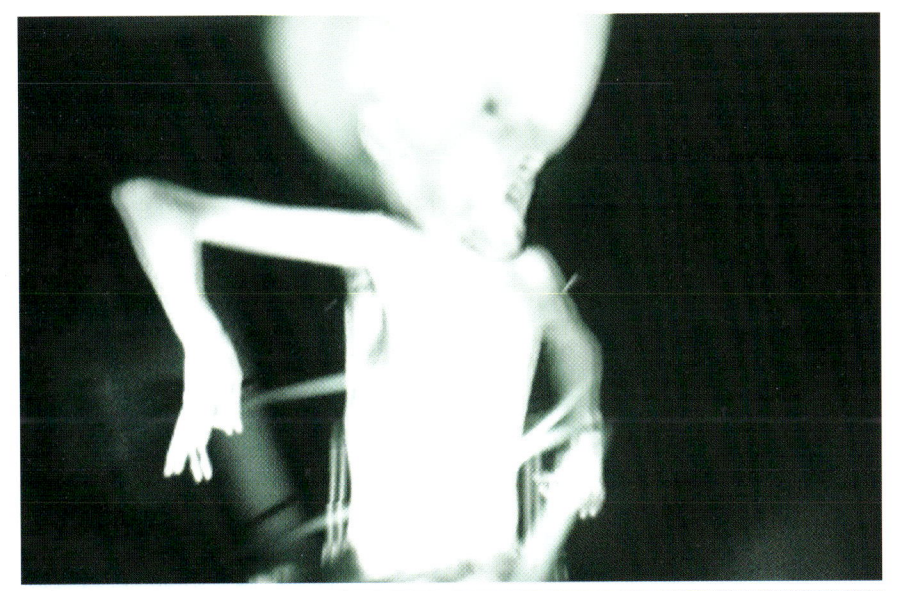

Stills from *Rubber Johnny*, 2005, directed by Chris Cunningham.

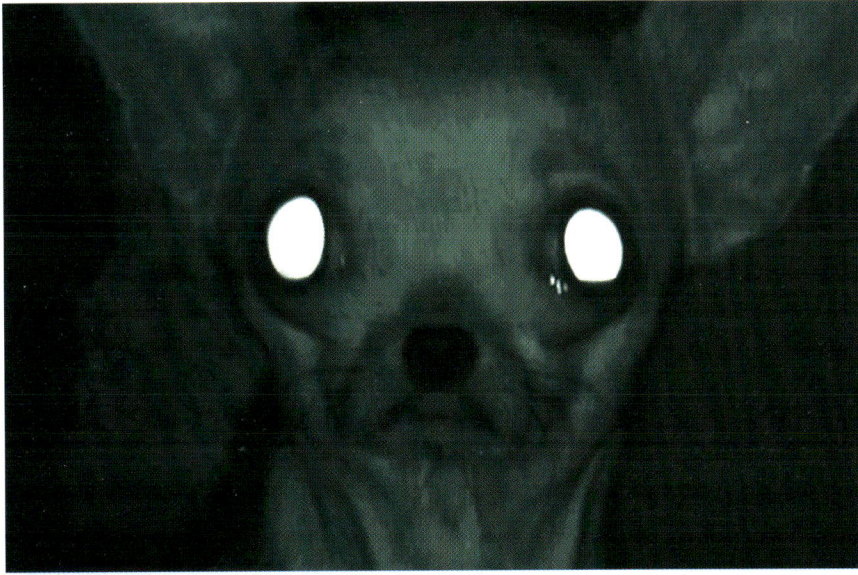

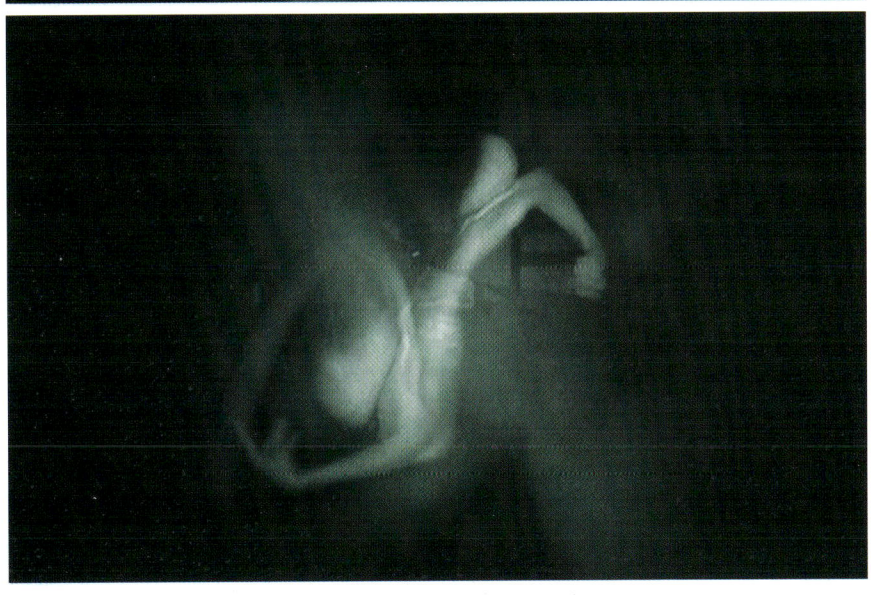

Stills and poster for Shane Meadows's
Dead Man's Shoes, Warp Films, 2004. Photo
left: Dean Rogers. Below: Optimum Releasing.

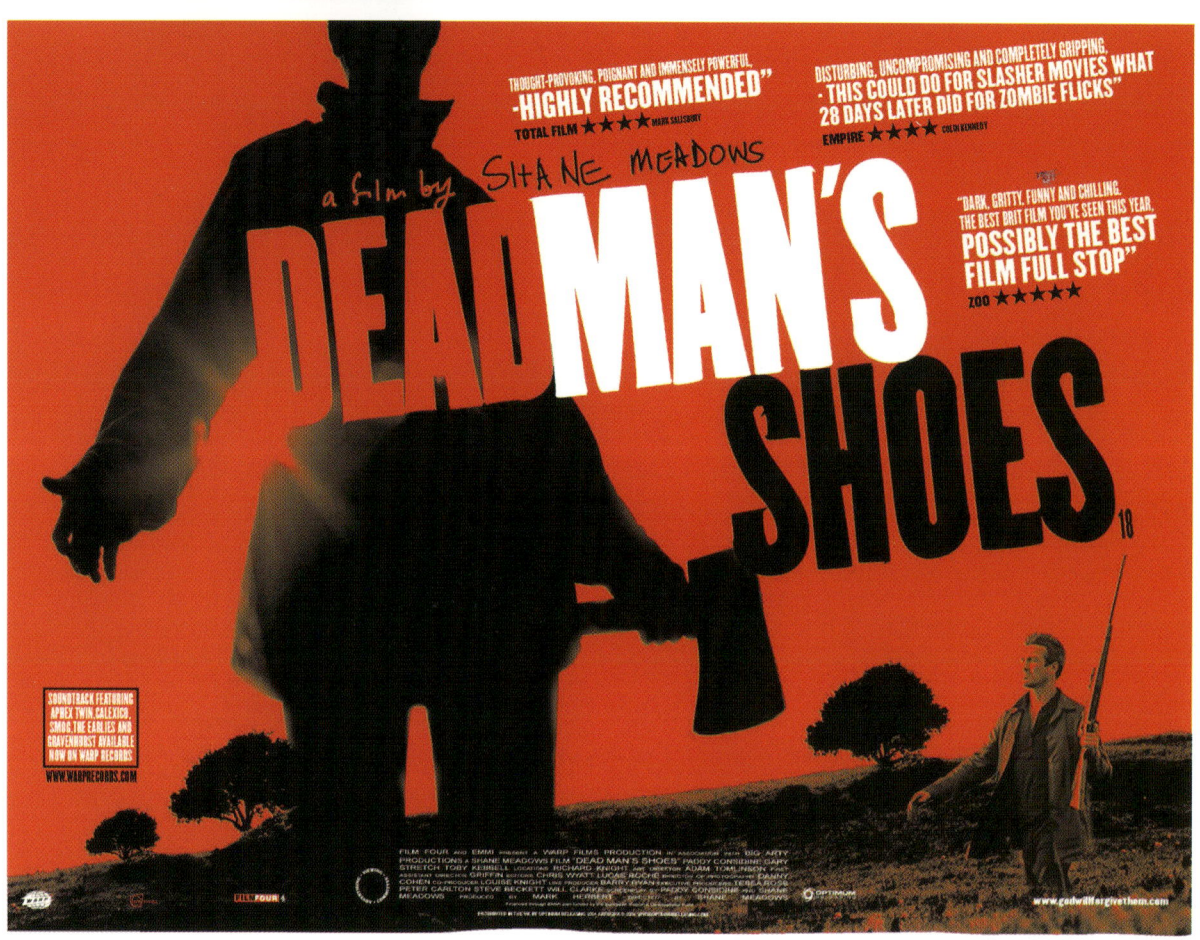

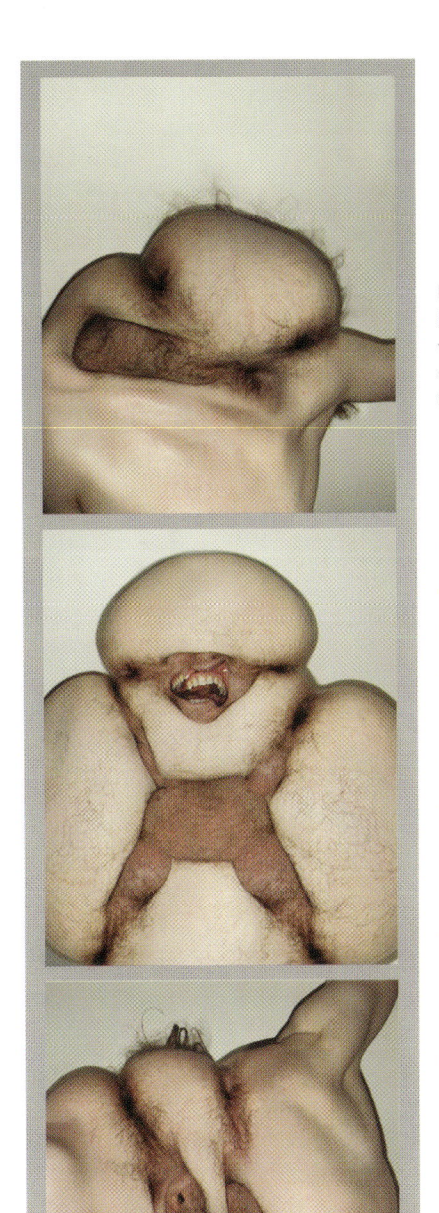

left: *Rubber Johnny* by Chris Cunningham, 2005. Italian printers delayed production of the DVD when they objected to imagery on the sleeve.
right: Paddy Considine and dog Rothko from Chris Morris's *My Wrongs #8245-8249 & 117*, 2003.

Chris Cunningham's *Rubber Johnny*, 2005, is literally a bedroom movie, filmed over several years in odd moments the director had to spare. Cunningham crams masses of visual information into his seven minutes, depicting a mutant child in a wheelchair morphing and splattering various body parts up against panes of glass, all to an Aphex Twin soundtrack. Cunningham used his own body and face as the source, but the microsurgical editing and rapid fire barrage of images pushes the medium towards a kind of grotesque abstraction.

In 2005 Warp Films distributed the documentary *Paradise Lost 1 & 2*, directed by Joe Berlinger and Bruce Sinofsky (*Blair Witch Project 2*, *Metallica: Some Kind Of Monster*), about the murders of three eight year old boys in Arkansas, allegedly inspired by heavy metal. At the same time the company had several projects in development: two features by Cunningham, who won't discuss any work that's not been finished; an existential horror picture by David Slade; a documentary about disinformation by John Lundberg and Mark Pilkington, and a second feature by Shane Meadows, *Bulldog*. Meanwhile their Warp X initiative was set to launch in early 2006: funded by the UK Film Council and FilmFour, its brief to discover and nurture innovative new film makers and writers is a natural extension of Warp's attitude to musical A&R.

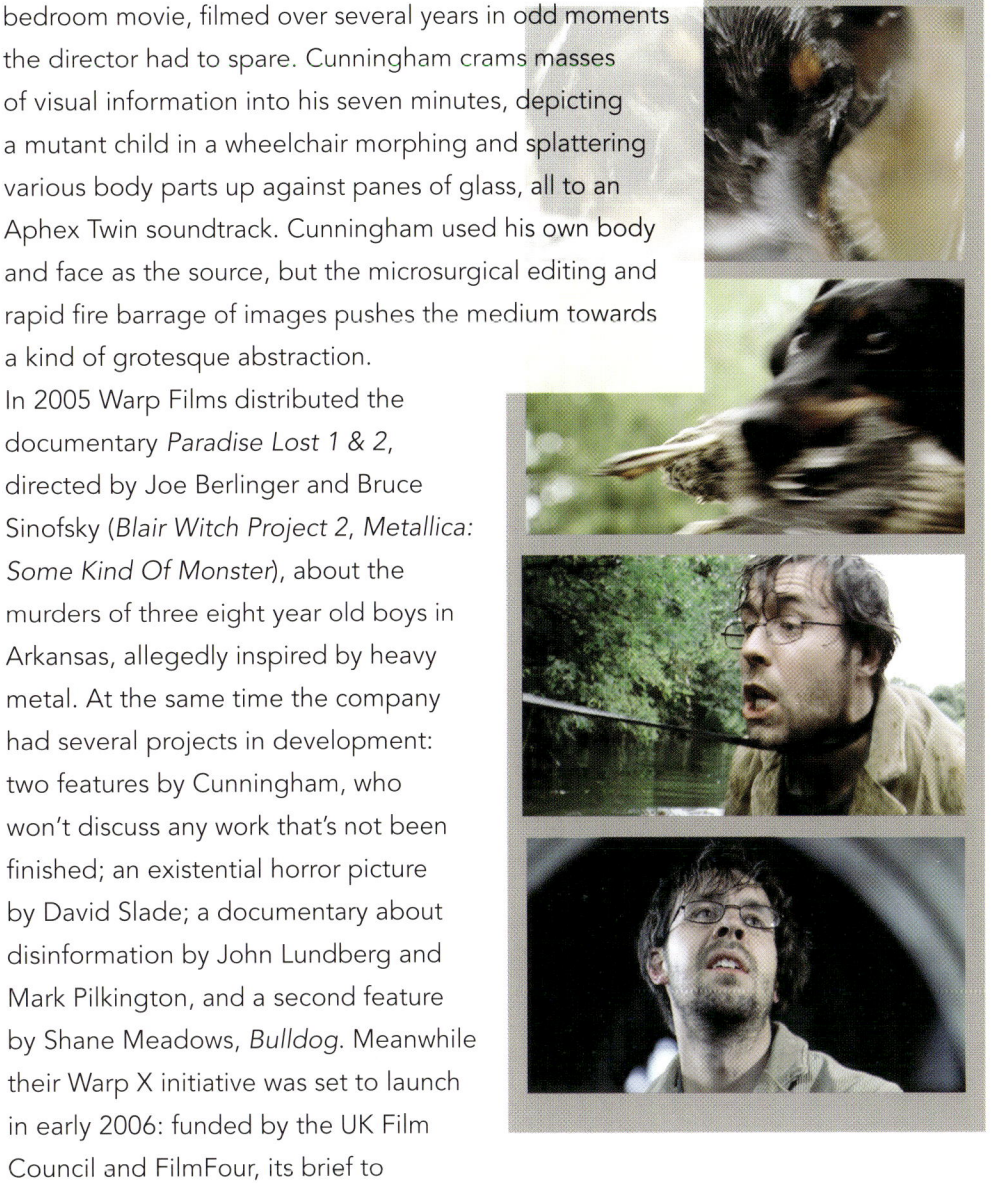

Q&A: Steve Beckett
co-founder, Warp Records

Rob Young: In the documentary The Corporation, companies get characterised with psychological profiles. How would you describe Warp's 'character'?

Steve Beckett: Well, I've just done a test online and this is what it says: 'You seem to have a Type B personality. Your personality draws characteristics from each of the other personality types, that is, Type A and Type C. Either you adjust your behaviour depending on the situation, or you tend to be moderated in your attitudes. In any case, you are the most balanced of the three personality types.'

Is there such a thing as a typical day for you? If so, what would it involve?

Not really – it has a general theme, which is, most of my actions are somehow related to music, film and art, but specifically it varies. So on Saturday I was at a video shoot from eight in the morning till 12 at night; on Sunday I spent the day with my MD of Warp USA, who had flown over to meet me and spend a few days with me and the company. Monday I have most of my staff meetings, so I meet the whole company at 10am and just go through anything that's pertinent; then I meet Warp's general manager for an hour; then I talk to the Warp Films MD for an hour; then I have a marketing meeting for an hour and a half; then I went through potential tracks for the Jimmy Edgar album with two other people from Warp till the end of day; then I went out for dinner with our Japanese licensee and the US MD till midnight.

Tuesday I did a film distribution meeting, looked at CVs for a new product manager role I am interviewing for, then I went to the Mercury Awards till 1pm.

Today I have been interviewing people for a job, and after this interview I'm having an A&R session with one of my scouts for the rest of the day. So yes, it varies quite a lot.

After what seems like a couple of years of the roster remaining more or less static, you seem to be on a roll of signing and developing new artists in 2004-2005. How actively are you out A&Ring for new music, and is it currently more important for you to introduce almost unknown artists onto the label rather than bringing in already established acts?

With signings and developing artists, it tends to go in waves, or maybe like a seesaw. So you look for new artists for a period and try to find just the right one that fits with what you want, then, when you finally find them and convince them to sign, it switches and all your effort goes into breaking them – there's no point just signing loads of artists if you aren't going to push them and do what you promised when you convinced them to sign. Then after a period – say, one to two years – you need to swing back to looking again.

I'm just moving into a signing period after I've been working solidly on breaking Maxïmo Park, which has just gone gold in the UK. I want to sign another two acts in the next six to eight months. We sign very few acts, as the ones we sign we want to work with to their fullest potential, and it's very time consuming to do that.

There's not really a preference for signing new or established artists. It's maybe personally a bit more satisfying to develop new artists, but it's easier to sell established acts, as they have an existing fanbase, so sometimes you have to get a balance between the two. Often with the established acts it's their label approaching you for certain territories, asking you to work with them as a licensee.

Is live presence becoming more important to you? Jamie Lidell, Jackson, Maxïmo Park, !!! and others are dynamic on stage as well as in the studio – is that what you are tending to look for at this point?

It's always been important. LFO used to go on tours, Nightmares On Wax went on tour, Autechre, Aphex, Squarepusher have all done hundreds of gigs. We've always seen that as crucial because it creates a genuine connection with the audience and gives the act longevity, rather than just being perceived as a faceless studio project.

Warp continues to be involved in a bunch of diverse live events and festivals; what are some of the highlights of those for you?

I think the Lighthouse Party we did [in October 2000 in London's Docklands] was chaos, but looking back on it, it was great. It's the only time me and Barry Hogan of All Tomorrows Parties fame actually nearly crumbled and cried. The Warp 10 parties [1999] were incredible, seeing the diversity of the label over a three day festival, as were the first ATP festivals, especially the Autechre-curated one with Public Enemy, Boards Of Canada and Bernard Parmegiani [2003]. But the events I've been really blown away by are the two

London Sinfonietta performances at the Royal Festival Hall, and the events we've done at the Vasarely Foundation in France.

How important has the internet been for your expansion?

It seems so strange to even think of a time before the internet, but it's relatively new and yet it moves so quickly. I remember Greg Eden coming to our office in Sheffield and plugging in a dial-up modem. As I got set to 'surf', I was expecting a virtual technology rollercoaster ride, but all I got was the sensation of being in a library. But I could instantly see the potential of the internet for getting our music directly to people without going through the filters of radio and press. Unfortunately, at that time I didn't see all the dangers, from our perspective, in terms of people being able to get the music for free.

But we did decide to embrace it fully, and we built our first site and then started selling CDs via Warpmart. Then we took on other labels and artists, and then set up Bleep.com and started selling downloads. Bleep is a tiny proportion of our total sales – say, one per cent – but I see it growing over the next five years in much the same way Warpmart sales have grown. A big seller on Bleep would do, say 1000 downloads, and the biggest week we've had was probably about 25,000 downloads of the whole catalogue.

Do you expect to be selling CDs in ten years time? How do you see the destiny of the recorded artefact?

I can't see CDs being relevant to people in the next ten years. I mean, how many people do you see carrying those clunky portable CD players around any more? Everyone is carrying iPods, and then eventually the phone will be the main portable gadget that will carry music, satellite navigation, email, calendar, computer, credit card facilities, etc., so I just can't see how the CD is going to survive. It will, oddly enough, be vinyl and digital formats.

When did you first start discussing the incorporation of a film company?

Warp Films is a completely separate standalone company with different shareholders, and it's headed and run day-to-day by a human cyclone called Mark Herbert. The idea just came from a meeting with NESTA [National Endowment for Science, Technology and the Arts], who said we had the right attributes as a company to win one of their awards. We realised we had great connections and relationships with many film makers via our various activities – Chris Cunningham, Chris Morris, Lynne Ramsay, Vincent Gallo. It didn't seem that different from what we do as a music label, so we gave it a shot.

Can you remember your first meeting with Richard James?

I think my first meeting with him was in a mastering session with Rob Mitchell for *Artificial Intelligence* at the Townhouse Studios. He'd brought in his Polygon Window DATs and the engineer was saying, 'it's glitching and distorting', and Rich was being stroppy and saying, 'That's how it's supposed to sound'.

What's not generally known by the public is that he's a loveable lion with an almost Zenlike control over his own life and destiny. He has no interest whatsoever in the music biz side of things, but will just dip his toe in it if he feels a need to fund his lifestyle by selling some records, and he does just enough to do this and no more, and then disappears again.

He loves chaos at times, and likes to have electric people around him – people that make the unexpected happen. He is extremely good company to be around, and definitely has a magnetic aura. Then at a moment's notice he gets bored and causes some trouble.

He genuinely makes music for himself, and doesn't care if people like it or comment on it. We once tried to get him to edit "Windowlicker" because we needed a shorter edit to get played on the radio, and he described it as 'we were trying to cut his child's arm off'.

When "Windowlicker" was breaking in the States, we set up a 20-date radio interview tour which would have smashed his career over there. He blew it out the night before because he wanted to go on a picnic with his girlfriend.

Like it or not, Warp has developed from underground label to an institution, with a reputation and a substantial history behind it. Criticisms of the label tend to come from those who still think of Warp as a 'sound' that has been abandoned – there are always people who will judge you against what has gone before. How do you deal with the pressure of expectations from so many different sides?

I don't really feel pressure from people's expectations, as I am living my life, not theirs. I can't possibly live my life by figuring out what someone else I don't even know would do – I just have to do what I do. When people criticise, they are just saying, 'Well, I wouldn't have done that', but I'm not walking their path – I'm going my path.

I just sign whatever genuinely moves or interests me, and that changes by the minute! I was working with Pulp in 1990 and released three of their records. We were selling Black Flag, Misfits and Danzig records in our shop in 87 before Acid House hit, so it's nothing new that I've worked with rock acts.

There is no 'Warp sound', there is no 'Warp': it's just a concept, like the equator. There's just what's happening: it's like pointing to a rainbow and saying, 'Hey, you've got too much red, not enough brown, and you curve too much.' The rainbow just turns round and says, 'What do you mean? I'm a rainbow – I'm supposed to be like this.' We are supposed to be just the way we are; we couldn't possibly be any other way.

Around 1992, was the move into the *Artificial Intelligence* series also connected with your exit from the distribution deal with Rhythm King? In other words was there a feeling that it was difficult making headway with explicitly 'dance' tracks, and that in order to survive it was necessary to diversify and promote a more album based form of electronic music?

Well, we always wanted album artists because we came from a rock background in retail, and we could see that the artists that had longevity were touring album artists and the ones that disappeared were one-off single producers.

Sweet Exorcist, LFO, Nightmares On Wax, all those early artists made albums and most of them toured, so that was always part of the vision, not a reaction to anything. The Rhythm King deal collapsed because we *were* selling *lots* of records and weren't getting paid, so we walked.

What were the advantages and disadvantages of the move to London? How did the running of the company change, once you were no longer a 'local' label as you had been in Sheffield?

Well, the advantages were, we had direct, close access to all the activities related to our business: distributors, radio, press, agents, gigs, international people were all based in or regularly visiting London. So me and Rob spent our lives going up and down the motorway or trainline, and Rob was away from his wife and kids a lot, so he wanted to be seeing them every evening. Also, we got bored with Sheffield, it just felt really small and often negative.

The disadvantages were that everything is more expensive, so I live in a place that is a fraction of the size of the place I lived in in Sheffield and three times the cost. There is a constant upward pressure on salaries down here, because everyone is fighting to afford the rent or mortgage, whereas in Sheffield a lot of the staff owned nice big houses and there wasn't that financial pressure. Things were easier and greener in Sheffield.

How did you first meet Rob Mitchell?

I met Rob in a rehearsal room, where a singer of our band had brought him in to try him out. My memories [of being in a band with him] are mainly of just getting wasted, taking local magic mushrooms and having intense trips listening to music – turning into animals, meeting Jesus, that kind of thing.

What effect did Rob's death have on the culture of the company, and how did you deal with it personally?

I don't really know how it affected the 'culture' – I think other people would have to answer that. I think they might say it became very serious for a period of time, and maybe became less of a family, as me and Rob were like brothers, really. The way it affected me was, I felt a lot more weight on my shoulders, as there was instantly twice as much work. With a really experienced person like Rob just evaporating, in six months it's irreplaceable.

Personally it was one of the key points in my life – I see everything as before and after that point. It was a privilege to be with him when he died. A few days before, he could hardly speak, but he thanked me very simply for everything I had done for him and his family, and that meant so much.

Ever since then my life has just opened up, and I'm just so grateful to be alive. I remember walking back to my house after he had died and looking at clouds and feeling how magical life is, but we spend so much time being dead to it all, wrapped up in our petty problems, and then we're gone and you've missed it. So the main purpose of my life now is just to be present, to be awake.

Were there any alternative names suggested for Warp in the beginning?

Yeah, things like Big Bass, Twisted Records, stuff like that. Crap names that showed we had loads of bass. We were originally called Warped Records, but every time we said it on the phone, no one could understand it, so we changed the name to Warp.

You and Rob Mitchell are usually referred to as the founders of Warp, but Robert Gordon has claimed the idea was all his. Can you describe from your perspective who was directly involved in setting up the label and what roles you all played?

I don't know who came up with the name. I remember us all talking about which name to use from a big list up at his house, and we decided on Warped... I thought it was more Rob Mitchell's idea.

I approached Rob Mitchell about setting up a label. We were driving in his car in Sheffield. And then I think me and Rob Gordon had a conversation, in this rave at a community centre, about setting up a label that he would contribute music to and be part of.

In terms of roles, I was just getting it going, getting tracks in, organising pressing, and so on. Rob Mitchell was organising things like distribution deals via contacts from the shop, and Rob Gordon was doing things like mixes, mastering... He taught us everything we knew about mastering. He used to get acetates cut and then listen to them in clubs and then go back down re-cut them over and over till they were perfect.

How did the split with Rob Gordon come about?

We were constantly arguing and not getting on, especially the two Robs. After one big row where he threw something at me – can't remember what – we said we wanted him out, so we did a deal and bought his shares for, at that time, a huge amount for us that we could barely afford.

What's your favourite Warp release, and why?

I can't pick just one – it's impossible for me. I would say Aphex Twin's *Selected Ambient Works II*, because it's a record I can still go back to over and over again. It's got a deep, emotional, primal magic. And his "Bucephalus Bouncing Ball" [from the *Come To*

Daddy EP], just for pure, heavy, intense mathematical genius. Squarepusher's *Music Is Rotted One Note*, especially "My Sound", which just shows the simple emotional beauty that many people miss in Tom's music. Autechre's *Chiastic Slide*, for its grainy, industrial purity, and memories of tripping to it for the first time with my friend Ashton Thomas. We were both in beanbags that turned into spaceships.

Loads of others – Nightmares On Wax, most of *A Word Of Science*; Boards Of Canada *Music Has The Right To Children*. I love all Broadcast's music, Antipop, Vincent Gallo, Black Dog's *Bytes*….

And your favourite Warp sleeve?

I reckon the DR-designed *Chiastic Slide* sleeve just feels perfect. When you pick it up you just have to keep holding it and looking at it. And the Boards' *Music Has The Right* just perfectly represents the music in the sleeve – nostalgic, dreamy and psychedelic.

Does Warp have any long term missions and goals at this point? Where do you see the label in five, ten years, if it's possible to think that far ahead?

I just want to sign, nurture and develop incredible new artists in whatever genre they may practise in. I want to run a tight, fun, adventurous, professional international organisation that still has a family feel or essence to it. I want the people who work for us, our audience and the artists we sign, to feel a genuine emotional connection with us. I want every object we put into the world to have a positive impact and have a reason for being there and to represent excellence.

If it wasn't for practical or financial constraints, what would you ideally like Warp to be doing at the moment?

Well, I'd be doing the above but hopefully a lot quicker and easier. I'd sign and develop ten new artists. I'd be TV-advertising Russell Haswell albums during *Big Brother*. I'd be doing huge high tech live events with specially built lasers for Autechre. I'd do a Warp tour of ports of the world on a boat with a venue on it. I'd put on a Boards Of Canada gig in Iceland and the desert. I'd be making £200,000 Chris Morris and Jake & Dinos Chapman videos for all our artists. I'd buy a huge office overlooking the Thames with Panton and Eames chairs and desks and a macrobiotic chef. I'd spend ten million on a Chris Cunningham feature film starring Sam Morton. I'd sign Kraftwerk and Radiohead, and all Neu!, Can, Eno, Fela Kuti and Steve Reich's back catalogue….

warp artists a-z

!!!

!!! (pronounced chk chk chk) officially formed in California in 1995 but have become inextricably linked with New York. Nic Offer (vocals) is also a member of Out Hud, and his !!! colleagues Mario Andreoni (guitar), Dan Gorman (horns/percussion/keys), Tyler Pope (guitar/electronic devices), John Pugh (drums/vocals), Justin Vandervolgen (bass), Allan Wilson (horns/percussion/keys) and Jason Racine (percussion) put a surrealistic spin on the early 80s No Wave funk sound of ESG and Liquid Liquid on tracks like "Me And Giuliani Down By The Old School Yard".

AFX
See Aphex Twin

Aphex Twin. Photo: Wolfgang Tillmans

Antipop Consortium

The motormouth avant hiphop trio of Priest, Beans and M Sayyid, plus producer Earl Blaize, emerged out of New York's rap and poetry scene at the end of 1997. Following an association with the Wordsound label, their debut album *Tragic Epilogue* appeared on Bill Laswell's 75Ark. Their highly literate, hyper-dense wordage, idiosyncratic delivery and experimental electronic beats came to Warp's attention at the end of 2001, but following two EPs and the album *Arrhythmia*, they reached an "amicable dissolution" in 2002.

See also Beans, Priest

Aphex Twin

Richard D James had already captured the attention of the new electronica community by the time he signed to Warp in 1993. Born on 18 August 1971 to Welsh parents, he grew up in Cornwall where he started DJing and making Acid House tracks as a teenager, attending clubs and illegal parties in the area around 1990 before attending Kingston Polytechnic. His many known aliases have included AFX, GAK and Polygon Window (all on Warp), Caustic Window, The Dice Man, Power Pill, Universal Indicator, Q-Chastic and Bradley Strider, and his label Rephlex, founded in 1992, enjoys success in its own right, but it was his album for Belgian label R&S, *Selected Ambient Works 1985-92*, that brought him wider recognition and was shortly followed by his first Warp release, *Polygon Window*. Since 1994's *Selected Ambient Works II* his music has fanned out into gritty beatless textures, hyperactive drill 'n' bass, Acid House influenced tracks and minimalist piano pieces, as well as the R&B makeover of "Windowlicker", 1999. Since film director Chris Cunningham made the notorious video for "Come To Daddy", 1997, they have regularly collaborated, with James making the soundtrack for Cunningham's first film *Flex*, 2000.

Autechre

Autechre formed in 1991 in Manchester, a product of Rob Brown and Sean Booth's shared passion for experimental hiphop and electro. As well as broadcasting on pirate radio, they formed part of the Gescom collective and were closely involved with the Skam label. Shortly after their debut album *Incunabula*, 1993, they relocated to Sheffield where they became one of the central Warp acts, refining and updating their industrially toughened music on albums including *Amber*, 1994, *Tri Repetae*, 1995, *Chiastic Slide*, 1997, and *LP5*, 1999. Now based in Suffolk and London, the duo continue to push the envelope with each release, coupling musical number crunching and digital rigour with a spirit of on the hoof improvisation and the spontaneity of old school street sounds.

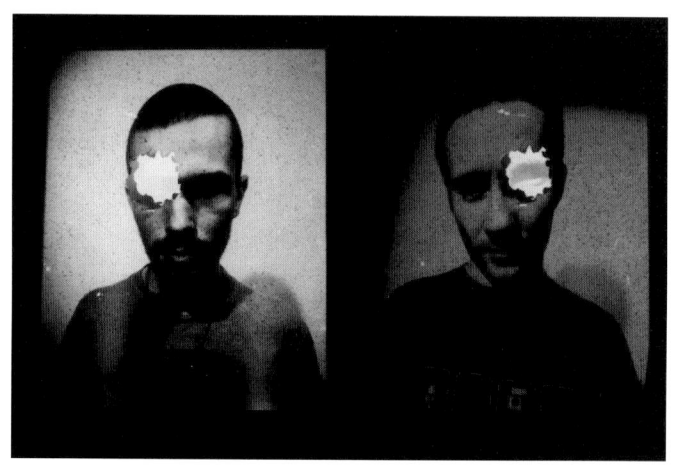

Autechre

B12

Romford based Mike Golding and Steve Rutter got together in 1989, working under aliases such as Redcell, Musicology and Cmetric, one of the earliest UK acts to convincingly respond to – and be respected by – the first wave of Detroit Techno practitioners. Signing to Warp in 1992, the publicity-shy duo's music came packaged with sci-fi imagery, dystopian visions and notions of robotics and time travel. *Electro-Soma*, 1993, collects the group's pre-Warp singles, and *Time Tourist*, 1996, and the *3EP*, 1998, became increasingly jazz inflected.

Beans

Beans grew up in White Plains, New York and took part in the legendary Brooklyn Boom poetry collective before co-founding Antipop Consortium with Priest and M Sayyid in 1997. After the group dissolved in 2002, he went solo and stayed with Warp; his two albums *Tomorrow Right Now*, 2003, and *Shock City Maverick*, 2004, crackle with his high-speed, literate raps (or 'orations', as he calls them) over beats by long-time producer Earl Blaize. He has also worked with Prefuse 73 and Def Jux's El-P and supported Radiohead on tour.

See also Antipop Consortium

Joey Beltram

The hugely influential New York based DJ/producer enjoyed success with early releases on New York labels Nu Groove, Atmosphere and New Street, as well as Trax Records in Chicago as Cold Six, before signing to Belgian label R&S, where he released the output of his project with Mundo Music, Direct, as well as under his own name. His track "Mentasm", 1992, featured a synth stab which was sampled in Hardcore drum 'n' bass for years afterwards. He made a brief, single appearance on Warp in 1994 with the EP *Caliber*, and has since released various recordings through Tresor. Beltram founded his own label STX in 1999, which has further cemented his position as a key mover in the dance scene.

The Black Dog

The Black Dog

Named after the Egyptian canine deity Anubis, The Black Dog was born around 1989 when former Naval recruit Ken Downie advertised for musical collaborators, which led to the addition of Ipswich friends Ed Handley and Andy Turner. Their fresh, oddly angular, Detroit-inspired electronic music, which also went out under the names Balil, Repeat, and IAO, was influenced by deep interests in ancient Egyptian and Mesopotamian mythology and the conspiracy writings of Robert Anton Wilson and William Burroughs. While building up a fearsome reputation in the early 90s, the group maintained a low public profile, preferring to communicate via email and the Black Dog Towers bulletin board. Following *Bytes*, 1992, and *Spanners*, 1995, on Warp (see also the *Age Of Slack* EP, and *Temple Of Transparent Balls* and *Parallel*, both on GPR) the trio disbanded following disagreements, with Downie retaining the Black Dog name and Handley and Turner morphing into Plaid. *Music For Adverts (And Short Films)* came out in 1996, after the release of which the Dog parted company with Warp. A new LP *Silenced* emerged in 2005.

www.dogsquad.co.uk

See also Plaid

Black Mojo
See Solitaire Gee

Boards Of Canada

British born Michael Sandison and Marcus Eoin's families temporarily relocated to Canada while they were growing up in the 1970s. Exposure to natural history documentaries made by the National Film Board of Canada during the period led to their adoption of the name for the music and visual work they ended up doing together once they had resettled in Scotland. Sandison and Eoin have been making music together since the mid 80s from within a large, floating community of friends and artists using the collective name Hexagon Sun. Now based near Edinburgh, the crew produce kaleidoscopic artwork, films and their signature electronic music which first emerged on Skam.

Slow but sure workers, their first Warp record, *Music Has The Right To Children*, came out in 1998, the *In A Beautiful Place In The Country* EP in 2000, and *Geogaddi* in 2002. All their output is notable for its uncanny blend of 70s electronica and timeless folk textures, almost familiar but just out of the reach of memory, and their incorporation of buried geometric patterns, backwards and treated voices (often sampled from their own home movies), and the use of organic, queasy sounds and acoustic instruments. Their third, guitar-heavy LP, *The Campfire Headphase*, appeared in late 2005.

www.music70.com

Boards of Canada

Broadcast

Birmingham's Broadcast has existed in various different line-ups since 1995. The core of Trish Keenan (vocals) and James Cargill (bass, keyboards) has been supplemented by Roj Stevens (keyboards), Tim Felton (guitar), Keith York and Steve Perkins (drums). Early tracks which appeared on the small indie Wurlitzer Jukebox were collected on Warp's *Work And Non Work*, 1997, but it took another three years before they delivered *The Noise Made By People*, quickly followed by a string of EPs including *Extended Play I & II*, *Come On Let's Go* and *Drums On Fire*. Influenced by the avant-garde pop of Stereolab, the Broadcast sound is a melange of echo chamber concrete pop, vintage analogue keyboards, driving rhythms and faux-naif stream of consciousness lyrics. After 2003's *Haha Sound*, Keenan and Cargill reverted to a duo for 2005's *Tender Buttons*.

www.broadcast.uk.net

Broadcast

BrothomStates

Finland's Lassi Nikko, also known as Dune, put out a single EP on Exogenic Records in 2000 before Warp tuned into his glitchy, complex beats and textures. Since his *Claro* album and *Qtio* EP just after the turn of the century, Nikko has remained relatively silent apart from one single on Warp's Arcola offshoot in 2004.

www.brothomstates.com

BrothomStates. Photo: Peter Iain Campbell

John Callaghan

Originally part of the Birmingham underground scene that included Pram, Broadcast and Plone, John Callaghan's maverick, unconventional one-man 'auto-karaoke' performances, specially conceived DJ sets and performance art set him apart from much of the Warp roster. The 7" release of "I'm Not Comfortable Inside My Mind" was accompanied by an excellent, surrealistic video which Callaghan directed himself. His second and last Warp appearance was on the 10" EP *You've Got Your Memories*,

I've Got My Dreams, 2000. More recently he resurfaced in London with an EP entitled Every Kiss Takes A Minute Off Your Life (Short Sharp Shock Records) and has performed regularly around the UK and Europe.

www.johncallaghan.co.uk

John Callaghan

Chris Clark

Chris Clark recorded his Warp debut Clarence Park, 2001, while still at University in Bristol, and its rough hewn, unfinished edges and frosty tundra sound placed him firmly in the lineage of Aphex Twin/Autechre abstract electronica. Appropriately, as well as early LFO, he has cited influences including Larry Young's fusion, Pavement's slacker-rock surrealism and the Rawkus label's hardscrabble hiphop. After moving to Birmingham, via a brief stay in Brighton, Clark's 2003 releases, the "Ceramics Is The Bomb" single and the album Empty The Bones Of You signalled a hardening and sharpening of his aural arsenal, with some tracks reaching a psychotic intensity.

Chris Clark

Chok Rock

Chok Rock is Gael Baillier, Camille Bazbaz, Cyril Kebellian and Check Morris (included in the group as graphic designer and video maker).

Chok Rock

Circle City

Little information is available on the personnel on this outfit whose sole Warp release was the Trance track "Moments Of Inertia" in early 1994.

Coco, Steel & Lovebomb

In the early 90s, Brighton DJ Chris Mellor ran the city's most popular underground Acid House night at the Zap club. The single "Feel It" was the Coco Club's' anthem, and as Coco, Steel & Lovebomb, with Lene Stokes and Craig Woodrow, he recorded increasingly Ambient flavoured dance tunes that incorporated sound effects taped on his travels. After Warp singles and albums including *Summer Rain* and *It!!*, both released in 1994, Mellor's time was increasingly occupied as editor of *DJ Magazine*, although he found time to release a track on Emit Recordings and a final album, *New World*, in 1997. He is now a prominent dance DJ on BBC Radio 1.

www.chriscoco.com

Richard Devine

Atlanta-born computer science graduate Devine is closely associated with Miami's Schematic Records, from whom Warp licensed his 2000 album *Lipswitch*. Devine's music is the product of intricate and obsessional programming, built up of layers of converging and dispersing arcs of scintillating beats and accelerated rhythmic play, with many micro-events compressed into short timescales, as heard on subsequent releases *Aleamapper* and *asect:dsect*. In 2005 Devine, who also uses the names Trapezoid and El Chino Maricon, released *Cautella* (Sublight).

www.richard-devine.com

Richard Devine

Disjecta

Named after a collection of essays by Samuel Beckett, Disjecta is a solo project of former Seefeel member Mark Clifford. Although he also subsequently worked with vocalists (such as Sophie Hinkley in the duo Sneakster), Disjecta is an outlet for his abstract constructivist electronica, evident on his two records for Warp, *Looking For Snags*, 1995, and *Clean Pit And Lid*, 1996. A newer Disjecta release, *True_Love By Normal*, appeared on Clifford's Polyfusia imprint in 2003.

www.polyfusiarecords.com

See Seefeel, Woodenspoon

Disjecta

DiY

The sprawling DiY collective of DJs and underground party organisers came together around 1989 in Nottingham. At the 1990 Glastonbury Festival they connected with a swelling illegal rave/traveller circuit and spent much of the next 12 months DJing around parties in the South West, culminating in an appearance at the infamous Castlemorton Festival in 1991. Digs and Woosh, the most visible members, compiled the *Serve Chilled* series which anticipated the early 90s' interest in Ambient electronic music, and they have kept the DiY flame burning with releases on their own labels Strictly 4 Groovers (also the title of their one Warp album in 1993) and, more recently, DiY Discs.

www.diydiscs.com

DIY

Drexciya

Detroit electro-Techno outfit Drexciya was conceived in 1989 but first swam into the public eye in 1994 with *Aquatic Invasion*, the first of a thematic series of releases – *Bubble Metropolis*, *The Unknown Aquazone* and (on Warp) *The Journey Home*. Drexciya's James Stinson and Gerald Donald remained hidden behind their alias for much of the group's existence (they also used the names Elecktroids, Transllusion, Glass Domain and LAM), communicating instead a complex personal mythology of the Drexciyan race of underwater dwellers, descended from pregnant slave women thrown overboard during transatlantic deportation. Within this sonic fiction, their music – which they claimed was recorded "live in the studio" rather than programmed, was imagined as a "dimensional jumphole" between their black African roots and the contemporary USA. Following *The Journey Home*, 1995, Warp released two works by their 80s synthpop tribute incarnation Elecktroids, the *Kilohertz* EP and *Elektroworld* album, both 1995. Drexciya continued into the late 90s on other Techno labels including Berlin's Tresor and Detroit's Submerge and Underground Resistance imprints, and Stinson's solo project, The Other People Place, put out the lyrical electro album *Lifestyles Of The Laptop Cafe* on Warp in 2001. Sadly Stinson died suddenly on 3 September 2002 of a heart condition. Donald continues to produce music under the names Dopplereffekt, Der Zyklus, Japanese Telecom and Arpanet.

DSR

Miami based act whose gospel/House crossover "Miami" was released on Warp in mid 1992.

Jimmy Edgar

Jimmy Edgar was born in Detroit, and was inevitably exposed to the city's influential electronic music from a young age. At 15 he was performing at raves alongside some of the scene's big names such as Juan Atkins and Derrick May, and developing an interest in a wide range of music, from experimental electronica to Goth rock. After early releases on Isophlux and Poker Flat, his debut album *My Mines I* appeared on Miami's M3rck label under the curious alias Kristuit Salu vs Morris Nightingale. After a low-key release as Michaux on audio.nl, Edgar signed exclusively to Warp where he now releases under his own name. The *Access Rhythm* EP appeared in 2004, followed by the *Bounce, Make, Model*, 2005.

Jimmy Edgar

Elecktroids
See Drexciya

Elecktroids

Eternal

Australian producer Mark James scored a hit in 1990 with Bass Culture's "Love The Life", a feel-good dance anthem used in a late 90s Coca-Cola advert. His Eternal single "Mind Odyssey" was a Top 20 hit in 1992 for Warp. He subsequently became a prominent producer of progressive House and Techno in his native country.

Forgemasters

The trio of Robert Gordon, Winston Hazel and Sean Maher achieved the distinction of releasing the first ever record on Warp in 1989 after their white label of "Track With No Name", recorded at Gordon's home studio in Sheffield, sold out its first edition of 1000 copies. Despite being one of Warp's founding directors, as well as an innovative and highly respected producer, engineer, remixer and musician, Gordon, whose career began in FON Studios, is strangely under-represented on record since WAP1. Significantly, he contributed mixes to Unique 3's 'original' bleep tune "The Theme" in 1989, but only two further Forgemasters singles were to appear, *Black Steel* (Network) and *Quabala* (Hubba Hubba). Gordon briefly collaborated with Ambient artist Pete Namlook on *Ozoona*, 1996 (Fax Records), and in the same year Source put out *Robert Gordon Projects*, a collection of his dextrous, acrobatic electronic funk tracks from the first half of the 90s. Hazel, a prominent Sheffield DJ since the mid 80s, was also part of The Step with DJ Parrot. He moved to London in the late 90s where he has pursued a successful career as a producer and DJ, associated with Ashley Beedle's Afro Art label (under the name Supafix), running his own Sotuff company, and working with drummer Ross Orton of the Fat Truckers. Maher appears to have left the planet.

Freeform

Born in 1977, Simon Pyke issued his first electronic experiments on the Worm Interface and Skam labels in the early 1990s. Influenced by 'headphone Techno' as well as dub, gamelan and electro, his music typically sculpts forests of tightly programmed clicks, chirps and fuzzed beats. He was picked up by Autechre as support on their 1995 tour, and a year later released his *Prowl* EP on Warp. He has also enjoyed associations with independent electronic labels such as Quatermass, Leaf and Sprawl Imprint. In 2000 he began a series of 'audio tourism' projects featuring material sampled on travels in Vietnam and China. More recently, now based in Brighton, he has embarked on sound design projects with Designers Republic and has been supplying sound bites for TV and film companies.

www.freefarm.co.uk

FUSE

Richie Hawtin was born in Oxford, UK, to British parents in 1970, but his family moved to Canada soon after, and he grew up in Windsor, Ontario, just across the border from Detroit. In his late teens he rapidly joined the front rank of DJs, and achieved worldwide credibility with the output of his own Plus 8 label. Although he is best known as Plastikman, purveyor of radically tweaked and manipulated Acid basslines, FUSE (Futuristic Underground Subsonic Experiments) is one of many aliases Hawtin has used over the years for his ultra-minimal, clinical Techno, first appearing on 1991's "Approach And Identify" single on Plus 8. The Warp releases *Dimension Intrusion* and *Train Tracs* helped secure Hawtin's reputation worldwide. Hawtin appeared as UP! on Warp's *Artificial Intelligence* compilation in 1993.

www.plastikman.com

GAK

See Aphex Twin

Vincent Gallo

Born in Buffalo, New York, in 1961, Vincent Gallo has pursued parallel paths through the worlds of film, art and music. As a teenager he played bass in New York City groups such as The Good, The Plastics, I'll Wear You, and The Nonsexuals, before hooking up with celebrated downtown painter Jean-Michel Basquiat and forming the short-lived Gray, who were given a brief residence at the legendary Mudd Club. He made his first released recordings with the group Bohack, and shortly afterwards, in 1983, was given a role on Eric Mitchell's independent film *The Way It Is*, for which Gallo also wrote music and produced the score. He appeared in around 20 movies over the ensuing years, before directing his first feature, *Buffalo 66*, in 1998, which included reworked versions of pieces from *The Way It Is* plus several songs by progressive rock group Yes. In 2001 Warp put out his solo album *When*, a clutch of fragile, moonstruck songs. All instruments were played by Gallo and taped on primitive analogue equipment at his University for the Development and Theory of Magnetic Tape Recorded Music Studios in LA. The following year's *Recordings Of Music For Film*, 2002, presented all the music he had ever made for the screen. He plays in the group Bunny with Lukas Haas, and in 2005 curated the All Tomorrows Parties festival in the UK.

www.vincentgallo.com

Laurent Garnier

From Boulogne, Laurent Garnier was one of the most influential and prolific European DJs during the 1990s. His spinning of House and Acid tunes at Manchester's Hacienda in the late 80s turned the heads of The Stone Roses and Happy Mondays, while his Wake Up club in Paris and F Communications label were focal points for the emerging electronic Trance scene. His one appearance on Warp came about in 1993 when his "À Bout De Souffle" single was licensed from FNAC.

www.fcom.fr

Gescom

The Gescom name provides cover for an amorphous electronic music collective based around the Skam label, active since the late 80s. The group includes Autechre's Sean Booth and Rob Brown, and its output is often more abrasive and loose than Autechre's music. Most of Gescom's releases have appeared via Skam, with notable exceptions including an EP for Clear, a minidisc-only album on Touch, and a collaboration with experimental artist The Hafler Trio. As well as various remixes for Warp, Gescom put out the *Keynell* EP in 1996.

Gravenhurst

Singer/songwriter Nick Talbot moved to Bristol in the late 90s, attracted by the fuzzed post-rock psychedelia of local groups such as Third Eye Foundation and Flying Saucer Attack. After a stint in My Bloody Valentine-influenced outfit Assembly Communications, he founded his own label Silent Age, on which he released two albums by Gravenhurst, his new trio with Dave Collingwood (drums) and Paul Nash (various instruments), blending dark folk-rock with explosive heavier passages. Warp rereleased their earlier LP *Flashlight Seasons*, plus the new *Black Holes In The Sand* in 2004, followed by *Fires In Distant Buildings*, 2005, on which the group was joined by Huw Cooksley (bass). Talbot also has a 'horror-tronica' side project with Guy Bartell, Bronnt Industries Kapital.

www.silentagerecords.co.uk

Gravenhurst

Harmonic 33

Harmonic 33 is Mark Pritchard (of Jedi Knights, Reload and Global Communication) and Dave Brinkworth, who met and began making music together in Cornwall in the late 90s. With a mixture of Easy Listening strings and vintage Moog and Optigan synth sounds, *Music For TV, Film & Radio Volume One*, 2005, mimics the functional 'library music' of the 60s and 70s created by anonymous session musicians for use as incidental music.

See Link

David Holmes

The Belfast born DJ and producer's best known work is inspired by film composers such as Ennio Morricone and John Barry – no wonder he's been chosen as soundtracker of movies such as *Out Of Sight*, *Analyze That* and *Ocean's Twelve*. *Johnny Favourite*, 1994 (Warp) was his first solo release following the break-up of his previous act, Disco Evangelists. At the same time he was involved in remix work with Andrew Weatherall's Sabres Of Paradise label, before signing with Go! Discs in 1995. Subsequent albums include *This Film's Crap*, *Let's Slash The Seats*, 1995, and *Bow Down To The Exit Sign*, 2000.

Home Video

Home Video's David Gross and Collin Ruffino originally hail from New Orleans, are based in New York, and had still to play their first show when Warp signed them in 2004. Their live/electronic hybrid has been compared to 80s electronic pop of Electribe 101 and M/A/R/R/S. Ruffino's obsession with collecting random film footage, nurtured while at New York University film school, gave the group its name.

www.homevideooffice.com

Home Video. Photo: Tim Siccanti

K Hand

Detroit's Kelli Hand is a well known name in Techno as producer of jazz inflected progressive House, remixer, label owner and DJ. Inspired by visits to Larry Levan's Paradise Garage nights in New York, she set up her label Acacia in 1988, before focusing on producing singles and albums in the 90s. Her "Global Warning" single on Warp in 1994 helped cement her quickly growing reputation. Since then she's carried on recording for a huge number of different labels including K7, Distance Records, Ausfahrt, Tresor and Loveslap.

K Hand

Mike Ink

Mike Ink is one of many alter egos of Cologne's Wolfgang Voigt. His post-Acid minimal click-Techno fell between Detroit's Motor City sound and the oceanic precision of Berlin's Basic Channel. He provided the impetus for Germany's awakening to Acid House in 1991-1992, by organising the 'Brotherhood of Structure' group of artists and labels, which included Dr Walker, Air Liquide, Bionaut, and Biochip C. Via his mid 90s imprints Studio 1 and Profan, he embarked on a quest to explore the deep soul of German machine music by stripping music to its rhythmic essence of kick, click and carefully sculpted sonic grain. Finely tuned variants on his sound have been produced under a spiralling array of names including M:I:5, Gas, Love Inc, Auftrieb, Dom, Freiland, Grungerman, Popacid, and more. Warp licensed his *Paroles* – unusually featuring breakbeats rather than Ink's customary 4/4 – in 1996, followed swiftly by the *Polka Trax* EP. Soon afterwards, Voigt rationalised his activities by setting up Kompakt, a Cologne based shop, label, distribution, promotion and artist agency that functions almost as an electronic musicians' commune.

www.kompakt-net.com

Mike Ink

Jackson And His Computer Band

French maverick Jackson Fourgeaud signed to Warp in 2005. He released several driving House tunes in the late 90s, but it was his 2003 glam/R&B-meets-electro single "Utopia" that caught the attention of DJs, and it is included on his 2005 album *Smash*, a brash and strident collection of angular electronic pop. Jackson's records are a family affair, with guest vocals from his mother (folk singer Paula Moore) and four year old niece.

Jaco
See Solitaire Gee

Kid Unknown

Paul Fitzpatrick had been immersed in Manchester's club scene since the early 80s. A regular Hacienda DJ who went on tour with 808 State, Public Enemy and others, he recorded Kid Unknown's breakbeat classic "Nightmare" in 1991, which came out on Warp the following year, closely followed by the equally punchy "Devastating Beat Creator". Immediately afterwards he took a year out in Thailand, then signed a deal with Polydor as Nipper. After a decade as a recording artist during which time he set up two studios, he established LCD Records with partner Ian Bland (ex-Dream Frequency).

Kid Unknown

Richard H Kirk

As a founder member of Cabaret Voltaire in 1973 with Stephen Mallinder and Chris Watson in Sheffield, Richard Kirk has impeccable credentials as a sonic pioneer reaching far back beyond the origins of punk rock. From their beginnings as an experimental noise combo in Watson's parents' attic, Cabaret Voltaire evolved into a titanic force in Industrial music, with their experimental use of cut-up tapes (inspired by the writings of William S Burroughs) and uncompromising use of abrasive electronics and heat-seeking beats that left a glaring scar on Sheffield's late 70s electronic music scene. As a solo artist in the latter half of the 1980s, Kirk's post-Industrial Techno slowly converged with the UK Acid House movement via releases on DoubleVision and Rough Trade, and he met Sheffield's DJ Parrot on the city's club circuit around the time Warp was getting going. Appropriate, then, that with such a history, Kirk's duo project with Parrot, Sweet Exorcist, should have become the third ever Warp catalogue entry. "Testone" is an all time classic of lo-fi bleep Techno and a huge influence on the later work of LFO, Aphex Twin and others. Kirk's two solo LPs on Warp, *Virtual State*, 1994, and *The Number Of Magic*, 1995, combined a sheen of metallic and plastic textures with rhythms that betrayed Kirk's interest in African and Latin American ethnic drumming. The 90s saw Kirk spreading his material across a raft of pseudonyms including Sandoz, Electronic Eye, and Citrus, some on the Touch label, others on his own Alphaphone imprint.

www.richardhkirk.com
www.thegreedyeye.com
See Sweet Exorcist

Ko-Wreck Technique

Collaboration between Bomb Hip-Hop's DJ Craze, a former World DMC turntable championship winner, and Push Button Objects, aka Edgar Farinas, the Miami based producer who has also recorded for Florida labels Chocolate Industries and Schematic, and Manchester's Skam. Warp released the four track *Ko-Wrecktion* EP, featuring the great "Metro Dade", awash with funk breaks, violin samples and turntable scratching (with remix by Plaid) in 1999.

Kenny Larkin

Kenny Larkin first discovered House music in the mid 80s while serving as a computer engineer in the US Air Force, but began his career in music in 1990. A Detroit resident, he soaked up the local clubs and released his early tracks on Plus 8 and Transmat and set up his own label, Art Of Dance, in 1992. His 1994 *Azimuth* album for Warp is a gem in the *Artificial Intelligence* series, with sleek bubbling rhythmic cross-hatchings and melancholy Ambient washes. Soon afterwards, on 17 November 1994, he was shot in the lower abdomen at his home after a bungled robbery attempt. Discharged after a lightning recovery, he was back on tour in Europe within two weeks promoting *Metaphor*, released on the Belgian R&S label. During a frenetic few years of international DJing, Larkin only released one LP, Dark Comedy's *Seven Days*, 1997 (Elypsia), before he became disillusioned with recording his own material. In 2002 he quit music and moved to Los Angeles in order to enter the realm of stand-up comedy, although he has since relented with *Narcissist*, 2004 (Peace Frog), and Dark Comedy's jazz/blues inflected *Funk Faker: Music Saves My Soul*, 2005 (Poussez).

Kenny Larkin

Lex Loofah
See Solitaire Gee

LFO

Low Frequency Oscillation was the key to the early sounds of Mark Bell and Gez Varley, who met at the 1980s breakdance clubs of their native Leeds. Their potent combinations of deep sub-bass and test tone inspired bleeps received rapturous reactions on the dance floors of clubs like the Warehouse, and their "LFO" theme, 1990, became Warp's first major hit, reaching number 12 in the UK with sales exceeding 100,000 – unprecedented for an underground, anonymous single. The *Frequencies* LP, 1991, quickly became a touchstone of British Techno. After a five year silence, "Tied Up" and their second LP *Advance* arrived packed with more hard and abrasive Techno, using the efficient design of Kraftwerk, sparse synth sounds and occasional distorted voices to hurtle from A to B. Although they got to work with their hero, Kraftwerk's Karl Bartos, and Depeche Mode's Alan Wilder, the pair split up (for unspecified reasons) in 1996. Varley pumped out scouring Techno on labels such as Swim and Leaf, while Bell took on creative production work, which has included Björk's *Homogenic*, the *Dancer In The Dark* soundtrack *Selmasongs* and her music for Matthew Barney's film *Drawing Restraint 9*, and Depeche Mode's *Exciter*. After another long wait came *Sheath*, 2003, by Bell sole trading as LFO.

LFO

Jamie Lidell

After releasing tracks on labels like Mosquito and Sativae, in 1998 Lidell formed Super_Collider as vocalist with prolific Techno producer Cristian Vogel. The group helped him reconnect with a soulful singing voice he had possessed since his childhood, although heavily processed in Vogel's edits. Lidell's solo *Muddlin Gear*, 2000 (Warp), buried his distorted singing in clouds of digital dust, but his increasingly frequent live performances and a move to the artistically vibrant city of Berlin helped him develop a set of new material where he could explore the imaginative flights of Marvin Gaye, Prince and Smokey Robinson – an approach that came to fruition on 2005's *Multiply*.

www.jamielidell.com

Jamie Lidell

Link

Like so many 90s electronica players, Wiltshire based duo Tom Middleton and Mark Pritchard employed a full deck of aliases and shifted across an astonishing range of generic styles, of which Link was one. Middleton knew Aphex Twin's Richard James from the Cornish raving days, and co-produced one of his early *Analogue Bubblebath* tracks. Pritchard was producing bedroom tracks and was a member of Shaft, whose "Roobarb And Custard", sampling a 70s children's cartoon over breakbeats, was a Top Ten rave hit. As Global Communication, their *76:13*, 1994 (Dedicated) was a brooding, immersive take on Ambient introspection; Reload exemplified early 90s 'intelligent Techno'; Chameleon explored intricate Jungle rhythms; The Jedi Knights allowed them to give rein to a retro-fetishism for old school electro on *New School Science*, 1996 (Clear). As Link they perfected a blend of progressive House and bleep Techno on the *Antacid* EP, 1995 (Warp). Many of their own productions and music by Wishmountain, Jak & Stepper and Danny Breaks came out on their labels Evolution and Universal Language. In 1995 Warp issued the definitive introduction to the productions of the duo and their associates with the *Theory Of Evolution* compilation. The duo had ceased working together by 2000; Middleton went solo as Cosmos. Pritchard continued producing under a wide range of names, and more recently formed the studio project Harmonic 33.

See Harmonic 33

Link

Maxïmo Park

They may be named after a recreational zone in Havana, Cuba, but guitar based quintet Maxïmo Park hail from Newcastle – a fact clearly audible in the Tyneside accent of singer Paul Smith. Bandmates Lukas Wooler (keyboards), Tom English (drums), Archis Tiku (guitars) and Duncan Lloyd (guitars) generate spiky, jangly Smiths/New Wave-style arrangements for Smith's songs of urban alienation. The single "Apply Some Pressure" was included on the 2005 LP *A Certain Trigger*.

DJ Maxximus

DJ Maxximus is Berlin's F Stader, also known as Himself and DIN-ST. Since 1994 he has issued his crunchy Bass and Hardcore sounds on many labels including Ambush, DHR, Tresor and Schematic. His one Warp showing is a split single with Something J, "Mercedes Bentley vs Versace Armani", 2001.

Milanese

Birmingham based 'digital Grimecore' producer Steve Milanese released his *Vanilla Monkey* EP on the Warp offshoot Arcola, and his second album "1Up" appeared on Warp in 2004.

DJ Mink

Mancunian Michael Naylor met Warp's Robert Gordon when aged only 17, and as a result his high tempo hiphop track "Hey! Hey! Can You Relate?" became the fourth Warp single in April 1990.

Mira Calix

Born in Durban, South Africa, Chantal Passamonte arrived in London to work as a photographer at the beginning of the 1990s, and quickly became caught up in the city's emerging Ambient party scene, DJing at clubs like Megatripolis, The Big Chill and helping to organise events under the banner Telepathic Fish, also a fanzine. She was given the job of Warp's press officer and moved to Sheffield in early 1995. Her first tentative electronic music experiments were released as the *Ilanga* 10", 1996, and *Pin Skeeling*, 1998, after which she left the job to concentrate on putting together her first album, *One On One*, 2000. Since then, and following a move to Saxmundham, Suffolk with husband Sean Booth (Autechre), she has become a frequent DJ at Warp events and clubs and her music – which often sounds like buzzing miniature sonic ecologies, has branched out into art installation work including the intriguing *NuNu* – sourced from work with the Geneva Natural History Museum's collection of insect noises, plus an orchestral version involving live insects; and an environmental sound work for London's Barbican Art Gallery in tandem with a Helen Chadwick retrospective, all of which are collected on the *3 Commissions* CD, 2004.

Mira Calix

Modus Vivendi

Ludovic Navarre's best known project is the smooth House grooves of St Germain on Laurent Garnier's F Communications label. As Modus Vivendi he issued one self-titled single on Warp in 1993.

Chris Morris

The creator of outstanding TV satire such as *The Day Today*, *Brass Eye* and *Nathan Barley*, Cambridgeshire-born Chris Morris started his career as a radio DJ. A collection of sketches from his Radio 1 comedy *Blue Jam*, laid over an Ambient background, was his first release on Warp. More recently Morris has ventured into direction, and his *My Wrongs Nos 8245-8249 & 117* was the first film to appear on a Warp Films DVD.

Move D

Based in Heidelberg, southern Germany, David Moufang's Source imprint is responsible for an eclectic series of electronica releases, characteristically loose, jazzy and executed with a lightness of touch. His own music has appeared on Fax and Compost, with alter egos including Move D, Conjoint, Deep Space Network (with Jonas Grossman) and Reagenz (with Jonah Sharp). The *Cymbelin* EP, 1996 (Warp) is classic, pristine Moufang.

Nightmares On Wax

George Evelyn (EASE, meaning 'Experimental Sample Expert') and Kevin Harper (Boy Wonder) met in Bradford in 1984 as young hiphop and breakdance fans, and by 1987 they had their own club, Downbeat, and a breakdance crew called Soul City Rockers. They

Nightmares on Wax

inaugurated their Poverty label in 1989 with a 12" featuring hiphop tune "Stating A Fact" on one side and "Let It Roll"/"Dextrous" on the flip. Remixed by Warp's Rob Gordon, "Dextrous" became the second Warp single and placed Nightmares On Wax firmly among the Northern bleep movement alongside Unique 3, LFO and Forgemasters. 1990's "Aftermath" crept into the UK chart at number 38 but following the *A Word Of Science* album (whose track "Playtime" featured the moans of a woman the duo had brought back to their apartment), Harper left to concentrate on DJing and Evelyn co-ran the Headz club in Leeds while collecting a massive databank of soul and funk samples.

These, coupled with live instrumentation, formed the primary ingredients of *Smoker's Delight*, 1995, the archetypal British downtempo chill-out record, whose slick veneer belied the complex rearrangements of sampled funk riffs and beats. That talent for reinventing familiar musical elements while respecting tradition has continued through Evelyn's subsequent releases, including *Carboot Soul*, 1999, the dub-inspired *Mind Elevation*, 2002, various singles (including a collaboration with De La Soul on "Keep On") and DJ mix CDs. In 2002 Evelyn, in the role of "spiritual conductor", took an 11 piece live incarnation of Nightmares On Wax on an international tour.

www.nightmaresonwax.com

The Other People Place

James Stinson, one of the founders of enigmatic Detroit duo Drexciya, created this one-off solo project on Warp in 2001 with *Lifestyles Of The Laptop Cafe*, an album of clipped, futuristic electro doused in obscure vocoded singing. Sadly, almost exactly a year after its release, Stinson died of a heart condition.

See Drexciya

Phoenecia

Miami based electronic producers Joshua Kay and Romulo Del Castillo made their first tracks as Soul Oddity, before kickstarting the new project Phoenecia in 1997 as a vehicle for their claustrophobic rhythmic chatter. The *Randa Roomet* EP, 1997 (Warp), was the project's first proper release, after which they focused on their work for local label Schematic.

Plaid

The duo of Ipswich friends Ed Handley and Andy Turner existed prior to their involvement in The Black Dog: witness their *Mbuki Mvuki* LP, 1991, and, as Balil, their appearance on Carl Craig's seminal Detroit label Planet E as far back as 1992. After a five year collaboration with Black Dog's Ken Downie ended with 1995's *Spanners*, Plaid was brought out of mothballs. Their *Angry Dolphin* EP, 1995 (Clear), suggested a lighter, warmer touch than the Black Dog productions, and as one of Warp's most prolific acts, they have pumped out a stream of perpetually inventive, sparkling and warm electronic music, often showing the influence of old school electro, Latin and Caribbean percussion on albums such as *Not For Threes*, 1997, *Rest Proof Clockwork*, 1999, and *Spokes*, 2003. *Trainer*, 2000, provided a handy sweeping-up of most of their early, out of print recordings. They frequently appear live or DJing, and in 2005 they developed a surround sound performance and DVD in collaboration with film maker Bob Jaroc.

www.plaid.co.uk

See The Black Dog

Plaid. Photo: Deidre O'Callaghan

Plone

Taking their name from an imaginary cartoon sound, Plone's Mike Bainbridge, Mark Cancellara and Michael Johnston formed out of the Birmingham scene that spawned Broadcast and Pram amongst others. The first recording of their analogue-fetishist synthesizer sound, the "Press Any Key" single, 1997, came out on the local Wurlitzer Jukebox label. The following year Warp picked up their *Plock* EP and *For Beginner Piano* album. The group have been subjects of a curious homage: an American computer content management system was named after them in 1999.

Plone

Polygon Window

See Aphex Twin

Prefuse 73

A native of Atlanta, Georgia who always seems to be on the move, (Guillermo) Scott Herren is a prolific production wizard who has displayed virtuosity spread across a number of differently named projects. As well as the experimental, slice 'n' dice hiphop Prefuse 73 (after his love of pre-fusion music around 1973), he crafts electronica as Delarosa And Asora, acoustically tinged electronic music as Savath + Savalas, and polemic-tinged projects as Piano Overlord. His Prefuse debut *Vocal Studies And Uprock Narratives*, 2001, introduced his rainbow of endlessly inventive cut-up skills, reducing hiphop's narrative flow down to infectious yet stuttering glitched samples and beats. Reconnecting with his Catalan roots, he temporarily moved to Barcelona in 2003 where he completed the bulk of the work on *Surrounded By Silence*, 2004, a monumental LP on which he secured the guest appearances of Ghostface, El-P, The Books, Aesop Rock, Masta Killa & GZA, Beans and more. On Prefuse 73's *Reads The Books* EP, 2005, he continued working with the intellectual Massachusetts post-rock duo.

www.prefuse73.com

RAC

Sheffield teenager Chris Duckenfield initiated a successful and popular DJ residency at the Limit club in 1989, where he met fellow DJ Richard Brown. As progressive House duo RAC (Richard And Chris), they produced the first single, "Monsoon/Yogomotion", on shortlived Warp sublabel Nucleus in 1991. During the 90s RAC released several 12"s and one LP, *Diversions*, 1994. Duckenfield worked as the dance records buyer at the Warp shop for five years until its closure in 1997, when he set up his own Primitive label and he and Brown renamed themselves SWAG. In this format the pair have enjoyed success with releases on the Junior Boys' Own label (including the album *Felony Funk*, 1998), and as sought after remixers and DJs.

See Rhythm Invention

RAC

Red Snapper

David Ayers (guitar), Ali Friend (double bass), and Richard Thair (drums) formed Red Snapper in 1993 in Manchester with the intention of combining their loves of jazz fluidity, instrumental funk, hiphop and newer dance music. Early singles, featuring saxophonist Ollie Moore and vocalist Beth Orton, appeared on the small Flaw Recordings, and eventually collected on the Warp release *Reeled And Skinned*, 1995. Developing their vibrant live sound on *Prince Blimey*, 1996, and adding Jungle MC Det, singer Alison David and jazz cornettist Byron Wallen on *Making Bones*, 1998, the group peaked with the deliciously eclectic confection of reggae, noir soundtracks, Charles Mingus-style bass acrobatics and hiphop on *Our Aim Is To Satisfy Red Snapper*, 2000. Although the group split in

2002, with Thair embarking on a new DJ career, he released new material as Red Snapper on Lo Recordings in 2003 as well as forming a new live project, TOOb.

Red Snapper

Req

Brighton's Ian Cassar developed an obsession for hiphop and its street art culture after films such as *Beat Street* and *Style Wars* crossed the Atlantic in the mid 80s. Known as Req One, he enthusiastically plunged into a world of B-boying, breakdancing, spraycan painting, DJing and music making, his activities focused around Brighton's Slip Jam B nights. He made the acquaintance of Norman Cook well before he adopted his Fatboy Slim persona, and accompanied Cook's group Beats International on a global tour that took in Europe, Africa and the US. As one of the UK's most respected graffiti artists, he created live artworks on stage at early Fatboy Slim shows, and he regularly shows his paintings outside Brighton's Ocean Rooms and Rounder Records shop. In the late 90s he began constructing his dense audio collages of fractured samples, drum machines and skilful, heavily processed turntable scratching. After two acclaimed LPs on Skint, he signed with Warp and delivered *Sketchbook*, 2002, and *Car Paint Scheme*, 2003.

www.req.net

Resoraz

See Solitaire Gee

Rhythm Invention

Richard Brown partnered Nick Simpson in this early 90s Sheffield based House act. The white label of their club anthem "I Can't Take It" was brought to the label by Warp employee Chris Duckenfield in 1992, which led to the formation of RAC. Brown also gave technical assistance to several early Warp artists including Nightmares On Wax and Solitaire Gee. They released the "Ad Infinitum" single and *Inventures In Wonderland* LP, 1993, before leaving to pursue other projects. Brown handled production for Björk, Rabbit In The Moon and Beaumont Hannant, and more recently has been working as Cherry Bomb and Barb Wired (with Billy Nasty). Simpson formed Hazed, a duo with Rabbit In The Moon's David Christophere, with a string of releases including a track for Plus 8, and has also released dance tracks under the name Slick.

See RAC

Rhythm Invention

Rubber Johnny

The mystery figure behind Rubber Johnny's burbling drill 'n' bass 12" *Jam Roly Poly*, 1997 (Warp), turned out to be Sheffielder Jason Buckle, a member – alongside Dean Honer (I, Monster) and DJ Parrot (Sweet Exorcist, The Step) – of The All Seeing I, the eccentric electronic trio who scored a chart hit with "The Beat Goes On" in 1998. As JP Buckle, his corrosive mash-ups appeared on the 1998 Rephlex LP *Flyin Lo-fi*; he has also recorded as National Bandit and is currently a member of Jarvis Cocker's post-Pulp group, Relaxed Muscle.

Sabres Of Paradise

DJ, producer and one of the most influential figures on the British electronica scene, Andrew Weatherall has enjoyed a long and fruitful relationship with Warp since the first Sabres Of Paradise releases in 1993. Hailing from Windsor, Weatherall has been manning decks across the planet since his swashbuckling rise to prominence at the end of the 80s when he provided the magic studio touch that transformed Primal Scream from rock revivalism to futurist visionaries on the *Screamadelica* LP. Henceforth, Weatherall's punishing work schedule has led to a colossal discography of releases and remixes, always one step ahead of the zeitgeist, and he has left a trail of labels including Sabres Of Paradise, Sabrettes, Emissions Audio Output and Rotters Golf Club. The group Sabres Of Paradise, featuring Jagz Kooner and Gary Burns, grew out of Weatherall's Sabresonic club in South London, and "Smokebelch" from *Sabresonic*, 1993, and the single "Wilmot", are classics of underground Trance. *Haunted Dancehall*, 1994, mutated Trance, Techno and electro into unfamiliar patterns, the latter shot through with dub and Caribbean echoes. The group downed swords in 1995, and Weatherall formed a new project, Two Lone Swordsmen.

See Two Lone Swordsmen

Andrew Weatherall

Satanstornade

Masami Akita and Russell Haswell gave Warp a welcome blast of cranium-scouring digital noise on their one and only self-titled album in 2002, assigned the beastly catalogue number WARP666. Akita is best known as Merzbow, the astonishingly prolific Japanese noise artist with several hundred releases and collaborations to his name dating back to 1984. Coventry-born Haswell has connections to the art world as well as the sonic realm: he has assisted British artists Jake and Dinos Chapman and exhibited his own work at galleries including London's Tate Modern. Haswell treats his noise work as sculpture rather than music, and has worked with a wide network of friends including Jimi Tenor, Aphex Twin, Pita and Doom/Heavy Metal group Cathedral. He curates the OR label and programmed the All Tomorrows Parties festival in the UK in 2005. More of Haswell's nihilistic art attack can be heard on *Live Salvage 1997-2000* (Mego).

Savath + Savalas
See Prefuse 73

Seefeel
Mark Clifford, Daren Seymour, Sarah Peacock and Justin Fletcher formed Seefeel in London in 1992 in the midst of the 'shoegazing' movement, writing dreamy songs with huge washes of effects-slathered guitar typified by their *Quique* LP, 1993 (Too Pure). Clifford became increasingly interested in pushing the music away from the live group format into studio processed electronic treatment, and they made a surprising appearance on Warp's *Artificial Intelligence II* compilation, followed by the *Starethrough* EP (1994) and *Succour* LP, 1995. The electronic approach was harder to sustain in performance, however, and tensions within the group led to an 'open-ended hiatus' in 1996 after the group released *CH-Vox* on Rephlex. Clifford released several recordings of solo electronic meanderings as Disjecta and Woodenspoon before forming Sneakster with vocalist Sophie Hinkley; the remaining three formed Scala and have all taken part in a number of different ventures.
members.iglou.com/artbear/seefeel.html
See Disjecta

Seefeel

Jake Slazenger
Mike Paradinas stormed the 'bedroom electronica' landscape with his lo-fi, distorted, Aphex Twin-influenced albums *Tango N' Vectif*, 1993, and *Bluff Limbo*, 1994, both on Rephlex under the name μ-Ziq. Born in 1971 in South London, Paradinas's early Techno experiments coupled abrasive clattering beats with deceptively innocent and simple melodic loops. Asked to remix indie rock group The Auteurs for Virgin Records, he practically drowned the original in distorted electronics. Virgin financed his own label, Planet Mu, which has continued as an uncompromising independent throughout his subsequent career. Paradinas's portfolio of aliases included Kid Spatula, Tusken Raiders, Gary Moscheles, and Jake Slazenger, who released the *Nautilus* 12" and *Das Ist Ein Groovy Beat, Ja?*

album on Warp in 1996. With stylistic nods to Detroit Techno and vintage jazz funk from the 1970s (Herbie Hancock a particular favourite), the Slazenger records consciously looked back with a nostalgia for the warmth of analogue music and old school electro, presented tongue firmly in cheek. There were no more Warp issues, but his discography has bulked up considerably in the interim, largely under the µ-Ziq banner.

www.planet-mu.com

Slum

Watford duo Danny Sargassa and Preston Mead's lone Slum release, *Twilight Mushrooms*, 1999 (Warp), predated their name change to Parsley Sound, when they signed to James Lavelle's hip London label Mo' Wax. So far they have released two more albums of their unique, psychedelic sample-palette.

Solitaire Gee

The collaborative hard House duo, John Gilpin and Raz Shamshed, are partners who run the Fourth Wave record shop and Phat As Phuck label in Huddersfield. The pair also release variations on their 4/4 based sound together as D-Tek and Jaco (with local artists Hotline). Over the years they have released a number of shortlived individual projects on Warp – Gilpin as Black Mojo and Lex Loofah; Raz as Resoraz.

Something J

Joel Amaretto was one of the original partners of Digital Hardcore Recordings, a vehicle for industrial strength breakbeat mayhem spearheaded by the productions of Alec Empire. Amaretto is a member of BlackJewishGays and Killout Trash, and has recorded as X-Ray Geisha. The name Something J was adopted for the one-off Warp split single with DJ Maxximus, "Mercedes Bentley vs Versace Armani", 2001.

www.digitalworldnet.com

Sote

Ata Ebtekar was born in Iran, educated in Germany and currently lives in the USA where he studied sonic art and music. Among his extremely sporadic appearances on record, his electronic project Sote left a single masterpiece in *Electric Deaf*, 2002, four tracks of fiendishly complex rhythm matrices. His only other recorded work is with Virgox, co-starring Safar Bake.

Speedy J

Rotterdam's Jochem Paap is one of the Netherlands' most innovative and enduring Techno musicians. The sleek modernism of *Ginger*, 1993 (licensed from Plus 8) and *G Spot*, 1995, were eventually replaced with grittier textures when he signed to Novamute in 1997 and unleashed *Public Energy No 1* and *A Shocking Hobby* albums.

Speedy J

Squarepusher

Hailing from Chelmsford, Essex, former art student Tom Jenkinson made his recorded debut as The Duke Of Harringay, whose *Allroy Road Tracks*, on Brighton label Spymania, introduced a twitchy, preposterous take on drum 'n' bass that has become almost synonymous with Squarepusher, the name he has used ever since. Typical tracks would couple his agile bass playing – recalling the slap-happy flights of Weather Report's Jaco Pastorius or Mahavishnu Orchestra's Rick Laird – with frenetic annihilations of Jungle's "Amen" drum break in a riot of distorted beats that pushed close to rhythmic meltdown. A meeting with Aphex Twin's Richard James led to the brain-boggling suburban realism of *Feed Me Wierd Things*, 1996 (Rephlex). Signed to Warp shortly afterwards, he produced a stream of records that piled on the breakbeat intensity: the *Port Rhombus* EP, *Hard Normal Daddy* album, 1997, and the mini-LPs *Big Loada* and *Vic Acid*. A move to Sheffield in 1998 brought a shift towards a looser electric jazz sound: *Music Is Rotted One Note* and *Budakhan Mindphone* featured Jenkinson playing live instruments and exploring unconventional acoustic arrangements. 1999's *Selection Sixteen* paid homage to vintage electronic composition, and releases over the ensuing years have seen Jenkinson combining all the elements of his music into a challenging, unpredictable, rich mix on *Go Plastic*, 2001, *Do You Know Squarepusher?*, 2002, and *Ultravisitor*, 2004 (recorded live on tour), all expressing his belief that "the composer is as much the tool as the tool itself, or even a tool for the machine to manifest its desires". His music featured in Sofia Coppola's film *Lost In Translation* and he has provided a new score for choreographer Darren Johnston's *Phase I, II and III*. In 2005 he collaborated with London Sinfonietta, accompanying their transcriptions of his music on his bass guitar.

Squarepusher

The Step

The Step began as a collaboration between Winston Hazel (Forgemasters) and Richard Barratt, aka DJ Parrot (Sweet Exorcist) – both influential DJs at clubs in Sheffield and Yorkshire in the late 80s – and singer Sarah Jay, who went on to work with Massive Attack, among others. Their track "Yeah You!" was the eighth Warp single in 1991. Several years later Barratt went on to join the successful All Seeing I while Hazel undertook a large number of different DJ, production and artistic projects.

See Forgemasters, Sweet Exorcist

Stereolab

Stereolab formed in 1991 in South London around a core of Tim Gane, Laetitia Sadier, Mary Hansen and Andy Ramsay. Their motorik trance-pop, with nods to French 60s bubblegum, Neu!-style Krautrock and avant garde electronica, has remained an enduring presence in independent music for nearly two decades. Most of their enormous catalogue has come out through their own label Duophonic UHF Disks, but the lone album *Aluminum Tunes* appeared on Warp in 1998.

www.stereolab.co.uk

Sweet Exorcist

Collaboration (named after a 1974 Curtis Mayfield LP) between former Cabaret Voltaire founder Richard H Kirk and DJ Parrot, who met on the Sheffield club scene and produced lo-fi 'northern bleep' tracks under the name Sweet Exorcist from 1989. "Testone", sampled from recordings of electronic frequencies used to check hi-fi equipment, was the third Warp single in 1990; 1991's *Clonk's Coming* LP was the first of the label's long players. A further release, *Spirit Guide To Low Tech*, appeared on Touch in 1994 before the pair went separate ways.

See Richard H Kirk, The Step

Sympletic

British DJ, producer and label owner Mark Broom has kept a relatively low media profile, which belies the extent of his subterranean influence on UK Techno. With the Plaid duo Ed Handley and Andy Turner, they formed the shortlived trio Repeat, and on tours he is a regular DJ accompanist of Warp related artists. Among many labels he has set up, the most significant have been Pure Plastic (which released his intelligent Techno classic *Angie Is A Shoplifter* LP), Ifach with UK Acid pioneer Baby Ford and Unexplored Beats. His early productions took place at UXB Studios, run by Dave Hill, who became a regular partner under a range of personae including Midnight Funk Association and Sympletic, whose *At Long Last* EP, 1996 (Warp), is one of only two extant works under that moniker.

Team SHADETEk

Team SHADETEk is SOZE.SHT and Zach Zigmore, aka M Schell and Zack Tucker. The pair grew up in the same area of downtown Manhattan and by 1999 were producing Autechre-style crunchy laptop tracks. They have released on their own SHADETEk label as well as Kid606's Tigerbeat6; the title of their *Burnerism*, 2004 (Warp), alluded to the duo's connections to the Change Agent Art Gang, a group of young graffiti artists. This influence can often be seen in their cover designs, several of which have been spraycanned by the New York street artist Swoon.

Jimi Tenor

While still a student in his home country Finland, Lassi Lehto rechristened himself Jimi Tenor and recorded four albums with his group The Shamans by the early 90s, whereupon he went travelling. As a photographer in New York, he began recording ironic nightclub-jazz songs on primitive synthesizers at his apartment – shared with German DJ/musician Khan – which emerged as *Sähkömies* on the minimalist Techno label Sähkö, run from Helsinki by artist Tommi Grönlund. On a live date in Vienna, after the release of *Europa*, Tenor caught the attention of Warp's

Steve Beckett, who promptly signed him. He went on to release three more albums on Warp, *Intervision*, 1997, *Organism*, 1999, and the orchestral *Out of Nowhere*, 2000. A consummate stylist and flamboyantly deadpan performer, Tenor currently lives back in Finland and has released two LPs for Kitty-Yo.

www.jimitenor.com

Jimi Tenor

THK

THK – German DJ Thomas Kukula – released House track "France" on Warp in 1992. Kukula has also released music under the names Candy Beat, DJ Red 5, DUG, and General Base.

Tomas

One of the last artists to be signed to Warp by Rob Gordon, Thomas Sylvanus Stewart surfaced with the three track, spacey Techno EP *Mindsongs* in 1991 before vanishing from the radar.

Tomas

Tortoise

An unprecedented combination of fluid jamming, rippling minimalist pulses and dub-heavy production brought this Chicago collective to worldwide attention in 1994. Dan Bitney, John McEntire, John Herndon, Jeff Parker and Doug McCombs have survived from an original line-up that also included Dave Pajo and Bundy K Brown. Closely associated with the Thrill Jockey label for their first releases, including the post-rock classic *Millions Now Living Will Never Die*, the group, always happy to hand their instrumental material over to electronic remixers, ended up on Warp in early 2001 for the album *Standards*, which marked a notable toughening of their exploratory, meandering sound.

www.trts.com/site.html

Tortoise

Tricky Disco

Michael Wells and Lee Newman had already had a hit with their group Greater Than One (aka GTO) by the time they set up one of many side projects, Tricky Disco, at the end of the 80s (the name occurred because, living in Berlin at the time, the pair used to substitute 'tricky' for words like 'cool' or 'fab'). Although not linked to the Sheffield Techno scene, Tricky Disco's self-titled theme tune was constructed from similar tones and frequencies to Sweet Exorcist and LFO. Shortly after releasing it in a private pressing (stamped with the number of a German professor friend who, if phoned, claimed to have discovered the Tricky Disco alien 'creature' in a nightclub), Warp made contact to express interest in releasing the track to a wider market. The track – the seventh Warp single – achieved chart success and saw the group's homemade video appear on BBC's *Top of The Pops* in 1990. 'Domestic rave anthem' "Housefly" was the second and last Warp release, following which they recorded for XL as John & Julie and for React as Technohead, whose "I Wanna Be A Hippy", 1995, reached number one in 12 different territories. Sadly, shortly after the release of the couple's album *Headsex*, Newman died of cancer. Wells has continued producing a wide variety of electronic music as Signs Of Chaos and currently lives in Spain. "Tricky Disco" was rereleased by Kompakt sublabel Speicher in 2005.

Tricky Disco

Tuff Little Unit

Two singles are all that survive of this Sheffield group featuring Glyn Andrews and Isaiah Hill – former school friends of Warp's Rob Gordon – and Forgemasters' Sean Maher. "Inspiration" and "Join The Future", both 1991, were bass heavy Techno with a warmer, jazzier atmosphere than the predominant Warp sound at the time.

Tuff Little Unit

Max Tundra

Classically trained pianist Ben Jacobs released the first of his charming bedroom productions on a primitive Amiga computer, "Children At Play", on Warp in 1998. He went on to join the Domino Records roster where he has since released *Some Best Friend You Turned Out To Be* (disjointed, angular electronica) and *Mastered By Guy At The Exchange* (quirky electronic pop songs sung by himself and his sister Becky Jacobs). A frequent live performer and DJ, he founded eclectic London clubs One Size Fits All and Rotogravure.

Two Lone Swordsmen

After hanging up his Sabres Of Paradise cutlass, Andrew Weatherall's next venture was the rapier-sharp Two Lone Swordsmen duo with Keith Tenniswood. Beginning their adventures with legendary six-hour DJ sets that prepared the way for the monumental triple LP *The Fifth Mission*, 1996 (Emissions Audio Output), the duo have been clashing blades ever since, with singleminded explorations of electro, downtempo Techno and minimalist digital funk that constantly defy expectations. Highlights of their Warp albums include *Stay Down*, 1998, *A Bag Of Blue Sparks*, 1998, *Tiny Reminders*, 2000, and *From The Double Gone Chapel*, 2004.

Two Lone Swordsmen. Photo: Steve Gullick, 2004

Ultradyne

From the same hermetic circle as Detroit's Drexciya, Ultradyne's Dennis Richardson and Alex Lugo recorded one science fiction-tinged EP for Warp, *E Coli* in 1995, followed after an interval of several years by scattered releases on their own Pi Gao Movement label (also home to Lugo's "neo-Detroit" solo project Vidrio), and a split record with Redshift (Jeff Mills) on Nu-Vorm in 2001.

www.pigaomovement.com

Ultradyne

Luke Vibert

Under the names Wagon Christ, Plug, Amen Andrews and Kerrier District, Luke Vibert has successfully channelled his mutual loves of Acid, deep funk, old school hiphop, mutated Ambient, Jungle breakbeats, 'cheesy listening' and quirky library music. From humble beginnings in Cornwall as drummer in jazz funk outfit The Hate Brothers, he befriended Richard James aka Aphex Twin at Cornish club events, and had produced his debut Wagon Christ album, *Phat.Lab Nightmare*, for London label Rising High by 1993. *Throbbing Pouch*, a masterpiece of addled funk, was followed by Plug's *Drum 'N' Bass For Papa*, a breakneck breakbeat collection whose manic spin on Jungle surfaced in later work by Aphex Twin and Squarepusher. He has recorded for a wide range of labels including Virgin, Ninja Tune, Mo' Wax, Rephlex and Lo Recordings, and in later years he has concentrated on simultaneous homages/rereadings of Acid House, including *YosepH*, 2003 (Warp), and early 90s rave under the name Amen Andrews on Rephlex.

VLAD

Little information is available about VLAD's true identity; rumours about a pre-Techno existence as an itinerant Heavy Metal guitarist are hard to square with the music on his "Motion Institute" single, 2000 (Warp), which displayed the clinical rhythms of Kraftwerk and Afrika Bambaataa. A new album, *Emo-Droidz*, came out on Laboratory Instinct in 2005.

Wild Planet

UK born Simon J Hartley released the analogue Detroit Techno inspired "Electron" and the *Blueprints* LP on Warp in 1993 before moving to Stockholm. He has issued tracks on Michigan imprint 430 West, and continues to record, produce and DJ.

Woodenspoon

See Seefeel, Disjecta

Discography

Warp Records Albums

WARP1 **Sweet Exorcist** Clonk's Coming 1991
WARP2 **Various** Pioneers Of The Hypnotic Groove 1991
WARP3 **LFO** Frequencies 1991
WARP4 **Nightmares On Wax** A Word Of Science 1991
WARP5 **Various** Evolution Of The Groove 1992
WARP6 **Various** Artificial Intelligence 1992
WARP7 **Polygon Window** Surfing On Sine Waves 1993
WARP8 **Black Dog Productions** Bytes 1993
WARP9 **B12** Electro Soma 1993
WARP10 **Various** Tequila Slammers And The Jump Jump Groove 1993
WARP11 **Wild Planet** Blueprints 1993
WARP12 **FUSE** Dimension Intrusion 1993
WARP13 no release
WARP14 **Speedy J** Ginger 1993
WARP15 **Rhythm Invention** Inventures In Wonderland 1993
WARP16 **Sabres Of Paradise** Sabresonic 1993
WARP17 **Autechre** Incunabula 1993
WARP18 **DiY** Strictly 4 Groovers 1993
WARP19 **Richard H Kirk** Virtual State 1994
WARP20 **Kenny Larkin** Azimuth 1994
WARP21 **Aphex Twin** Selected Ambient Works II 1994
WARP22 **RAC** Diversions 1994
WARP23 **Various** Artificial Intelligence II 1994
WARP24 **Coco, Steel & Lovebomb** It! 1994
WARP25 **Autechre** Amber 1994
WARP26 **Sabres Of Paradise** Haunted Dancehall 1994
PUP1 **The Black Dog** Spanners 1995
WARP27 **Speedy J** G Spot 1995
WARP28 **Seefeel** Succour 1995
WARP29 **Various** Theory Of Evolution 1995
WARP30 **Aphex Twin** I Care Because You Do 1995
WARP31 **Sabres Of Paradise** Versus 1995
WARP32 **Richard H Kirk** The Number Of Magic 1995
WARP33 **Red Snapper** Reeled And Skinned 1995
WARP34 **Sabres Of Paradise** Sabresonic II 1995
WARP35 **Elecktroids** Elektro World 1995
WARP36 **Nightmares On Wax** Smoker's Delight 1995
WARP37 **B12** Time Tourist 1996
WARP38 **Autechre** Tri Repetae 1995
WARP39 **LFO** Advance 1996
WARP40 **Various** Blech 1995
WARP41 **Disjecta** Clean Pit And Lid 1996
WARP42 **Jake Slazenger** Das Ist Ein Groovy Beat, Ja? 1996
PUP2 **The Black Dog** Music For Adverts (And Short Films) 1996
WARP43 **Aphex Twin** Richard D James 1996
WARP44 **Various** Blech II: Blechsdottir 1996
WARP45 **Red Snapper** Prince Blimey 1996
WARP46 **Various** Eurowarp 1996
WARP47 **Jimi Tenor** Sähkömies 1999
WARP48 **Jimi Tenor** Intervision 1997
WARP49 **Autechre** Chiastic Slide 1997
WARP50 **Squarepusher** Hard Normal Daddy 1997
WARP51 **Autechre** Radio (Promo) 1997
WARP52 **Broadcast** Work And Non Work 1997
WARP53 **Squarepusher** Burningn'n Tree 1997
WARP54 **Plaid** Not For Threes 1997
WARP55 **Boards Of Canada** Music Has The Right To Children 1998
WARP56 **Red Snapper** Making Bones 1998
WARP57 **Squarepusher** Music Is Rotted One Note 1998
WARP58 **Two Lone Swordsmen** Stay Down 1998
WARP59 **Stereolab** Aluminum Tunes 1998
WARP60 **Jimi Tenor** Organism 1999
WARP61 **Nightmares On Wax** Car Boot Soul 1999
WARP62 **Squarepusher** Budakhan Mindphone 1999
WARP63 **Plaid** Rest Proof Clockwork 1999
WARP64 **Plone** For Beginner Piano 1999
WARP65 **Broadcast** The Noise Made By People 2000
WARP66 **Autechre** LP5 1998
WARP67 **Various** 10+1 Influences 1999
WARP68 **Various** 10+2 Classics 1999
WARP69 **Various** 10+3 Remixes 1999
WARP70 **Boards Of Canada** Twoism 2002
WARP71 **Jimi Tenor** Europa 1999
WARP72 **Squarepusher** Selection Sixteen 1999
WARP73 **Mira Calix** One On One 2000
WARP74 **Plaid** Trainer 2000
WARP75 **Jamie Lidell** Muddlin' Gear 2000
WARP76 **Jimi Tenor** Out Of Nowhere 2000
WARP77 **Two Lone Swordsmen** Tiny Reminders 2000
WARP78 **Red Snapper** Our Aim Is To Satisfy Red Snapper 2000
WARP79 **Chris Morris** Blue Jam 2000
WARP80 **Savath + Savalas** Folk Songs For Trains, Trees And Honey 2000
WARP81 **Tortoise** Standards 2001
WARP82 **Various** Routine 2001
WARP83 **Prefuse 73** Vocal Studies And Uprock Narratives 2001
WARP84 **Plaid** Double Figure 2001
WARP85 **Squarepusher** Go Plastic 2001
WARP86 **Chris Clark** Clarence Park 2001
WARP87 **Vincent Gallo** When 2001
WARP88 **Brothomstates** Claro 2001
WARP89 **Req** Sketchbook 2002
WARP90 **The Other People Place** Lifestyles Of The Laptop Cafe 2001
WARP91 **Two Lone Swordsmen** Further Reminders 2001
WARP92 **Aphex Twin** drukqs 2001
WARP93 **Priest** (unreleased)
WARP94 **Antipop Consortium** Arrythmia 2002
WARP95 **Nightmares On Wax** Mind Elevation 2002
WARP96 **Vincent Gallo** Recordings Of Music For Film 2002
WARP97 **Squarepusher** Do You Know Squarepusher? 2002
WARP98 **Various** Morvern Callar 2002
WARP99 no release
WARP100 **Warp Magic Bus Tour** Magic Tracks 2002
WARP101 **Boards Of Canada** Geogaddi 2002
WARP102 **Aphex Twin** 26 Mixes For Cash 2003
WARP103 **Beans** Tomorrow Right Now 2003
WARP104 **Mira Calix** Skimskitta 2003
WARP105 **Prefuse 73** One Word Extinguisher 2003
WARP106 **Broadcast** Haha Sound 2003
WARP107 **Chris Clark** Empty The Bones Of You 2003
WARP108 **Req** Car Paint Scheme 2003
WARP109 **Squarepusher** Budakhan Maximised (no date)
WARP110 **LFO** Sheath 2003
WARP111 **Autechre** Draft 7.30 2003
WARP112 **Luke Vibert** YosepH 2003
WARP113 no release
WARP114 **Plaid** Spokes 2003
WARP115 **Savath + Savalas** Apropa't 2004
WARP116 **Jimmy Edgar** album tbc
WARP117 **Squarepusher** Ultravisitor 2004
WARP118 **Chris Morris** Blue Jam II (not released)
WARP119 **Two Lone Swordsmen** From The Double Gone Chapel 2004
WARP120 **Gravenhurst** Flashlight Seasons 2004
WARP121 **!!!** Louden Up Now 2004
WARPD122 **Various** Warp Vision: The Videos 1989-2004 2004
WARP123 **Boards Of Canada** The Campfire Headphase 2005
WARP124 **Mira Calix** 3 Commissions 2004
WARP125 **Beans** Shock City Maverick 2004
WARP126 **Various** Dead Man's Shoes OST 2004
WARP127 **Harmonic 33** Music For TV, Film And Radio Vol 1 2005
WARP128 **Autechre** Confield 2001
WARP129 **Prefuse 73** Surrounded By Silence 2005
WARP130 **Maxïmo Park** A Certain Trigger 2005
WARP131 **Jamie Lidell** Multiply 2005
WARP132 **Gravenhurst** Fires In Distant Buildings 2005
WARP133 tbc
WARP134 **On The Hour** Series One (no release date)
WARP135 **On The Hour** Series Two (no release date)
WARP136 **Broadcast** Tender Buttons 2005
WARP137 **Jackson & His Computer Band** Smash 2005
WARP138 **AFX** Hangable Auto Bulb 2005
WARP180 **Autechre** Untilted 2005
WARP666 **Satanstornade** Satanstornade 2003

Warp Records Singles/EPs

WAP1 **Forgemasters** Track With No Name 1989
WAP2 **Nightmares On Wax** Dextrous 1989
WAP3 **Sweet Exorcist** Testone 1990
WAP4 **DJ Mink** Hey! Hey! Can U Relate? 1990
WAP5 **LFO** LFO 1990
WAP6 **Nightmares On Wax** Aftermath 1990
WAP7 **Tricky Disco** Tricky Disco 1990
WAP8 **The Step** Yeah You! 1991
WAP9 **Sweet Exorcist** Clonk 1990
WAP10 **Tomas** Mindsongs 1991
WAP11 **Tricky Disco** Housefly 1991
WAP12 **Tuff Little Unit** Join The Future 1991
WAP13 no release
WAP14 **LFO** We Are Back 1991
WAP15 **Nightmares On Wax** A Case Of Funk 1991
WAP16 **Tuff Little Unit** Inspiration 1991
WAP17 **LFO** What Is House? 1992
WAP18 **Coco, Steel & Lovebomb** Feel It 1992
WAP19 **DSR** Miami 1992
WAP20 **Kid Unknown** Nightmare 1992
WAP21 **Rhythm Invention** I Can't Take It 1992
WAP22 **Wild Planet** Electron 1992
WAP23 **Kid Unknown** Devastating Beat Creator 1992
WAP24 **Nightmares On Wax** Set Me Free 1992
WAP25 **Coco, Steel & Lovebomb** You Can't Stop The Groove 1992
WAP26 **THK** France 1992
WAP27 **Eternal** Mind Odyssey 1992
WAP28 **Nightmares On Wax** Happiness 1992
WAP29 **Jaco** Show Some Love 1992
WAP30 **Warp Party at Sheffield Leadmill** 1993
WAP31 **DiY** Hothead 1993
WAP32 **Solitaire Gee** Slumberland 1993
WAP33 **Polygon Window** Quoth 1993
WAP34 **Rhythm Invention** Ad Infinitum 1993
WAP35 **Modus Vivendi** Modus Vivendi 1993
WAP36 **Laurent Garnier** A Bout De Souffle 1993
WAP37 **Resoraz** Art Of Time 1993
WAP38 **FUSE** Train Tracs 1993
WAP39 **Aphex Twin** On 1993
WAP40 **Circle City** Moments Of Inertia 1994
WAP41 **Lex Loofah** Freak Deaky 1994
WAP42 **David Holmes** Johnny Favourite 1994
WAP43 **Black Mojo** Mojo's Working 1994
WAP44 **Autechre** Basscadet Mixes 1994
WAP45 **Seefeel** Starethrough 1994
WAP46 **Speedy J** Pepper 1994
WAP47 **Coco, Steel & Lovebomb** Set Me Free 1994
WAP48 **GAK** GAK 1994
WAP49 **Joey Beltram** Caliber 1994
WAP50 **Sabres Of Paradise** Wilmot 1994
WAP51 **Coco, Steel & Lovebomb** Summer Rain 1994
WAP52 **RAC** Tangents 1994
WAP53 **Seefeel** Fracture/Tied 1994
WAP54 **Autechre** Anti 1994
WAP55 **K Hand** Global Warming 1994
WAP56 **LFO** Tied Up 1994
WAP57 **Drexciya** The Journey Home 1995
WAP58 **Autechre** Garbage 1995
WAP59 **Link** Antacid 1995
WAP60 **Aphex Twin** Ventolin 1995
WAP61 **RAC** Doublejointed 1995
WAP62 **Sabres Of Paradise** Versus 1995
WAP63 **Aphex Twin** Donkey Rhubarb 1995

WAP64 **Autechre** Anvil Vapre 1995
WAP65 **Elecktroids** Kilohertz 1995
WAP66 **Ultradyne** E Coli 1995
WAP67 **AFX** Hangable Auto Bulb 1995
WAP68 **Disjecta** Looking For Snags 1995
WAP69 **AFX** Hangable Auto Bulb 2 1995
WAP70 **Red Snapper** Mooking 1996
WAP71 **RAC** Structures 1996
WAP72 **Autechre** (Untitled) 1996
WAP73 **Freeform** Prowl 1996
WAP74 **Squarepusher** Port Rhombus 1996
WAP75 **Jake Slazenger** Nautilus 1996
WAP76 **Nightmares On Wax** Still Smokin' 1996
WAP77 **Woodenspoon** Souff Souff 1996
WAP78 **Aphex Twin** Girl/Boy EP 1996
WAP79 **Sympletic** At Long Last 1996
WAP80 **Move D** Cymbelin 1996
WAP81 **Mike Ink** Paroles 1996
WAP82 **Mike Ink** Polka Trax 1996
WAP83 **Mira Calix** Ilanga 1996
WAP84 **Red Snapper** Loopascoopa 1996
WAP85 **Jimi Tenor** Take Me Baby 1996
WAP86 **Jimi Tenor** Can't Stay With You Baby 1996
WAP87 **Jimi Tenor** Outta Space 1997
WAP88 **Gescom** Keynell 1996
WAP89 **Autechre** Envane 1997
WAP90 **Squarepusher** Vic Acid 1997
WAP91 **Rubber Johnny** Jam Roly Poly 1997
WAP92 **Squarepusher** Big Loada 1997
WAP93 **Jimi Tenor** Sugardaddy/Take Me Baby 1997
WAP94 **Aphex Twin** Come To Daddy 1997
WAP95 **Plaid** Undoneson 1997
WAP96 **Autechre** Cichli Suite 1997
WAP97 **Mira Calix** Pin Skeeling 1998
WAP98 **Phoenecia** Randa Roomet 1997
WAP99 unique mitDR™ artwork donated to Chantal Passamonte/Mira Calix
WAP100 **Various** WAP100 1998
WAP101 **Max Tundra** Children At Play 1998
WAP102 **B12** 3EP 1998
WAP103 **Plaid** Booc 2000
WAP104 **Red Snapper** Bogeyman 1998
WAP105 **Aphex Twin** Windowlicker 1999
WAP106 **Two Lone Swordsmen** A Bag Of Blue Sparks 1998
WAP107 **Plone** Plock 1998
WAP108 **Red Snapper** The Sleepless 1998
WAP109 **Jimi Tenor** Venera 1998
WAP110 **John Callaghan** I'm Not Comfortable Inside My Mind 1998
WAP111 **Red Snapper** Image Of You 1998
WAP112 **Autechre** Peel Session 1999
WAP113 no release
WAP114 **Boards Of Canada** Peel Session 1999
WAP115 **The Black Dog** Peel Session 1999
WAP116 **Jimi Tenor** Year Of The Apocalypse 1999
WAP117 **Slum** Twilight Mushrooms 1999
WAP118 **Nightmares On Wax** Les Nuits 1999
WAP119 **Plaid** Peel Session 1999
WAP120 **Autechre** EP7 1999
WAPEP7.1 **Autechre** EP7 1999
WAP121 **Jimi Tenor** Total Devastation 1999
WAP122 **Squarepusher** Maximum Priest 1999
WAP123 **Nightmares On Wax** Finer 1999

WAP124 **Autechre** Splitrmx12 1999
WAP125 **Broadcast** cho's Answer 1999
WAP126 **Two Lone Swordsmen** A Virus With Shoes 1999
WAP127 **Two Lone Swordsmen** Receive Tactical Support 1999
WAP128 **Ko-Wreck Technique** The Ko-Wrecktion EP 1999
WAP129 **Broadcast** Extended Play 2000
WAP130 **VLAD** Motion Institute 2000
WAP131 no release
WAP132 **Broadcast** Come On Let's Go 2000
WAP133 **Nightmares On Wax** Keep On 2000
WAP134 **Prefuse 73** Estrocaro 2000
WAP135 **Jimi Tenor** Spell 2000
WAP136 **Broadcast** Drums on Fire 2000
WAP137 **John Callaghan** You've Got Your Memories, I've Got My Dreams 2000
WAP138 **Slum** Keys For Frobisher 2000
WAP139 **Richard Devine** Lip Switch 2001
WAP140 **Mira Calix** Peel Session 2000
WAP141 **Broadcast** Extended Play Two 2000
WAP142 **Red Snapper** Some Kind Of Kink 2000
WAP143 no release
WAP144 **Boards Of Canada** In A Beautiful Place Out In The Country 2000
WAP145 **Mira Calix** Prickle 2001
WAP146 no release
WAP147 **Squarepusher** My Red Hot Car 2001
WAP148 no release
WAP149 **Vincent Gallo** So Sad 2001
WAP150 **Autechre** Peel Session 2 2001
WAP151 **Brothomstates** Qtio 2001
WAP152 **Something J/DJ Maxximus** Mercedes Bentley Vs Versace Armani 2001
WAP153 **Antipop Consortium** Ghost Lawns 2002
WAP154 **Antipop Consortium** The Ends Against The Middle 2001
WAP155 **Squarepusher** (Untitled) 2001
WAP156 **Prefuse 73** The 92 vs 02 Collection EP 2002
WAP157 **Sote** Electric Deaf 2002
WAP158 **Plaid** P-Brane 2002
WAP159 **Nightmares On Wax** Know My Name 2002
FLY1 **Mira Calix** NuNu 2003
WAP160 **Nightmares On Wax** 70s 80s 2003
WAP161 **Chris Clark** Ceramics Is The Bomb 2003
WAP162 **Broadcast** Pendulum 2003
WAP163 **!!!** Me + Giuliani Down By The School Yard 2003
WAP164 **Prefuse 73** Extinguished 2003
WAP165 **Luke Vibert** Synthax/I Love Acid 2003
WAP166 **LFO** Freak 2003
WAP167 **Beans** Now Soon Someday 2004
WAP168 **Nightmares On Wax** Destiny 2003
WAP169 **Broadcast** Microtronics Volume 1 – Stereo Recorded Music For Links and Bridges 2004
WAP170 **Team SHADETEk** Burnerism 2004
WAP171 **Jimmy Edgar** Access Rhythm 2004
WAP172 **Squarepusher** Venus No 17 2004
WAP173 **Home Video** That You Might 2004
WAP174 **Two Lone Swordsmen** Sex Beat 2004
WAP175 **Milanese** 1 Up 2004
WAP176 **!!!** Hello? Is This Thing On? 2004
WAP177 **Savath + Savalas** Manana 2004
WAP178 **Beans** Down By Law 2004

WAP179 **Home Video** Citizen 2004
WAP180 **Jimmy Edgar** Bounce, Make, Model 2004
WAP181 **Gravenhurst** Black Holes In The Sand 2004
WAP182 **Two Lone Swordsmen** Big Silver Shining Motor Of Sin 2004
WAP183 **Maxïmo Park** The Coast Is Always Changing 2004
WAP184 **!!!** Me + Guiliani Down By The School Yard (LFO Remix) 2005
WAP185 **Maxïmo Park** Apply Some Pressure 2005
WAP186 **Prefuse 73 with Ghostface & El-P** Hideyaface 2005
WAP187 **Maxïmo Park** Graffiti 2005
WAP188 **Chok Rock** Big City Loser 2005
WAP189 **Prefuse 73** Reads The Books EP 2005
WAP190 **Maxïmo Park** Going Missing 2005
WAP191 **Jamie Lidell** When I Come Back Around 2005
WAP192 **!!!** Take Ecstasy With Me/Get Up 2005
WAP193 **Broadcast** America's Boy 2005
WAP194 **Jackson And His Computer Band** Rock On 2005
WAP195 **AFX/LFO** 4 Track EP (Waprmart exclusive) 2005
WAP196 **Gravenhurst** The Velvet Cell 2005
WAP256 **Autechre** Gantz Graf 2002

Warp Films

WF001DVD **Chris Morris** My Wrongs #8245-8249 & 117
WF002BK **Anjan Sarkar** Dead Man's Shoes Graphic Novel
WF003DVD **Chris Cunningham** Rubber Johnny
WF003DVDN **Chris Cunningham** Rubber Johnny US Version
WF004DVD **Joe Berlinger And Bruce Sinofsky** Paradise Lost 1 & 2: The Child Murders at Robin Hood Hills

Lex Records

LEX001 **Disflex6** Hot Season 2001
LEX002.1 **Various** Lexoleum Part 1 2001
LEX002.2 **Various** Lexoleum Part 2 2002
LEX002.3 **Various** Lexoleum Part 3 2002
LEX002CD **Various** Lexoleum (Album) 2003
LEX003 **Boom Bip** Mannequin Hand Trapdoor I Reminder 2002
LEX004 **Disflex6** Lazerus Jackson 2002
LEX005 **Danger Mouse & Jemini** Take Care Of Business 2002
LEX006 **Boom Bip** Seed To Sun 2002
LEX007 **Mummy Fortuna's Theatre Company** Born Of Man & Flies 2002
LEX008 no release
LEX009 **Tes** New New York 2003
LEX010 **Danger Mouse & Jemini** Ghetto Pop Life 2003
LEX011 no release
LEX012 **Tes** X2 2003
LEX013 no release
LEX014 **Boom Bip** From Left To Right 2003
LEX015 **Prince Po** Hold Dat (Richard X Mixes) 2004
LEX016 **Danger Mouse & Jemini** Conceited Bastard EP 2003
LEX017 **Hymie's Basement** Ghost Dream On Fairmont tbc
LEX018 **Non Prophets** Hope 2003
LEX019 **Hymie's Basement** Hymie's Basement 2003
LEX020 **Boom Bip** Morning And A Day 2004
LEX021 **Boom Bip** Corymb 2004
LEX022 **Danger Mouse & Jemini** Twenty Six Inch 2003
LEX023 **DJ Signify** Winters Going 2004
LEX024 **DJ Signify** Sleep No More 2004
LEX025 **Prince Po** The Slickness 2004
LEX026 **Non Prophets** Damage 2004
LEX027 **Subtle** FKO 2004
LEX028 **Subtle** Long Vein Of The Law 2004
LEX029 **Subtle** A New White 2004
LEX030 **Subtle** Swan Meat tbc
LEX031 **Prince Po** Bump Bump 2004
LEX032 **Fog** We're Winning tbc
LEX033 **Fog** Tenth Avenue Freakout 2005
LEX034 **Boom Bip** Blue Eyed In The Red Room 2005
LEX035 **Boom Bip & Gruff Rhys** Do's And Don'ts 2005
LEX036 **Dangerdoom** The Mouse And The Mask 2005

Nucleus
Shortlived sublabel for progressive House and dance 12"s during 1992

NUKE01 **RAC** Monsoon/Yogomotion 1992
NUKE02 **Rhythm Invention** Crunch 1992
NUKE03 **Freak Sisters** The Freak Boutique 1992
NUKE04 **On (2)** Applegas 1992
NUKE05 **RAC** Neo Rio 1992
NUKE06 **Anon** Alright/OK Armando 1992
NUKE07 **RAC** Hula Loops 1992
NUKE08 **Coco, Steel & Lovebomb** Work It/Run Free 1992
NUKE09 **Whistle** Whistlers Brother 1992
NUKE10 **Anon** Horny Honkies 1992
NUKE11 **Pio Bio** The Best Time To Go Swimming 1992
NUKE12 **Anon** Jammin' The Doughnut 1992
NUKE13 no release
NUKE14 **Nightmares On Wax** Alive 1992

Arcola
Sublabel named after a street in Dalston, East London, set up in 2003 with uniform 12"s aimed at the dancefloor

ARC000 **Anon** I Know You Got Soul/Uptown 2003
ARC001 **Dub Kult** Stop The World 2003
ARC002 **Denis Rusnak** Working Sister 2003
ARC003 **Louis Digital** Insurgency Soul 2003
ARC004 **Brothomstates** Rktic EP 2003
ARC005 **Cane** Teknotest/Fall 2003
ARC006 **Milanese** Vanilla Monkey 2003